BUILDING SUSTAINABLE HOME

Skyhorse Publishing books may be purchased in bulk at special discounts for sales promotion, corporate gifts, fund-raising, or educational purposes. Special editions can also be created to specifications. For details, contact the Special Sales Department, Skyhorse Publishing, 307 West 36th Street, 11th Floor, New York, NY 10018 or info@skyhorsepublishing.com.

Skyhorse® and Skyhorse Publishing® are registered trademarks of Skyhorse Publishing, Inc.®, a Delaware corporation.

Visit our website at www.skyhorsepublishing.com.

10 9 8 7 6 5 4 3 2

Library of Congress Cataloging-in-Publication Data is available on file.

Cover design by Mona Lin
Cover image by Paul Crosby

Print ISBN: 978-1-51073-344-2
Ebook ISBN: 978-1-51073-345-9

Printed in China

BUILDING A SUSTAINABLE HOME

Practical Green Design Choices for Your Health, Wealth, and Soul

MELISSA RAPPAPORT SCHIFMAN

Foreword by Thomas Fisher, Assoc. AIA

Skyhorse Publishing

Contents

Foreword   vii

Prologue

Chapter 1: Introduction   3
Chapter 2: All About LEED   8

Part I: For Our Health

Chapter 3: Clean Water   17
Chapter 4: Clean Air   26
Chapter 5: Clean House   47

Part II: For Our Wealth

Chapter 6: Energy   63
Chapter 7: Water Efficiency   116
Chapter 8: Durability   130

Part III: For Our Soul

Chapter 9: Materials   137
Chapter 10: Landscaping   168
Chapter 11: Location   186

Epilogue

Chapter 12: The Worst Green Decisions
   We Made   193
Chapter 13: The Bottom Line   200
Chapter 14: Beyond LEED: Moonshot   203

The LEED Checklist   208
Acknowledgments   211
Index   213

Photo credit: Karen Melvin

Foreword

The voice of the informed homeowner has, until now, been a missing part of the publishing world. There exists sizable literature about sustainable home building and design from the point of view of experts: people who make their living doing this work as well as teaching and writing about it. And all too often, that perspective lapses either into technical jargon that leaves the ordinary reader behind or into dry evaluations of performance measures that puts all but the most dedicated enthusiast to sleep.

Melissa Rappaport Schifman avoids both of those pitfalls in this book. She writes clearly and succinctly in a prose style that holds the reader's interest and conveys content in words that even those who have no prior experience with sustainability will understand. Her perspective also shows how homeowners have as much responsibility for decision-making as their architects and builders, needing to know when to support a design idea or technical solution and when to say no to it.

That give-and-take between homeowner and architect/builder differs from the way in which we typically consume products and services. When buying something, we usually choose from existing options already determined by their designers and producers, whom we may never meet and who rarely have an opportunity to tailor their offerings to fit our individual needs. Building or renovating a home does not work that way. A home's creation involves an interaction between homeowner and architect/builder that always results in a custom solution for a specific site and program. Because of that, the more informed the homeowner, the better the results.

This is what makes this book so valuable to homeowners wanting to live in healthier, less wasteful, and, as Schifman phrases it, more soulful ways. Who doesn't want to live like that? And yet despite all the progress we have made in cleaning up our physical environment in the developed world, we remain exposed to unhealthy conditions, from contaminants in our drinking water to pollutants inside our buildings; wasteful systems, from inefficient appliances to leaky windows; and unpleasant surroundings, from fake materials to flamboyant facades.

This book serves as an excellent antidote to that excessiveness. In a series of tables labeled "dollars and sense," Schifman lays out the sustainability strategies in a number of areas and summarizes their cost implications and whether it makes sense to invest in them. The text in those tables has a refreshing directness, with capital letters letting the reader know, in no uncertain terms, that something is not warranted or has too long a payback period and that other ideas have huge benefits and ample reasons to just "DO IT!"

These tables make the book useful as a quick reference not just for homeowners, but also for architects, landscape architects, and contractors looking for justification—or not—for their sustainability decisions. These summaries also let the reader skim the book to see what sections to read in greater depth or to review after having read the book to remember its high-level recommendations. In our hyper-speed, time-starved world, such synopses serve a real purpose.

If you have the time, though, the text of this book will reward your reading. Schifman writes in a fluid, first-person style that carries the reader along through content that in lesser hands could get awfully dry. She has plenty of numbers to back up her claims, for example, but manages to explain the data and tie it to the larger story in a way that makes it digestible for even the most mathematically challenged.

She also doesn't hesitate to talk about her own learning process and how some of what she once thought true turned out to be unfounded or at least unwise. That self-critical sensibility sets this book apart from those of most professionals, who typically do not share what they do not know or what they formerly advised and no longer recommend, as if expertise equals unassailability. Schifman's candor provides a refreshing alternative to that culture. She leads the reader through her own discoveries and draws conclusions that make sense in her context, acknowledging that in other climates or with other constraints, a homeowner might make a different decision.

In the end, the reader comes away from this book not only better informed, but also more inspired to learn more about what it has to offer. The best books treat readers with respect and invite them into a conversation that they can contribute to—if only in their imagination—with the author, and this book does that. Schifman has left me convinced that we will only really achieve the sustainable future that we—and future generations—deserve if we can cut through the technical mumbo jumbo that sometimes characterizes the books written by specialists and convey this important content in a way that an ordinary person can understand and apply to the one environment in which most people have some degree of control: their own homes.

—Thomas Fisher, Assoc. AIA

Thomas Fisher, Assoc. AIA, is a professor in the School of Architecture and the director of the Minnesota Design Center at the University of Minnesota. He is a graduate of Cornell University in architecture and Case Western Reserve University in intellectual history, and was previously the Editorial Director of *Progressive Architecture* magazine. Recognized in 2005 as the fifth most published writer about architecture in the United States, he has written nine books, over fifty book chapters or introductions, and over four hundred articles in professional journals and major publications. Named a top-twenty-five design educator four times by Design Intelligence, he has lectured at thirty-six universities and over 150 professional and public meetings. He has written extensively about architectural design, practice, and ethics.

Fisher has written two books (*Salmela Architect* and *The Invisible Element of Place: The Architecture of David Salmela*; University of Minnesota Press, 2005 and 2011) profiling the works of David Salmela, who ranks as one of the best residential architects in the country, having won dozens of design awards and having had his work published all over the world. Schifman's home is the only LEED gold certified Salmela-designed home.

PROLOGUE

CHAPTER 1:
INTRODUCTION

In 2006, my husband Jim and I embarked on a journey that would take almost three years and more of our time and energy—and money—than either of us had ever imagined. Anyone who even considers building or remodeling a home knows that the number of decisions a homeowner has to make, from architects and builders to styles, materials, windows, and furnishings, can be mind-numbing.

From the beginning, we were very interested in building a "green" or "sustainable" home; I also wanted to explore LEED for Homes certification. LEED, an acronym for Leadership in Energy and Environmental Design, is the nationally accepted high-performance green building rating system. I was intrigued by LEED and wanted to understand the costs and benefits of building a LEED certified home. (See chapter 2, *All About LEED*.)

Why was I so interested in building a green home? I am not an architect, builder, or interior designer. I can only explain that it is part of who I am. My maternal German heritage dictates a certain efficiency in the way I live; wastefulness is not in my DNA. My Jewish upbringing taught me to engage in *tikkun olam*, a Hebrew phrase for *repairing the world*. My love for nature and the outdoors, the place where my soul is nourished, necessitates caring for Mother Earth. So the seeds of a "green" lifestyle were sown in my genes and my upbringing. But it was when I became a mother that a new, fiercely focused dedication to creating a healthy home for my family sprouted.

I believe it is our moral obligation to help make the world a better place. It's an investment in our future and our children's future. After we had our first child in 2004, it became even more important to think about our health as well as the long-term effects of our purchasing and consumption choices. What kind of life will our children have on this earth? In twenty or thirty years, will they be asking us what we did to stop the destruction of our resources upon which we depend? It seemed like not just the responsible route to take, but really the only route for me and our family.

So, we decided that any house we built would be as healthy and sustainable as possible *and* fit within our budget and program requirements. I had already been educating myself on sustainable design, going to workshops and trade shows, and subscribing to magazines and newsletters on green building. This was my opportunity to find out how the "green" products available in the marketplace would play out in a real home.

While the hundreds of books and websites that provide expert advice on green building have been indispensable at times, they did not make the process much easier. Pick up any book on green building, and your eyes will glaze over with the sheer number of things that you *should* do to "go green," on a wide variety of topics: get an energy-efficient boiler, add insulation, buy recycled materials. It was overwhelming and confusing!

I pored through my extensive library of green home building guides, but I found that they were all missing something: *the real story.* By that I mean the process of decision-making, prioritizing against financial constraints. I had heard that building green costs more—typically 2 to 5 percent more than traditional building costs, on average. But I really wanted to know: which parts cost more? Is there anything that does not cost more, or actually costs less? And if something that costs more ends up saving us money year after year, is it worth it? How do you prioritize among those components? I began my quest to answer these questions.

Our architect and builder could give advice, but they stood to benefit financially from "green" choices that cost more up front, because their fee was a percentage of total construction costs. So they were motivated,

My green building library.

consciously or subconsciously, to encourage us to spend *more*. To me, that seemed like a conflict of interest, at least in the area of objective advice. And while they were quite skilled in their field, they did not perform cost/benefit analyses for me. They are not trained to do that. I have my MBA from the University of Chicago Booth School of Business and spent several years in finance in the airline industry, so I am trained to do exactly that. So, it was only natural that I would conduct the cost/benefit analyses for my own home. Besides, we would be the ones paying the utility and maintenance bills for the next several decades.

Once our home was well underway, a local builder who was designing his own home called me for guidance. When I asked why he wanted *my* advice (he had LEED Accredited Professionals on staff, who were well trained in green building), he answered, "Because you write the checks. As a homeowner, you are the one who has to make the decisions and prioritize them. I have a dozen friends who can give me green advice, but you have *experienced* green building. And that is where the rubber meets the road."

Let's back up: What does "going green" mean, anyway? So many companies have been jumping on the bandwagon and claiming that their product is "green." Well . . . compared to what? Compared to "standard construction practice"—which is what? Is it green because it uses less material? Or does not stink so much it gives you a headache? Is it made from recycled material, or is it simply recyclable? And how do we know? Is it certified by one of the hundreds of certifying bodies? Can I trust that certification? Is being made "locally" better than being made from "rapidly renewable resources"?

And the most important questions for *all* of our choices: is it functional, and do we like it?

Then there's the massive topic of "sustainability." Sustainability, which is quickly becoming an overused word like "green," is much more holistic than green. Sustainable development is most commonly understood as defined by the United Nations (UN): "meeting the needs of the present without compromising the ability of future generations to meet their own needs." Most of us do not know how our actions might have any effect on sustainability. In the context of building a home, it means choosing a location, technologies, and materials that do not pollute or harm our health, do not waste natural resources, are durable, and decrease the costs of operating the home. It is impossible to call one technology or material truly "sustainable" by itself. It always has to be compared to the alternative and understood in context of its use.

Why is the current state of the world *not* sustainable? That is the focus of many other books. Suffice it to say that while the industrial revolution brought a huge improvement in living standards, it also brought exponential human population growth—from about 2.5 billion in 1950 to over seven billion today. At the same time, our pattern of extraction, use, and waste disposal has depleted our natural resources and degraded our ecosystem that supplies us with clean air, clean water, and food—the very things we all need to survive.

While there are some examples of homes in the United States that have achieved or come close to achieving true sustainability (think zero energy, zero waste homes), it is rare, difficult, and expensive. We did not aspire to achieve this BHAG (Big Hairy Audacious Goal)[1] because frankly, it sounded too hard, too expensive, and too unrealistic. Going for LEED certification seemed extremely aspirational to us at the time.

I knew I had a mountain of work ahead of me, but as I worked to prioritize our choices, I soon realized that building a sustainable home as an end goal by itself was not all that helpful. We needed a *framework* to guide our decision-making process. What do we really care about? What are our values? Only then could we establish goals and figure out strategies to meet those goals.

So, a homeowner first needs to decide *why* he or she wants to build green. Our reasons were simple and utilitarian; we had just three. I would argue that these are the *only* three reasons to go green—and are the cornerstones of building a sustainable home: *for our health, wealth, and soul.*

For Our Health. Our family's health is our number one most important value. Our decisions were framed around three goals to ensure our home would not make us sick: clean water, clean air, and clean house. After having two babies in three years, we had learned a great deal about what is healthy and what is not—from food to personal care products to bedding, clothing, furniture, and paint. As with many consumer products that contain harmful ingredients, it was astounding to me how many "standard" construction practices have detrimental effects on our health, particularly for young children, whose little bodies are more at risk. My four-year-old daughter so wisely asked, when I told her to stay away from some hazardous cleaning chemical, "But Mommy, if it's bad for you, why do they make that?" Good question. Animals by instinct know what not to eat. My sister's cats would not even go in the same room as her new memory-foam petroleum-based mattress because it stunk.

For Our Wealth. Reducing annual energy, water, and maintenance costs was our secondary goal. This was a big deal to me, for three reasons. First, on the energy side, I have been fascinated by solar energy; when I lived in sunny Arizona I could not understand why we did not harness more of the sun's clean energy—it is free and abundant. The thought of free energy got me thinking that I wanted lower utility bills. (Who wouldn't? It just means more money to live your life!) Second, I have spent a great deal of time in my career doing cost/benefit analyses for large projects that would have a positive net present value (NPV)—meaning it is a good deal from a cash flow perspective and for our time horizon. So, here was my chance to find positive NPV projects for our house. Third, the house needed to be built to last. I have a wonderful husband who happens to *not* be the fix-anything handyman. So, I was convinced that the more things we could incorporate that would require very little, if any, maintenance, the more harmonious our marriage would be. (In reality, we have learned that nothing about a home is low maintenance, so that should not be anyone's expectation.) The financial benefit is that we spend less money and time replacing things

---

1   A business term coined by James Collins and Jerry Porras in their book *Built to Last: Successful Habits of Visionary Companies* (New York: HarperCollins, 1994).

that wear out quickly. The green piece is that fewer resources are wasted.

For Our Soul. This category is about doing the right thing for the environment, and feeling good about it. The green strategies discussed here—material purchases and waste, landscaping, and location—provide neither immediate health benefits nor financial paybacks. Like separating out trash for recycling, it just makes us feel better knowing that we are reducing our ecological footprint. And to be honest, it lessens the guilt factor in building a new home. We know that collectively, if we all make changes, it can make a tangible difference. Feeling like we are part of something bigger—and part of the solution, not the problem—can feed our soul.

"Feeling good about it" rests on the premise that there is something to feel bad about how we, as humans, have been behaving as it pertains to consumption choices. While not quite pervasive across the entire American psyche, this consumption guilt is a growing trend as people become more educated about global climate change, air pollution, scarce natural resources, water pollution, and how all of this affects our food supply and health. This is where "environmentalism" actually becomes "public health-ism."

The fact that doing the right thing *is* a motivating factor reflects a fundamental optimism in our future. Not only do we have to believe that one's individual purchasing decisions *can* make a difference, we have to believe that humans can exist in harmony with nature. And that philosophical outlook is possibly the single best thing about the sustainability movement.

As I write this book, I know full well that building a new home is not a "green" endeavor, as it consumes so many resources to do so. There are greener methods: remodeling an existing home, for example. I do not wish to compete for a trophy in sustainability. I am only trying to unravel the layers that can overwhelm and intimidate most homeowners in trying to make more sustainable choices. Yet for all I have learned, I am still a mother and a wife and a human being, and as that person I struggle to come to terms with the damage we are doing to the very planet that sustains us.

It is my belief that change begins in the home. Our homes are extensions of who we are—from our decorating styles to eating habits to tolerance for clutter. So, as I have committed myself to sustainability for the rest of my career, I wanted to start with my own home. By having the opportunity to cultivate my passion, I have learned about the costs, the benefits, the good, the bad, and the ugly. And now, we get to live with those choices— another new perspective. So I write to share my conclusions, and hope that this makes your journey of building or remodeling your home a little easier.

CHAPTER 2:
ALL ABOUT LEED

The built environment has a profound impact on our natural environment, economy, health, and productivity. —The very first sentence of the *LEED for Homes Reference Guide* (First Edition, 2008)

On May 18, 2011, our home became the eleventh LEED certified home in Minneapolis and the thirty-second in the state of Minnesota. I had appointed myself as the LEED project manager because I wanted to understand how it all worked. We had registered the project with the United States Green Building Council (USGBC), the organization that runs LEED, and performed all the necessary requirements during the design and construction process. But even after we moved into our home in early 2009, we still needed to figure out which points we earned and submit all the documentation for final review and approval. And by "we," I mean "me," because I was the only one who really wanted a LEED certified home.

So, I had to develop a plan for myself. Getting through LEED can be daunting: there are eighty-five performance standards to be met (referred to as "credits," each with different point values); eighteen of the performance standards are prerequisites—meaning they are mandatory, and there are no points associated with them. Since I had no deadline and no boss, I decided to start a blog to write about each of the eighty-five LEED credits, deciphering what they meant and whether we earned any of the associated points. The blog, I figured, would hold me publicly accountable, so I couldn't just quit. As I wrote about it, I would learn more, and maybe others could learn as well—that was my rationale. Plus, it would provide me the discipline I needed to get it done. To structure my time, I laid out a calendar whereby I addressed one LEED credit per day, Monday through Thursday, until I got through the whole rating system. This took about five months. Though I did not know it then, those five months of blog posts are the seedlings of this book.

Through all of my research, LEED classes and workshops, and time spent making our choices while our home was being built, I never once came across anything remotely helpful in identifying the true costs and benefits of a LEED certified home. The *LEED for Homes Reference Guide* (First Edition, 2008), to which I refer quite often, is a 342-page manual that could only be purchased for $249 through the

USGBC website. The *LEED for Homes Reference Guide* lays out the rationale and performance requirements of the eighty-five LEED credits and prerequisites. There is nothing that says: "Don't do this credit—it's too expensive." Or, "This credit gives you an easy two points," or "Very expensive, but worth it." You get the idea—I needed something like that and could not find it, so you'll find it here, for a lot less than $249.

LEED Background

The United States Green Building Council (USGBC), a member-based nonprofit formed in 1993, created and manages all LEED rating systems. Initially targeting the commercial building market, the first LEED rating system was developed and unveiled in the year 2000 to help new construction become greener. Why? Buildings contribute greatly to resource depletion, accounting for 40 percent of US energy consumption, 13.6 percent of potable water use, and about 40 percent of municipal

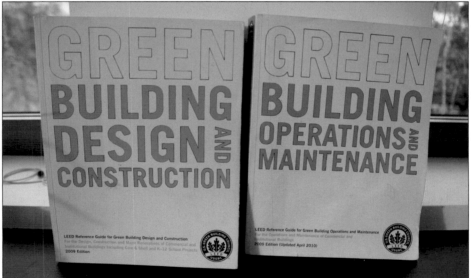

Each LEED rating system has its own thick reference guide. These two are for commercial buildings.

solid waste.[2] The USGBC subsequently introduced LEED for Existing Buildings, LEED for Core and Shell, LEED for Interior Design, and LEED for Neighborhood Development. Each rating system has its own reference guide and requirements, though the process for each is similar. As of October, 2017, the USGBC has overseen the certification of over 92,000 buildings in 167 countries, and the trend continues to grow.[3]

LEED for Homes was introduced in 2008 in recognition of the environmental impact of the *residential* sector, as distinct from the commercial sector—homes consume 22 percent of the nation's energy. The LEED for Homes Rating System applies to homes that are newly constructed as well as existing homes that are going through a major remodel.

The LEED for Homes Rating System is built around eight credit categories of sustainable design: Innovation and Design, Location and Linkages, Sustainable Sites, Water Efficiency, Energy and Atmosphere, Materials and Resources, Indoor Air Quality, and Awareness and Education. Each of these eight categories carries a different weight in the rating system, energy being the largest (with thirty-eight points, as shown in the pie chart) and therefore most important. The weight of each credit category is driven by a point system for certain planning, design, and building decisions.

Certification can be achieved at four levels, with a minimum of 45 points for base-level certification, 60 points for silver, 75 points for gold, and 90 points for platinum, out of 136 total possible points. (The newer version of LEED for Homes matches up better with the commercial rating systems, with 100 possible points, 40 needed for certification, 50 for silver, 60 for gold, and 80 for platinum.) The larger the home, the more points required to get to each threshold; conversely, the smaller the home, the fewer points needed to get LEED certified. It should be noted that *any* level requires that *all* eighteen prerequisites be met. If even one prerequisite is not met, the building cannot be certified.

When we started this process in 2008, only about five hundred homes had been LEED certified. As of October 2017, more than twenty thousand homes have been LEED certified,

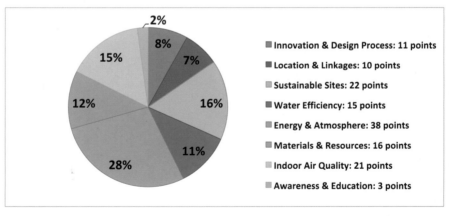

LEED for Homes version 2008 categories and points.

■ Innovation & Design Process: 11 points

■ Location & Linkages: 10 points

■ Sustainable Sites: 22 points

■ Water Efficiency: 15 points

■ Energy & Atmosphere: 38 points

■ Materials & Resources: 16 points

■ Indoor Air Quality: 21 points

■ Awareness & Education: 3 points

2   *LEED Reference Guide for Building Operations and Maintenance* (2013), 4, 133, 306.

3   "USGBC Statistics," published July 1, 2016 and revised October, 2017, https://www.usgbc.org/articles/usgbc-statistics.

with 30 percent at the certified level, 30 percent at silver, 23 percent at gold, and 17 percent at platinum. My goal for our home was to reach at least silver, hopefully gold, but never platinum. I figured that those homes that reach the platinum level were simply spending too much money—paying a lot more for relatively minor benefits, just to achieve the highest level. I wanted to be at the top of the curve, not at the point of diminishing marginal returns. Ultimately, we ended up with 94 LEED points—beating the gold threshold by two and a half points (see *The LEED Checklist* at the end of this book for details).

Two clarifications are needed in talking about LEED. First, *products* are *not* LEED certified, but they may qualify for LEED points (often called "LEED compliant" products). If someone tells you that the product they are selling is LEED certified, they are misinformed. Second, *people* are *not* LEED certified; they are *accredited*—as in, I am a LEED Accredited Professional (there are over 200,000 "LEED APs"). Only buildings and neighborhoods can be LEED certified. The LEED process requires registering the project through the USGBC website and establishing a relationship with a local LEED for Homes Provider before beginning construction.[4]

Why LEED Certification?

The questions I am usually asked are, first, did you get anything for it? No, we did not get anything other than a paper certificate. (New Mexico has a wonderful sustainable building tax credit, and I am hoping other state legislators will follow suit. Our home would have given us almost $23,000 in tax credits, more than paying for the cost of LEED certification.[5])

If we did not get anything for it . . . then why did we do it? Our three reasons for building a sustainable home—for our health, wealth, and soul—could have been pursued *without* LEED certification. So why not just build green and save the hassle and cost of actual certification? Again, three reasons:

First, the LEED for Homes Rating System is an extremely robust set of guidelines and green building principles developed by experts from many different fields in the building industry. It is holistic in both breadth and depth, but more importantly, it provides *metrics* by which we can define and measure our performance. These metrics help us wrap our brain around what we actually mean by building green.

Second, LEED certification requires third-party verification—which means you get the peace of mind knowing that the builder is doing what he says he'll do. Having an owner's advocate like that is truly beneficial, as homes are typically the biggest investment we ever make. And the truth is, if you don't go through the certification process, you will miss something—guaranteed. In my work, I have led

---

4   LEED for Homes Providers can be found through the USGBC website.

5   In New Mexico, a new Sustainable Building Tax Credit program was signed into law in April 2015 (Senate Bill 279) replacing the current program that had been in place since 2007. The new program reduces the amount per square foot a homebuilder or home-buyer receives. See http://www.emnrd.state.nm.us/ECMD/CleanEnergy TaxIncentives/SBTC.html.

the LEED certification of over two million square feet of commercial projects, and we *always* found improvements that the architect, builder, or facilities manager had missed.

Third, many studies have shown that LEED certification increases a building's resale value by 3 to 5 percent. Why? Because LEED certification *communicates* that the first two things above have been accomplished. While difficult to prove with a single-family home, it could make the difference between selling and not selling a home.

The real question everyone wants to know: How much more did you *pay* for LEED certification? There are really two parts to this answer. The first concerns the actual LEED fees: registration, third-party testing and verification, and certification. Those costs came to $3,075, which was paid by our builder, Streeter & Associates. In the USGBC's list of LEED certified projects, Streeter gets the accolades for building a LEED certified home, so it made sense to them to absorb it as a marketing expense; they did not pass the cost on to us directly. Since LEED was new at the time, they were excited about being one of the first ones to go through the process. The fees are broken down as:

- USGBC: $150 registration and $225 for certification = $375.
- Green Rater: $1,800 for all third-party testing and verifications through an organization called the Neighborhood Energy Connection. Jimmie Sparks was our Green Rater; I refer to him often in this book. This included several site visits and inspections, a blower door test, a duct leakage test, a local exhaust test, a supply airflow test, irrigation verification, and energy modeling. (chapter 6, Energy explains this all in more detail.)
- LEED for Homes Provider: $900 to Building Knowledge Inc., who verified all documentation from me, the builder, and the Green Rater. (This fee would have been substantially higher if we had used their consulting services and if I hadn't been the project manager.)

The bigger part of the answer relates to the cost of all the green technologies and features of the home that helped us reach the gold level of LEED certification. How much more did *that* cost? The truth is, some materials cost less than traditional products, some cost more, and for some there was no difference. Many things that did cost more reduced our operating costs so much that we got an easy return on our investment. A few things cost more and have no financial benefit whatsoever. You'll read more about the specific materials and their costs in subsequent chapters.

Architects and builders can be LEED's worst enemy: they say you have to jump through all kinds of hoops, they tell the homeowner it's going to cost 30 percent more (which is false), and they may tack a fee on top of their own just to cover their time to get up the learning curve. This is a shame, I think, because it discourages building owners from ending up with a much better product in the long run. In fact, studies have shown that LEED certified buildings have 34 percent lower CO_2 emissions, consume 25 percent less energy, 11 percent less water, and cost 19 percent less to operate.[6] Every study I have seen and every LEED project I have analyzed has shown a meaningful return on investment.

Now that we have lived in our home for eight years (and through some of our worst winters ever), I can actually say whether our investments that cost more have been worth it. I also know about the things we paid more for but did not get any LEED points for, but were worth it anyway. Conversely, there are things we decided against in order to keep costs down (which may or may not have given us more LEED points); in hindsight I can say which of those things I wish we had invested in, or I'm glad we did not.

So, this book is for you if you want to build to LEED standards—with or without going through the process of getting certified. It is for you if you are interested in how to prioritize green features for your own remodel; maybe you want to understand more about healthy home choices, or focus on those investments that pay for themselves. And it is certainly for you if, like me, you want to do all these things and make the world just a little bit better in the process.

---

6   US Department of Energy Study: "Re-Assessing Green Building Performance: A Post Occupancy Evaluation of 22 GSA Buildings, September 2011," xv. http://www.pnl.gov/main/publications/external/technical_reports/PNNL-19369.pdf.

Photo credit: Karen Melvin

PART I
FOR OUR HEALTH

Who wouldn't want a healthy home? Of course we all do. The US Environmental Protection Agency (EPA) estimates we spend 90 percent of our time indoors, and much of that time is in our homes. But figuring out how to make our homes healthy can be overwhelming. As busy moms, dads, and working professionals, we do not need more on our to-do lists, especially when it concerns house projects.

In 2013, I gave a "Healthy Home" talk to a group of about a hundred women. I lined up some speakers, and we spoke about how cleaning products, home furnishings, and personal care products can all cause health problems. By the end, I think many were in the "ignorance is bliss" camp and wished they hadn't come.

The healthy home topic is one of the most difficult to wrap our brains around, for two reasons. First, it is about our own health, and can often be tied directly to illnesses—which is scary. There are many unknowns with respect to how chemicals and toxins affect our health. Why? One issue is that manufacturers of products (other than food) are not required to reveal what ingredients are included in their products. So, they often don't, leaving us in the dark about what we are buying. Even if products were properly labeled, though, we do not fully understand the *effects* they have on our health. What makes a chemical poison? It can be the amount of exposure at one time (acute toxicity), or minimal exposure over a long period of time (chronic toxicity). Many are bio-accumulative—meaning they build up in our bodies over time, resulting in illnesses for which it may be difficult or impossible to definitively pinpoint a cause. According to the EPA, of the 83,000 chemicals introduced since 1915, only a very small percentage has been tested for adverse health effects.

The second reason is the very topic itself: our own homes, which are full of very personal choices and almost daily purchasing decisions. Most people do not want to tackle the healthy home issue, because they do not want their personal choices evaluated or judged. So, if you are still reading, congratulations! You have made an important step toward a healthier and more sustainable home.

Diet and exercise are often considered the primary influencers of our health. But three other components also have a significant effect: the water we drink, the things we touch that absorb into our skin, and the air we breathe. The LEED for Homes Rating System addresses only the latter under a section called "Indoor Environmental Quality," and offers three types of strategies: source removal, source control, and dilution. Did that last sentence make your eyes glaze over? That's what I thought, which is why I am addressing it differently. My three chapters are actually goals that provide a framework for guiding decisions, and cover more than just indoor air quality: clean water, clean air, and clean house. LEED standards are woven in where relevant.

Photo by Manki Kim on Unsplash

CHAPTER 3: CLEAN WATER

Because of water's pervasiveness, clean water was my number one goal in having a healthy home. We cannot live without water. The human body is more than 60 percent water. Blood is 92 percent water, the brain and muscles are 75 percent water, and bones are about 22 percent water.[7] We drink water, we wash our clothes in water, and water is the main ingredient in many things like coffee, tea, and soups. We bathe in water, and absorb it into our skin.

The fact that we can go into the kitchen, turn on the faucet, and be able to safely drink the water that comes out of the tap all day, every day, without worrying, is really quite amazing. This phenomenon was practically unheard of in our not-so-distant past (like, 140 years ago), and is still merely a dream in many other countries. We can consider ourselves lucky. But that is not to say that we should *not* pay attention to our water and question whether or not it contains contaminants that may be harmful to our health. The Flint, Michigan, water crisis in 2014 is one example, when residents were exposed to dangerous levels of lead in their drinking water.

Where does your drinking water come from? You don't actually have to know this to take action, but if you are curious, just check your city's website. In Minneapolis and many of its surrounding areas, the water comes from the mighty Mississippi River. The City of Minneapolis takes water from the river and runs it through a number of processes, including filtration, disinfection, and sedimentation, in order to reduce impurities. Fluoride is added to tap water to help prevent tooth decay. A variety of tests are performed on our water throughout the treatment process. On average, five hundred chemical, physical, and bacteriological examinations are done each and every day.[8]

The good news about water quality is that there are federal safety standards prescribed by the EPA that limit the amount of certain contaminants in water provided by cities or municipalities. (The US Food and Drug Administration regulates bottled water.) Thanks to the Safe Drinking Water Act of 1974 (and its amendments), the EPA sets national standards, or maximum contaminant levels, to protect

---

7   The Water Information Project, sponsored by the Southwestern Water Conservation District (no date), retrieved January 6, 2016, available: http://www.waterinfo.org/resources/water-facts.
8   The City of Minneapolis website, "About Minneapolis Water," http://www.minneapolismn.gov/publicworks/water/water_waterfacts.

against health risks. Cities and municipalities that supply water must comply with these regulations. The bad news is that the standards allow for some contamination and do not address every possible contaminant.

Every year, the City of Minneapolis releases a Water Quality Report. The results of their tests show that the water quality is high and meets regulations. However, it also shows that there *are* a certain number of contaminants still in the water, and it does not test for everything. According to the City of Minneapolis Water Department, common contaminants include:

- *Microbial contaminants*, such as viruses and bacteria, which may come from sewage treatment plants, septic systems, agricultural livestock operations, and wildlife.
- *Inorganic contaminants*, such as salts and metals, which can be naturally occurring or result from urban stormwater runoff, industrial or domestic wastewater discharges, oil and gas production, mining, or farming.
- *Pesticides and herbicides,* which may come from a variety of sources such as agriculture, urban stormwater runoff, and residential uses.
- *Organic chemical contaminants*, including synthetic and volatile organic chemicals, which are by-products of industrial processes and petroleum production, and can also come from gas stations, urban stormwater runoff, and septic systems.

- *Radioactive contaminants*, which can be naturally occurring or be the result of oil and gas production and mining activities.

Pretty gross, right?! So, what can you do? To begin with, you can test your water. A digital TDS ("Total Dissolved Solids") meter, also known as a PPM ("parts per million") pen, reads the overall purity of your water. The lower the TDS, or PPM, the purer the water is. A reading of zero is pure H_2O. Unfortunately, it does not test for biological contaminants or non-dissolvable solids, like floaties (which you might be able to detect yourself). Floating particles come in two types: inorganic, like silt or clay (which is dirty, but not all that harmful), and organic, like algae and bacteria (which can be quite harmful). The cost of a TDS meter is about $15, and it is reusable. You can also buy a full water testing kit for about $20. This is a one-time-use kit that tests the levels of pesticides, chlorine, nitrates, lead, pH level, and hardness. Either of these will help determine whether further action is needed. Your budget and construction or renovation project timing might also determine what you can do, so here are three different options.

Low Cost/Just the Basics Option: Filter just your drinking water on an as-needed basis. A Brita five-cup water filter that you keep in your fridge is about $11, and a single filter (about $5 each) can replace up to 300 bottles of water. (I am using Brita as an example; there are other good products on the market as well.) The filtration system decreases chlorine taste and odor, as well as zinc, copper, mercury, and cadmium often found in tap water. It is not designed to remove fluoride, or to purify water, but it does make water taste better.

Medium Cost Option: Get a reverse-osmosis filter for your kitchen sink and a chlorine filter for your showerhead. A reverse osmosis (RO) system is a process of purifying water through a semipermeable membrane. RO systems do the best job of getting your water closest to pure H_2O, though results vary greatly across different systems. It takes time for the RO system to work and can only produce a limited amount of RO water each day—though it should be enough for drinking and cooking. RO systems have separate faucets, because the water pressure is lower and the plumbing is separate, so you would need to have the space on your counter for another water dispenser. A basic General Electric system that can be installed under a sink is $147 at Home Depot; a fancier one at Costco is $289. This should take care of your drinking water, as long as the filters are changed regularly.

For bathing, the biggest concern is the chlorine that water treatment centers add to water to eliminate bacteria. Chlorine is very damaging to skin and hair and is unhealthy to breathe in. There are many options available that attach to the showerhead (or bathtub faucet) and filter the chlorine directly, avoiding more costly whole-house filtration systems. Shower filters range in price from $20 to $40 and are fairly easy to install. (And while you're at it, make it a low-flow showerhead to conserve water and save money.)

Highest Cost/Most Thorough Option: Whole-house carbon filtration systems filter chlorine and many other contaminants from your water at the point at which the water source is plumbed into your house. The benefit of this is that you do not need to install individual filters at each shower, bath, sink, and laundry outlet. A once-a-year service takes care of all the filtering issues at the same time, so you don't have to worry about it the rest of the year.

This does involve hiring someone, unless you are a stellar do-it-yourselfer; hence the higher cost. The upside is that the installer will do the water testing for you to ensure the equipment is appropriately filtering your water. If the installer is any good, he or she will provide you with before and after results. Before hiring, make sure water testing is part of their standard protocol—otherwise, how will you know it works?

The cost of these systems is between $1,000 and $1,500, depending on your subcontractor. The systems come with a carbon filter to remove the organics in the water, which is primarily chlorine. What remains is about one hundred parts per million of minerals, and fluoride stays in the water. This should take care of all water needs, except drinking water.

For drinking water, a whole-house RO system can be used instead of individual under-the-counter systems. It is an additional step that can be done during construction; it's especially nice for icemakers. Doing this for your whole house requires that the installer run the pipes to the different sinks where you want drinking water.

The Fluoride Controversy

Those of us who did *not* live in the first half of the twentieth century should thank our lucky stars! In those years, tooth decay was common, there was no known method of prevention, and the only treatment was tooth extraction—which was painful and could lead to disease. Fluoride has been credited with the reduction of the prevalence and severity of dental caries, another word for tooth decay. Adding fluoride to drinking water, a practice that began in the 1940s and 1950s, has been touted as one of the top ten great public health achievements of the twentieth century.[9]

According to the Centers for Disease Control and Prevention, 75 percent of the US population served by community water systems receives fluoridated water. The idea that we still need fluoride in our drinking water continues to be challenged by a whole host of activists, conspiracy theorists, and just plain old health advocates.

I have pored over the research on this controversial topic. It seems that fluoride *may* help in preventing tooth decay, but mostly due to the tooth itself being exposed to fluoride topically. It is unclear from the research whether *ingesting* it would still be the preferred method. Initially, the thought was that by adding it to the water supply, everyone would be better off—not just those who could afford it or had access to better dental care. Now, though, fluoride is prevalent in toothpaste and mouth rinses, and regular dental checkups for kids include fluoride treatment. Additional research still questions whether the decline in dental caries is due to the fluoridation of drinking water, or some combination of greater use of antibiotics, improved vitamin and mineral consumption, and overall improved dental and health care.[10]

Similar to many vitamins and minerals that claim health benefits, too much of a good thing can pose a risk. What is the risk of too much fluoride? The American Dental Association (ADA), the primary advocate for adding fluoride to drinking water, says it can cause mottled enamel, or fluorosis—white patches or streaks across the tooth enamel—as well as bone weakness or fractures. But these risks are low, because fluoride levels in drinking water are very low—less than the maximum allowed 4.0 milligrams per liter, and generally at the 0.7 milligrams per liter level required by some state laws (the "optimal" level). The ADA warns consumers: "Be aware of misinformation on the Internet and other junk science related to water fluoridation."[11]

---

9   Centers for Disease Control and Prevention, "Ten Great Public Health Achievements in the 20th Century," https://www.cdc.gov/about/history/tengpha.htm.

10 Eugenio D. Beltran, DDS, MPH, and Brian A. Burt, BDS, MPH, PhD, "The Pre- and Post-eruptive Effects of Fluoride in the Caries," *Journal of Public Health Dentistry* (vol. 48, no. 4, Fall 1988).

11 American Dental Association, "Fluoridation Facts," http://www.ada.org/~/media/ADA/Member%20 Center/FIles/fluoridation_facts.ashx.

This topic continues to be studied outside the confines of the ADA, some of which does not appear to be "junk science." According to the Harvard T.H. Chan School of Public Health, exposure to higher levels of fluoride causes neurotoxicity in adults.[12] More concerning, a research study in China found that children who lived in areas with high fluoride exposure had significantly lower IQ scores than those who lived in low-exposure areas.[13]

What I find most puzzling is how we treat children under six years old: dentists and pediatricians recommend that we *add* fluoride back into our filtered water, yet at the same time they tell us to not let them have toothpaste with fluoride in it, because they might swallow it. Where is the logic?

Then there's the "gross" factor. The City of Minneapolis Water Quality Report says that the State of Minnesota requires all municipal water systems to add fluoride to the drinking water to promote strong teeth. Where does the City of Minneapolis source its fluoride? It comes from the discharge of fertilizer and aluminum factories.[14] That just sounds disgusting—and was my final straw in deciding to thoroughly filter our water and rid it of fluoride.

---

12 Harvard School of Public Health, "Impact of Fluoride on Neurological Development in Children," https://www.hsph.harvard.edu/news/features/fluoride-childrens-health-grandjean-choi/.

13 Choi AL, Sun G, Zhang Y, Grandjean P. 2012. "Developmental Fluoride Neurotoxicity: A Systematic Review and Meta-Analysis." *Environ Health Perspect* 120:1362–1368; http://dx.doi.org/10.1289/ehp .1104912.

14 The City of Minneapolis Water Quality Report, http://www.minneapolismn.gov/www/groups/public /@publicworks/documents/webcontent/wcms1p-093798.pdf.

Despite our pediatrician and dentist recommending that we *add* fluoride to our children's drinking water, we have made the decision that we do not want to *drink* fluoride—or any other contaminant, for that matter—pure H_2O is what we want. So, we installed a reverse osmosis plus deionizer (RO/DI) system for drinking water only. (Water distillation also removes fluoride.) RO/DI is a proprietary technology made by Aquathin Corporation. It removes fluoride as well as other dissolved solids and chemicals that are suspended.

We were lucky enough to have met Richard Grassie of Richard's Water Systems to help us through the process and explain the differences. Most passionate about water quality, he's my go-to source for healthy water. When the City of Blaine, Minnesota, tested for *E. coli* in the water, Richard's clients were the only ones that did not have to worry, since the multi-barrier RO/DI system removes disease-causing micro-born organisms.

The downside of RO systems is that they do waste water. For every one gallon we drink,

	MULTI-BARRIER RO/DI	REVERSE OSMOSIS	CARBON FILTER	DISTILLATION MACHINE
MICRO-ORGANISMS				
Fecal Coliform	A+	F	F	A+
Cysts - Crypto, Giardia	A+	F	F	A+
Virus	A+	F	F	A+
INORGANIC				
Heavy Metals	A+	B+	F	A
Asbestos	A+	B	F	A
Arsenic	A+	B-	F	A
Flouride	A+	B-	F	A
Nitrate	A+	C	F	A
Sodium	A+	B-	F	A
Hardness	A+	B	F	A
Iron	A+	F	F	A
Total Dissolved Solids	A+	B	F	A
ORGANIC				
Chemical Solvents	A+	C	A-	B-
Pesticides	A+	C	A-	B-
Herbicides	A+	C	A	B
QUALITY				
Taste	A+	B	B	B
Odor	A+	B	B	B

Source: Richard's Water Systems.

three gallons go down the drain. But compared to what? If we would otherwise purchase bottled water for drinking, there is hardly any comparison—bottled water is much worse from a wastefulness perspective. In considering your budget, it is important to factor in the reduction in bottled water that you would otherwise need to buy. These single-use bottles are a major trash and recycling issue, not to mention costly. Bringing our own water with us, in our own reusable water bottles, is one of the best things we can do to have a positive impact on the environment *and* ensure we are reducing our exposure to potentially harmful contaminants. And, substituting our own

clean filtered water for bottled water saves money.

Reverse osmosis has gotten a bad reputation among some purists who think that we are killing the water and removing all the "beneficial" minerals water normally carries, like calcium and magnesium. The health of our drinking water quality can be very confusing, and it is difficult to know whom to trust.

One way to look at it is to assume that there are fifty different things in the water, and only five of them are beneficial. No technology exists that eliminates the forty-five harmful contaminants and leaves only the five beneficial ingredients. So, wouldn't you rather get

Separate RO faucet for drinking water, on the left.

Our RO/DI filtered drinking water test result: 5 PPM.

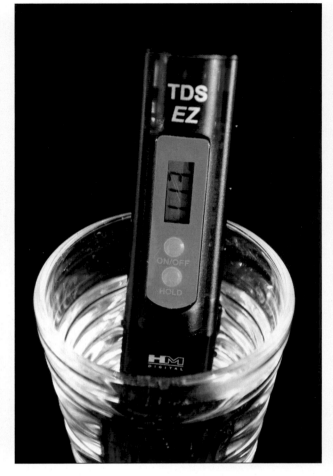

Our whole-house filtered water (non-drinking) test result: 113 PPM.

rid of *all* fifty non-H_2O particles, and have pure water? Then, if we are missing beneficial minerals, we can get them from our food (as opposed to dissolved rock).

We ended up installing one seven-gallon RO/DI system that serves the whole house for drinking water. We have small faucets in our upstairs bathrooms in addition to one in our kitchen. It is, perhaps, one of my favorite things about our house, because I don't have to go downstairs to get drinkable water at night, and I know our drinking water is safe.

The cost of the system was $1,500, and annual maintenance runs between $130 and $300. But the real question is: does it work? I have a water tester that shows the parts per million (PPM) of anything other than pure H_2O in the water. A recent testing of our RO/DI water demonstrated only 5 PPM—practically pure H_2O. The whole-house filtered non-RO/DI water (for washing, etc.) got us to 113 PPM, still well below the maximum EPA level of 500 PPM.

Having great drinking water delivered through the infrastructure of pipes is much more sustainable than getting big jugs of bottled water delivered, or worse, purchasing cases of bottled water for home drinking. I'm not going to go into all the deleterious effects bottled water has on our planet, but just read Elizabeth Royte's *Bottlemania: Big Business, Local Springs, and the Battle over America's Drinking Water* and you, too, will become morally opposed to bottled water.

The LEED for Homes Rating System does not address water *quality* at all, only water efficiency. In other LEED rating systems (for commercial or multi-family buildings), you can earn one LEED point as an innovation credit for adding a whole building water filtration system, thereby reducing or eliminating the need for bottled water.[15] But you'd have to have researched it yourself; LEED does not offer it up as an important strategy, unfortunately. So for the number one most important component of a healthy home, we did not achieve any LEED points.

Seven-gallon reverse osmosis drinking water tank.

---

15 USGBC, "Credit Interpretation Ruling number 2551," made April 22, 2009, https://www.usgbc.org/leed-interpretations?clearsmartf=true&keys=2551.

CHAPTER 4: CLEAN AIR

The EPA estimates that air inside homes can be three to five times more polluted than outdoor air, even in large industrialized cities. Why? Home building products, furnishing, cleaning supplies, and just day-to-day living can produce many pollutants. At the same time, homes have gotten tighter and more energy-efficient, so outdoor air cannot seep through and ventilate the indoor air. Because we are exposed to the air that we breathe 100 percent of the time, clean air was my second highest priority.

In green building literature, the primary aspect of a healthy home is indoor air quality. How many times have you walked into a home and smelled a peculiar odor? Does your own home have a smell? That can be a sign of an unhealthy home. Clean air has no smell at all, so that's the goal.

My two primary resources for healthy home decisions were Athena Thomson's *Homes That Heal and Those That Don't*, and Paula Baker LaPorte's *Prescriptions for a Healthy Home*. As I am not medically trained, I do not have much to add to those books, except to share the part that those books do not help you with: the effect on our bank account, living with the decisions we made, and whether they had

anything to do with getting our home LEED certified.

Many people think that if they have odors in their home, the best thing to do is to use air fresheners or scented candles. Aren't we all pummeled with advertisements to make us think we will be happier if we spray air freshener in our home? This actually worsens the problem, because air fresheners do not actually freshen the air—they just cover up other odors and make it harder to find the source to eliminate it. Additionally, many air fresheners contain toxic ingredients that are bad for human health. The Environmental Working Group's (EWG) online *Guide to Healthy Living* examined 277 air fresheners, and of those, over 82 percent got a D or F in terms of high concern for causing harm, mostly in the areas of developmental and reproductive toxicity, with some concern for skin irritation and asthma/respiratory issues. The EWG emphasizes the importance of choosing products whose labels say "fragrance free" and giving up air fresheners.[16]

According to the EWG, scented candles, like air fresheners, release mixtures of undisclosed fragrance chemicals into the air to

---

16 Environmental Working Group, "EWG's Healthy Living Home Guide."

cover up other odors. Even unscented candles can be harmful to your health. Most candles on the market today are made of paraffin wax, which is a petroleum-based product manufactured as a by-product of oil refining. So basically, you're burning a fossil fuel in your home without venting it outside. Candles made from paraffin, when burned over time, leave black soot stains on ceilings, walls, and furniture. And guess what? Those tiny black soot particles that leave stains are easily inhaled and can cause respiratory illnesses. If you want to burn candles, choose fragrance free candles made from soy or beeswax. If you want scents in your home, consider an aromatherapy diffuser, and use essential oils derived from plants.

This section actually lends itself well to LEED's prescribed three strategies of clean air: source removal, source control, and dilution. Starting with source removal makes sense, because it means *not* introducing materials in the house that off-gas in the first place. LEED refers to this as category as "low emission" materials; I like to call it "off-gassing."

Off-gassing

You may be skeptical: how do you know if the things in your house are off-gassing and that they are harmful to your health? Fair question. First, do the smell test: hold a sample of whatever it is up to your nose and breathe in deeply. If it stinks, it is off-gassing. It may even give you an immediate headache. Builders will tell you that it airs out: the solution to pollution is dilution! Well, yes, the smell does tend to go away, but inhabitants also tend to get used to it.

We have firsthand experience with installing new shades in our previous home, which caused severe headaches for my husband and me. We actually moved out of our home while they aired out, because I was pregnant at the time and was worried about the effects it would have on our baby. It turns out that those shades contained vinyl—that was the cause of the smell. So now, we are careful to choose products that do not contain vinyl!

If the smell doesn't get you, try to find the ingredients of the building material or furnishings. Every building material is required to have a Safety Data Sheet (SDS; formerly "MSDS"—Material Safety Data Sheet). Safety Data Sheets are designed to provide both workers and emergency personnel with the proper procedures for handling or working with a particular material. SDS sheets include information such as physical data (e.g., melting point, boiling point), toxicity, health effects, first aid, storage, protective equipment, and disposal. What is interesting is that Safety Data Sheets are meant for *employees* who may be exposed to a hazard at work—not for consumers. An SDS for paint, for example, is supposedly only important to someone who paints all day, every day. That does not sit well with me. Even if my family will not be exposed to something toxic all day every day, we will still have *some* exposure. Who is to say what is a tolerable level of poison? And, I actually do care about the workers who are building our house; it's not okay if they are exposed to toxic products due to our choices.

If you still do not know whether a product off-gasses, there are ways to measure indoor air quality. Find a building biologist in your area, and he or she most likely has appropriate testing equipment. Or just invite over a friend who has allergies or asthma—we can tell you right away.

While hundreds of products off-gas, I'm focusing on the two highest priority issues that all of my research, and the LEED for Homes Rating System, deem to be most important: formaldehyde and volatile organic compounds (VOCs).

FORMALDEHYDE

According to the Centers for Disease Control and Prevention, formaldehyde is a colorless, pungent-smelling gas. Sources of formaldehyde in the home include fiberglass, carpets, permanent press fabrics, paper products, and manufactured, pressed wood products. Pressed wood products made for indoor use include: particleboard (used as sub-flooring and shelving and in cabinetry and furniture); hardwood plywood paneling (used for decorative wall covering and in cabinets and furniture); and medium density fiberboard (used for drawer fronts and cabinets).

What happens when someone is exposed to elevated levels of formaldehyde (above 0.1 parts per million)? Symptoms include sore throat, cough, scratchy and watery eyes, nosebleeds, nausea, fatigue, and difficulty breathing. Additionally, formaldehyde is known to cause cancer, primarily of the nose and throat. Scientific research has not yet shown that a certain *level* of formaldehyde exposure causes cancer; however, the higher the level and the longer the exposure, the greater the chance of getting cancer.[17]

The technical term for the additive is "urea formaldehyde" (UF), as formaldehyde itself can be naturally occurring. UF resins are the primary adhesives for wood products because of their high tensile strength, low cost, ease of use, versatility, lack of color of the cured product, and because they are some of the fastest curing resins available.[18]

In July 2006, just after we bought our property and were starting the planning process, a very disturbing piece of news came out about the Federal Emergency Management Agency (FEMA) trailers that were housing Hurricane Katrina victims:

> For nearly a year now, the ubiquitous FEMA trailer has sheltered tens of thousands of Gulf Coast residents left homeless by Hurricane Katrina. But there is growing concern that even as it staved off the elements, it was exposing its inhabitants to a toxic gas that could pose both immediate and long-term health risks.
>
> The gas is formaldehyde, the airborne form of a chemical used in a wide variety of products, including composite wood and plywood panels in the thousands of travel trailers that the Federal Emergency Management Agency purchased after Katrina to house hurricane victims. It also is considered a human carcinogen, or cancer-causing substance, by the International Agency for Research on Cancer and a probable

---

17 Centers for Diseases Control and Prevention, "What You Should Know About Formaldehyde," https://www.cdc.gov/nceh/drywall/docs/WhatYouShouldKnowaboutFormaldehyde.pdf.

18 Polymer Properties Database, CROW 2015.

human carcinogen by the US Environmental Protection Agency.

Air quality tests of forty-four FEMA trailers conducted by the Sierra Club since April have found formaldehyde concentrations as high as 0.34 parts per million—a level nearly equal to what a professional embalmer would be exposed to on the job, according to one study of the chemical's workplace effects.

And all but four of the trailers have tested higher than the 0.1 parts per million that the EPA considers to be an "elevated level" capable of causing watery eyes, burning in the eyes and throat, nausea, and respiratory distress in some people.[19]

While it was devastating that victims of Hurricane Katrina were getting ill from FEMA trailers, it may have helped change public policy. Due to the prevalence of UF in the wood products industry[20] and the health concerns over formaldehyde emissions, the Formaldehyde Standards for Composite Wood Products Act was passed in 2010. This law, now Title VI of the Toxic Substances Control Act (TSCA), is designed to establish limits for formaldehyde emissions from composite wood products. It has taken the EPA several years to issue rulings on implementing and enforcing this new law, though; the new formaldehyde emission standards go into effect beginning December 12, 2018.

But we were choosing cabinetry back in 2008, before any legislation was passed to reduce exposure to formaldehyde. To specify that we did not want it in our home, we had to ask for "non-added urea formaldehyde," or NAUF. We actually chose our cabinetmaker, Damschen Wood, because they were one of the few subcontractors who did not look at us like a deer in headlights when we asked to use only NAUF particleboard and medium-density fiberboard (MDF), common panels for cabinetry. They were on board with this health issue and had already found suppliers for NAUF wood. But in 2008, that cost us! An analysis of our proposal showed that for raw MDF, NAUF cost us 16.5 percent more, and for raw particleboard, NAUF cost us a whopping 44 percent more. On average, NAUF cabinetry core for our entire home cost us 30 percent more.

Our choice for cabinetry on the main level was vertical grain fir, which, with the NAUF specification, cost $111.30 per 4x8-foot ¾-inch sheet. That made for some expensive cabinetry. But for our entire lower level (which we decided to partially finish about midway through our project), we decided to go with clear-coated NAUF MDF, which was $29.90 per sheet—a *much more* affordable solution. Clear-coated MDF actually looks great and so far has worn extremely well. It has no more nicks or dents than any other vertical grain fir piece of cabinetry. I would not recommend it for horizontal surfaces, though, because if it

---

19 Mike Brunker, MSNBC.com, "Are FEMA Trailers Toxic Tin Cans?" http://www.nbcnews.com/id/14011193/ns /us_news-katrina_the_long_road_back/t/are-fema-trailers-toxic-tin-cans/#.WgjC9WWbzKk.

20 The global formaldehyde market was worth almost $11 billion in 2012 and is expected to reach $18 billion by 2018, according to Transparency Market Research.

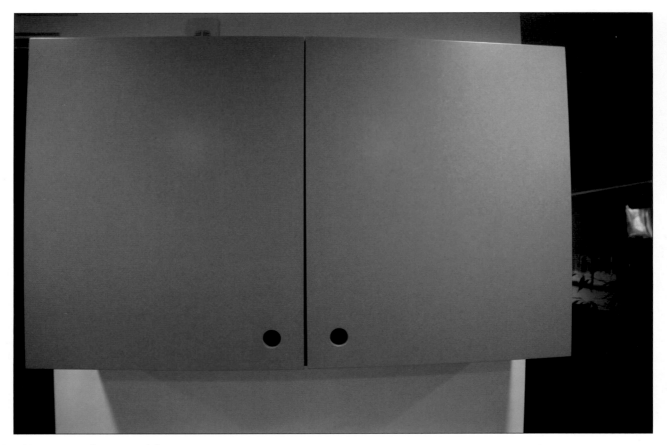

Clear-coated MDF cabinetry.

gets wet, it expands significantly. Given what I knew about formaldehyde, this was an added cost that we deemed necessary.

Thankfully, because of Title VI of the Toxic Substances Control Act, it should be easier to find cabinetry that does not off-gas formaldehyde, and the price has come down. However, consumers still need to be on top of this issue. The EPA is recommending that, when shopping for composite wood products or finished goods containing composite wood products, consumers should look for products that are labeled *TSCA Title VI compliant*.[21] Yet another difficult term to remember—I wish they had stuck with NAUF!

While LEED recognizes the importance of cabinets, counters, and trim containing no added urea formaldehyde, it only awards points if these *also* meet its broader definition "environmentally preferable products"—that is, made out of recycled content or forest stewardship council certified wood. Our trim and countertops met both definitions, but our cabinets did not qualify (see *Materials* chapter 9).

21 US Environmental Protection Agency, "EPA's Rule to Implement the Formaldehyde Standards for Composite Wood Products Act," July 2016 (Revised January 2017), EPA-950-F-17-001.

VOCs

Volatile organic compounds (VOCs) are a class of carbon-based compounds that readily become volatile under ordinary atmospheric conditions. In other words, they are gases that are emitted from certain solids or liquids, and they can have adverse health effects.

According to the EPA, VOCs are emitted by thousands of products. Examples include paints and lacquers, paint strippers, cleaning supplies, pesticides, building materials and furnishings, office equipment such as copiers and printers, graphics and craft materials including glues and adhesives, permanent markers, and photographic solutions.

There are many known health risks to VOC exposure: eye, nose, and throat irritation; headaches, loss of coordination, nausea, memory impairment; damage to liver, kidney, and central nervous system; allergic skin reaction; fatigue and dizziness. Similar to exposure to other toxins, the health effects vary dependent on the length of time exposed, the concentration of the substance that contains the VOCs, and the overall level of toxicity. VOCs are also large contributors to pollution and smog. In Southern California, the South Coast Air Quality Management District (SCAQMD), estimates that 13 percent of the ozone-forming pollution comes from VOCs from paints and solvents.

To understand what you are buying, the best thing to do is read the label on the product. VOCs are characterized as grams per liter, or g/L, excluding any water or tinting added at the point of sale. There are federal limits that define "low" and "no" VOCs, as regulated by the EPA.

Many states and regions have required even lower VOC levels (from federal regulations) for paints that can be legally sold in their areas. Southern California's SCAQMD, for example, has one of the most stringent standard for VOCs; these are the same standards adopted for LEED certification across all rating systems (homes as well as commercial buildings). Different standards apply to different types of products; the following discusses five home construction categories where we had to pay attention to VOCs.

Flooring

The Carpet and Rug Institute (CRI) Green Label Plus program sets high standards for indoor air quality and ensures carpets with this label have very low emissions. According to LEED, low-emissions flooring is attained if at least 90 percent of the flooring is CRI Green Label Plus carpet with CRI Green Label pad, or at least 90 percent of the flooring is hard surface flooring (or some combination of these). It was not difficult to find carpet that meets this standard, and the options keep expanding. Carpet padding that complies was slightly more difficult to find, and if you do not ask for it, you probably won't get it, because carpet padding is one of those hidden things that once everything is installed, you can't see it. But if it does off-gas—you'll notice it, and not in a good way!

We chose a wool carpet that is CRI certified, and we love it. Wool carpeting is more expensive than non-wool; this is a design feature that we believe is well worth the extra cost for its look, feel, durability, and because it is a natural material. The rest of our flooring

Carpet is Green Label Plus certified for low emissions.

is hard surface (slate tile, unfinished concrete, and cork), so we got a half point there.

For hard surface flooring, FloorScore is the trusted certification to meet LEED's indoor air quality performance standards. Our slate flooring is not FloorScore certified, because stone has no emissions, other than the potential for radon. The FloorScore low emissions rating is more important for flooring types that typically do have emissions: engineered hardwood, bamboo, rubber, and laminate.

Interior paints and coatings

Paints, coatings, and primers applied to interior walls and ceilings have VOC standards: they must be a maximum of 50 grams per liter (g/L) for flats and 150 g/L for non-flats. This was (and still is) a very easy standard to meet—but we got there in a roundabout way. We were attempting to find alternatives to paint, because I honestly do not believe "environmentally friendly" paint exists (well, maybe milk paint—a potentially good option for those who want a more rustic, antique look).

During one of my visits to Natural Built Home, a local store that carries natural building supplies, I learned about a product called American Clay. American Clay is a plaster, an alternative to paint and other types of plaster for walls. It comes in all kinds of earthy colors and has a warm, homey feel. It also has amazing features: it is made of only natural materials, has

Sample colors of American Clay plaster.

zero VOC, and helps regulate humid air inside buildings by absorbing and releasing moisture naturally. So of course I wanted American Clay on all of our walls. In fact, the more I learned about paint, the more I could not understand why anyone would want paint anywhere near their home! It is, after all, a toxic chemical. It cannot be put down the drain; it has to be disposed of at a toxic waste dump.

I bought a lovely box of all the American Clay sample colors. Our architect was somewhat disturbed that there was no pure white, but I thought we could work through that. We were going to have fir ceilings and many windows, so I figured it would not be that much money to plaster the remaining walls.

Then the estimate came back. It was going to cost us almost twice as much as paint to have American Clay plaster on all of our walls. So, we thought, maybe we don't need it in the garage, or the bedrooms, or the ceiling (which we decided to paint instead of installing fir strips–both because it cost too much and it seemed like unnecessary use of materials). How about just the main room? What about the trim? Wouldn't it start looking a bit odd if we chose just a few walls for the clay plaster?

Ultimately, our budget did not allow for the clay plaster. I was disappointed, but also somewhat relieved, due to a few unknowns. Like, what happens when you rub up against it—will your clothes get dirty (because they seemed to with the sample we had)? How easily is the finish nicked or damaged? How would we do touch-ups? Our architect was thrilled—he loves the pure white paint, as well as some of the other colors that real paint offers, but clay plaster does not.

Environmentally-friendly paint is a bit of an oxymoron, but conventional wisdom says that it is simply just low- and no-VOC paint. So I researched a little more. I learned that you could buy no-VOC white and light colored paint, but any paint with a strong color tint cannot be no-VOC; it can only be low-VOC at a minimum. In the end, we acquiesced and went with more standard construction practices for "environmentally-friendly" paint. All of our paints were no-VOC Benjamin Moore Aura, so we met that requirement, earning a half point for LEED, and our house did not stink when we moved in.

The obvious next questions: do no- and low-VOC paints work as well, and do they cost more? For interior paints and sealants, it has been my personal experience that there is absolutely no difference in quality, and there is an enormous difference in smell. It is truly amazing to walk into a home that was just painted that day with no-VOC paint, and there is virtually no smell, no headaches, and no dizziness.

What's more, the painters appreciate it! They have to work every day with exposure to toxins, and they can really tell the difference. The times I have had work done on our house, the painters have specifically thanked me for choosing those types of paints and sealants. They have also confirmed there is no difference in quality. According to Consumer Reports' *Paint Buying Guide,* "earlier low-VOC paints lacked the durability of higher-VOC finishes, but now all of the paints in our tests are claimed to have low or no-VOCs and many performed very well."

It is difficult to compare costs of paint, because branding, distribution, quality, the number of coats you'll need, etc. have a lot to do with pricing. Yolo paints sell at Home Depot and Amazon for $36 per gallon, and they have no-VOC plus other added low-toxic benefits. A competing product, Jeff Lewis Color brand at Home Depot, is "ultra low VOC" (less than 15 grams per liter), so not "no-VOC" but still pretty good. This sells for about $40 per gallon at Home Depot: $4 more per gallon, and a little less healthy. So while this is just one example, I would definitely say that low- or no-VOC products *do not cost more*. Besides, paint is one of those things *not* to skimp on, because low-quality paint will just require refinishing more frequently, costing more in the long run.

Another paint selection tip is to look for products that carry one of the recognized green stamps of approval: the Green Seal or GREENGUARD certification mark. GREENGUARD certification has strict emissions criteria and focuses primarily on healthy indoor air quality.[22] Green Seal, a nonprofit organization formed in 1989, seeks to help consumers find truly green products by certifying household products, construction materials, paints and coatings, paper, and personal care products. Beyond low

---

22 GREENGUARD certification is part of UL Environment; all GREENGUARD certified products are listed in the UL SPOT Sustainable Product Database.

VOC emissions, Green Seal also ensures that a product has a safer formula, reduced packaging, user instructions, and many other significant qualities that are specifically defined within each of its thirty-two environmental leadership standards—so it is a more holistic green label.[23] Ultimately, because no- and low-VOC paints and sealants perform just as well, are better for your health and the environment, *and* do not cost more, there is absolutely no reason to choose anything else.

If we were to actually *not* use paint anywhere, there is still the issue of wood finishes. Wood cannot really be left without a finish, because it can  rot, splinter, and generally decay. Finishes help preserve the wood and keep it beautiful. Yet, like paint, most finishes are high-VOC and solvent-based. We talked with our paint subcontractor, and they agreed to try a new water-based product for all of our interior reclaimed wood.

The LEED requirement is that clear wood finish lacquers must be less than 550 g/L, 350 g/L for varnishes, and sealers must be 250 g/L. (There are more standards for shellacs, stains, floor coatings, and antirust paints. Some are based on Green Seal standards, some on South Coast Air Quality standards; we did not use them, so I won't go into those details.) The interior wood finish we used on the window trim was Agualente, which is GREEN-GUARD certified and has a VOC level of 100 g/L, easily beating the requirement for low emissions. For the reclaimed wood stairs, we used BioShield Hard Oil #9, made primarily of linseed oil and tung oil, and also low VOC (though just meeting the 250/L VOC limit for LEED).

I went to our house while the workers were applying the finish. Matt, a twenty-something painter, was for the first time working *without* a mask covering his face. I was concerned about the performance of these "non-standard" products I insisted on using. So, I asked Matt how the BioShield and Agualente products hold up over time. He replied, "I don't know. This is the first time we've used them. But it's nice to go home without heartburn every night." I groaned. "No, really? You have heartburn every night using the [petroleum-based] finish you normally use?" "Yeah. But a job is a job!" I went home distressed, wondering why we humans make stuff that is so bad for us.

Now, I can answer how it holds up over time: so far so good. After eight years of no maintenance, we do need to reapply the finish around some of the wood window trim, but the stairs are fine. We've had several painters look at them, and they are in much better condition than they expected. And it never stunk. We earned a half LEED point here for low emission paints and coatings.

Adhesives and sealants

The rules for adhesives and sealants are more confusing; they must comply with a long list of VOC content levels that adhere to the South Coast Air Quality Management District Rule

---

23 Information from Doug Gatlin, CEO of Green Seal. *Green Seal-certified paints and coatings, and the Green Seal Standard for Paints, Coatings, Stains, and Finishes* can be found at www.greenseal.org/GS11.

#1168.[24] *Sealants* were a whole new ball of wax for me, as I did not know what needed to be sealed. Apparently our concrete floors in our basement and garage did need sealing, but the exposed concrete walls in our basement did not. Our slate floor tiles on the main level *could* be sealed, but did not have to be. It seems that once you seal something, it will need to be *resealed* at some point. So, we chose *not* to seal anything where our builder thought it was optional.

For the concrete flooring, we used a product made by Green Building Supply, an environmentally friendly home store out of Fairfield, Iowa. Our builders had never used a sealant like this before, and they complained and moaned while installing it. *Not* because it stunk, or didn't seem to work, but because it

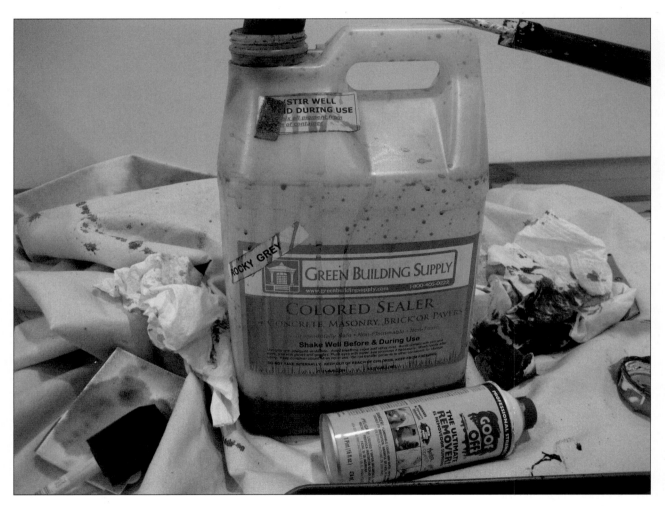

Concrete floor sealant from Green Building Supply.

24 See www.aqmd.gov for more information.

went on a little haphazardly—not smooth like the oil they were used to applying. It looked fine—just like exposed concrete. Our garage has a few small pits in it and does need resealing, but that is to be expected after eight years of living and driving in the wintery salted streets of Minneapolis.

While we were quite clear what we wanted in terms of non-off-gassing adhesives, there were so many different types of caulking, foams, etc. that served some function unknown to me but essential to the subcontractor, it was impossible for me to verify that every one of them complied with the standards. I would have had to be at the house every day (I almost was), examining every little tube each worker was using. We did not pursue this LEED point, as I did not deem these smaller products important and impactful enough to spend the time it would have required.

Insulation

To ensure low emissions, products must comply with California's Practice for Testing VOCs from Building Materials Using Small Chambers.[25] The only way to know that is to just ask the manufacturer or installer; ours had no idea. We used closed-cell polyurethane spray foam, which is highly toxic while it is being installed, so I had to assume it did not comply. I have been assured that once the insulation is sprayed, it becomes completely inert, and that there is no off-gassing. So while we did not get the LEED credit, the insulation we chose was worth it for the energy savings (see chapter 6, Energy).

Exterior finishes

All of these standards are for the inside of the home; the outside is not regulated by LEED, because this section only addresses *indoor* environmental quality. But I still care about *not* polluting the outdoors, so I looked into the finishes.

Our house is supported by steel columns that hold up the beams that span across our twenty-four-foot-wide home. That steel also needed to be sealed, according to our builders, or it would rust. The builders were quite concerned about the possibility of rust, and rightly so—the entire structural integrity of the house would be compromised if these columns decomposed. Our architect wanted to paint the columns. Our builder said that we would need to reapply paint at least every five years to prevent rust, and once the house was built, it would be really hard to ensure paint covered all sides of the steel column. So, our builder suggested we galvanize the steel. What does that mean? It means that the steel is dipped in zinc, which protects the steel from corrosion, and it will never need painting. It would look like street sign posts. I liked that idea, so we went with it. Our architect decided that not painting them is more "honest." I'm happy we found one application to *not* use paint. And since both steel and zinc are abundant and 100 percent recyclable, galvanized steel is a great building material.

---

25 Updated in January 2017, this product emissions testing protocol provides a basis for testing indoor air emissions; it is fully transparent and has become the accepted standard. See standards.nsf.org.

Steel columns under construction.

(Having said that, there is an environmental tradeoff: metals are mined, and the operations and waste products of mined metals can cause physical site disturbances and soil and water contamination. In this case, a strong, virtually rust-proof product that lasts a very long time outweighs these concerns—though that is a matter of opinion.)

For exterior wood sealants, I have yet to find a low-VOC product that works well. The problem is that most water-based paints and sealants do not provide a protective coating for exteriors that ward off rain and snow. We had to resort to solvent-based products, and they do stink. It's not a huge deal, because it is outside and can air out fairly quickly. And, as standards become more stringent, more products that *can* do the job well are becoming available. I would just say that if you can live without the beautiful aesthetic of wood on your exterior, then avoid it. It is a maintenance issue every year. It is a big expense every

Steel columns support the home. Photo credit: Paul Crosby.

summer. And if we miss a summer, like we did in 2017 (only for part of the house, while we tried to figure out a new product), the wood looks pretty bad—and I get bawled out by my father-in-law for neglecting my home.

So, under my category of off-gassing, which LEED refers to as "low emissions," we earned one LEED point—a half for the carpet and a half for the paint—neither of which cost more.

Radon

Another important component of clean air is radon prevention. Radon—that scary, silent, odorless gas—is, according to the EPA, responsible for 21,000 lung cancer deaths per year and is the second leading cause of lung cancer after cigarette smoking. Additionally, nearly one out of every fifteen homes in the United States is estimated to have elevated radon levels, and elevated levels of radon gas have been found in homes in every state. Radon comes from the natural, yet radioactive, breakdown of uranium in soil, rock, and water, and it gets into the air we breathe.

Weathered cedar window boxes.

LEED for Homes takes the precautionary route by requiring radon-resistant construction in high-risk areas as a prerequisite. Hennepin County, where we live, is rated as Zone One—a high-risk area, so this was mandatory for us.

Radon-resistant construction techniques involve five components: a gas-permeable layer, heavy-gauge plastic sheeting, sealing and caulking of all penetrations through the concrete slab, and a vent pipe to exhaust gases from under the home. Our builders knew about this requirement and designed and built

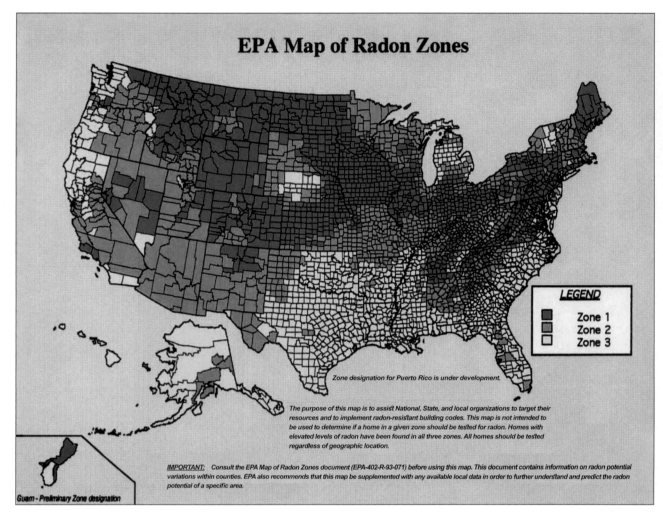

EPA Map of Radon Zones

LEGEND
- Zone 1
- Zone 2
- Zone 3

Zone designation for Puerto Rico is under development.

The purpose of this map is to assist National, State, and local organizations to target their resources and to implement radon-resistant building codes. This map is not intended to be used to determine if a home in a given zone should be tested for radon. Homes with elevated levels of radon have been found in all three zones. All homes should be tested regardless of geographic location.

IMPORTANT: Consult the EPA Map of Radon Zones document (EPA-402-R-93-071) before using this map. This document contains information on radon potential variations within counties. EPA also recommends that this map be supplemented with any available local data in order to further understand and predict the radon potential of a specific area.

Guam - Preliminary Zone designation

EPA Map of Radon Zones (higher risk is darker red, zone one). Source: US EPA.

to these specifications. (Elevating the home by at least two feet is another method of radon protection, but that presents other issues with design, plumbing, etc.)

Fortunately, radon-resistant construction techniques are not only simple, but have been proven effective. The method primarily used is a vent pipe system and fan, which pulls radon from beneath the house and vents it to the outside. In our home, we have a vent pipe system but no fan. Our builders assured us that since it is the only hole in our foundation, that's where the radon will go naturally—up and out.

Does it work? I bought a radon test kit from Home Depot to test if our builder's assurance was accurate. Testing radon is fairly easy. The kit itself cost about $10. You get two little bottles, and you are supposed to set them out near each other, on the lowest level of livable space. It needs to sit there for three full days; then you cap the bottles and send them to Pro-Lab,

Passive radon ventilation in our mechanical room.

Inc., the accredited laboratory for this type of testing. The test fee is $30, and you get your results within ten to fourteen days.

The test results showed an average of 2.1 picocuries of radon gas per liter (pCi/L), with one test as low as 1.8 pCi/L and one at 2.4 pCi/L. This was curious, given that the two samplings were placed only six inches away from each other—one was 33 percent higher.

The EPA recommends that you "fix your home" if the radon level is 4 pCi/L or more. The email I received back let me know a little more about our results: "The average level of

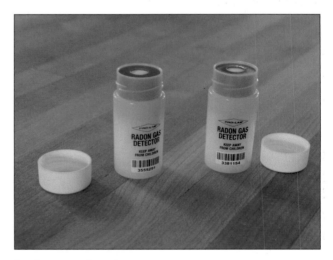

Radon test bottles.

radon in America's homes is 1.3 pCi/L. Radon levels less than 4 pCi/L still pose a risk, and in many cases may be reduced. You should retest your home in one year to make sure the radon level continues to be low." The EPA information guide goes on to list the risks of lung cancer tied to radon exposure over a lifetime, for smokers and nonsmokers. Where do we come in at around 2 pCi/L? As nonsmokers, our risk getting lung cancer is four in one thousand, or 0.4 percent, equivalent to the risk of dying from poison. That does not seem too bad. And apparently, it can be quite difficult to get radon levels below 2.0 pCi/L.

There are many homes in Minneapolis that do test higher for radon, and according to a realtor in the area, it costs about $1,500 to fix the problem. That's on top of the $40 per year for the test kit and lab results to ensure your home is not killing your family.

Air Filtration

Good, better, or best? This LEED credit addresses air filtration, which falls under the category of *source control*, assuming we will not be entirely successful at *source reduction* (the previous section). We do, after all, have four people and two cats living in the house. (I won't count the crayfish, weird tiny water frogs, hermit crabs, or guinea pig, as they were short-lived.)

The prerequisite for air filtration requires installation of "good" air filters, offers one point for "better" filters, or two points for "best" filters. The intent is clearly to filter the air—but from what? Called "particulate matter," it's stuff in the air that we can't really see,

but we breathe it in, and it can have adverse health effects. Particularly in homes located near highways, homes with pets, or for anyone allergic to dust or pollen, air filters can make a big difference. (You just have to make sure you change out those air filters regularly.)

Air filters have what is called a MERV rating on a scale of one to sixteen. MERV stands for minimum efficiency reporting value, and the higher the MERV rating, the more efficient your filter is at removing particles from the air. The most common MERV filters are rated at eight; critical areas of hospitals use MERV 14. Filters rated MERV 8, for example, filter out human hair, carpet fibers, dust mites, and plant spores. But they do not do a good job of filtering out tobacco smoke, smog, cooking oil, and many dust particles. To remove those particles, we would have to move up to at least a rating of MERV 11.

A standard 20x20x1-inch MERV 8 filter at Home Depot retails for $8.97 or less if purchased in volume. Higher prices usually go with higher ratings—the same size 3M Filtrete with a MERV 12 rating is currently $19.97 at Home Depot, so you have to weigh the value of clean air against your budget.

The prerequisite MERV rating is a rating of at least eight; we could get one point for installing air filters of at least MERV 10 and two points for at least MERV 13.[26] Our current air filters are rated at MERV 11, which would have earned us one LEED point and easily meet the prerequisite.

But there is a caveat to this credit: having a true HEPA filter (not a "HEPA-type" filter) counts as equivalent to a MERV 16 rating,

---

26 *LEED for Homes Reference Guide*, 311.

and is therefore worth two points. Air filtration was an important component of our goal of having a healthy home, so we purchased a whole-house HEPA filter. Supplied by Pure Air Systems, it is designed to remove 99.97 percent of all particles. The American Lung Association also recommends it.

Because we live in Minnesota, we do not open our windows for many months out of the year. In the winter, air can get pretty stale pretty quickly, and so can smell! The HEPA filter ensures it is really clean air. It cost an incremental $1,500. The two LEED points were a bonus, because we would have purchased it anyway. To me, investing in good air filtration is preventive health care—like going to the doctor for annual well visits. It just makes sense.

Outdoor Air Ventilation

After trying to reduce the source of pollutants by ensuring that only no- and low-emissions products make it into your home, then trying to control the source through air filtration, this credit addresses the third strategy: *dilution*. Ventilating with outdoor air is definitely a cornerstone of a healthy home. It's a tradeoff with energy efficiency, though, because ventilation requires energy. The *LEED for Homes Reference Guide* recognizes this balancing act: from a health perspective, it is important not to under-ventilate a home. From an energy perspective, it is important not to over-ventilate.

There are three parts to this LEED credit: basic outdoor air ventilation (a prerequisite), enhanced outdoor air ventilation (worth two points), and third-party testing (one point). The prerequisite is basically that the HVAC contractor should follow the requirements of ASHRAE Standard 62.2–2007, sections four and seven (the more recent version of LEED for Homes references ASHRAE Standard 62.2–2010). Homes located in mild climates are exempt; Minnesota is not exactly mild, so we are not exempt. What is that standard? It lays out minimum airflow levels for various sized homes. For our home, we need a CFM (cubic feet per minute) airflow of at least 105. There are various strategies to meet the prerequisite: exhaust-only ventilation (not good for hot and humid climates); supply-only ventilation (not good for cold climates); and balanced ventilation with both supply and exhaust fans that ensure an exchange of air between the inside and outside. Since we live in an area that is both very hot and very cold, the balanced ventilation system works best. We have it—our variable-speed fan has a continuous blower rating of 575 CFM—well over the 105 minimum. Does that mean our system is vastly oversized and we are wasting energy? Likely, but I'm not sure what to do about that!

For enhanced outdoor air ventilation, we need to have either an HRV or ERV installed. An HRV is a heat recovery ventilator; an ERV is an energy recovery ventilator. Both HRVs and ERVs supply air to the home and exhaust stale air while recovering heat from the exhaust air in the process. The difference is that HRV only transfers heat; an ERV transfers heat and moisture.

We have a Venmar Heat Recovery Ventilator. I like to think of it as an air pre-heater. If you bring in outdoor air through the whole-house ventilation system in the middle of winter (which is good for a healthy home), it would be freezing cold. Heating it up would

Houseplants Are Good for Your Health

One thing LEED does not address but which is helpful for healthy indoor air: houseplants. Plants act as natural air filters that remove pollutants. NASA conducted a study on this phenomenon, and not only do plants provide oxygen, they also do a good job of eliminating formaldehyde, benzene, and trichloroethylene. The top two plants in overall purifying performance are the peace lily and chrysanthemum. Other strong performers are mother-in-law's tongue, English ivy, spider plant, bamboo palm, and rubber plant.[27] Additionally, plants add an aesthetic that make homes more beautiful (though that is personal preference). According to a Consumer Product Safety Commission (CPSC) report, though, "there is no evidence that a reasonable number of houseplants remove *significant* quantities of pollutants in homes."[28] So, while houseplants help, they should not be *relied upon* entirely for healthy indoor air quality.

Pretty chrysanthemums help filter indoor air.

---

27 B.C. Wolverton, Willard L. Douglas, and Keit Bounds, "A Study of Interior Landscape Plants for Indoor Air Pollution Abatement," July 1, 1989.
28 US Consumer Product Safety Commission, "The Inside Story: A Guide to Indoor Air Quality," https://www.cpsc.gov/Safety-Education/Safety-Guides/Home/The-Inside-Story-A-Guide-to-Indoor-Air-Quality.

require a lot of energy. But if you run it through the ductwork that already has warm air, it basically pre-heats the cold air before it gets to the furnace that then heats the air to the set temperature. Complicated? A little, but if you think about it long enough it does make sense from an efficiency standpoint. And from our perspective, we can save on energy bills—so we wanted an HRV with or without the two LEED points awarded for this.

This was also a quality assurance credit, because we could get a point for third-party testing. Our Green Rater from the Neighborhood Energy Connection, Jimmie Sparks, verified that our ventilation system did move the air in our home at least 105 CFM, thereby complying with building code. So, we got two points for planning and designing for a certain minimum air flow, and another point for proving that it actually works.

Whether you have ductwork or not, you need to get some air circulation in the house for it to be healthy. That can mean ceiling fans, regular fans, and/or opening the windows periodically. There are other "air cleaners" on the market that can be effective at removing particles, but they are not designed to remove gaseous pollutants.

Another important component of outdoor air ventilation is a one-time pre-occupancy

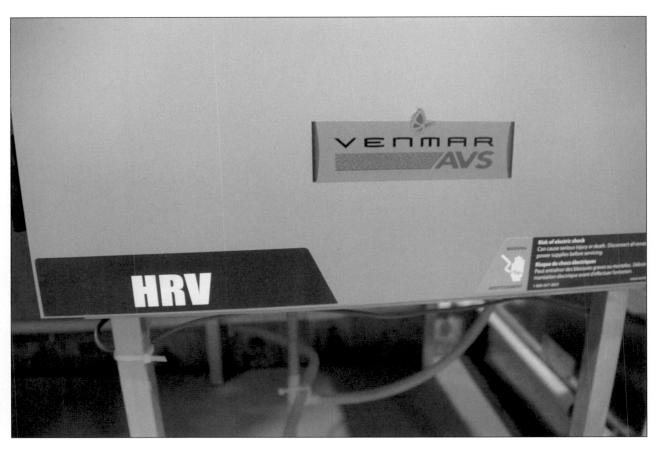

Heat Recovery Ventilator.

flush. LEED offers one point if the home is flushed with fresh air before we move in. This has to occur after all phases of construction are completed, for all areas of the home, for forty-eight hours, by keeping all windows open while running the HVAC system fan, and the HVAC filters have to be cleaned or replaced afterward. I was not at the home for this "flush," but our builder says they always do this as a matter of course. It helps clear the air—and the house—of construction debris and dust; we earned another LEED point for this.

Indoor air was flushed-out before we moved in.

CHAPTER 5: CLEAN HOUSE

This is the third of the three goals for a healthy home: Clean Air, Clean Water, and Clean House. This chapter is broken down into two strategies: Mold Prevention and Contaminant Control, which are addressed by the LEED for Homes Rating System under the Indoor Environmental Quality category. I also include a section on cleaning products, which is not covered in LEED for Homes, because cleaning products do not relate to the building design and construction of a home. (Green cleaning policies and purchases are, however, addressed in the commercial rating system LEED for Existing Buildings.) I am including it because it is an important element of a healthy home.

Mold Prevention

I only have breathing issues when I am around mold, and then I am miserable. The house we bought and had intended to remodel, in fact, had to be torn down due to too much mold in the basement. The LEED credit related to mold prevention is titled "Moisture Control," which is much broader in scope than just mold prevention. Its intent is to control indoor moisture levels to provide comfort and increase the durability of the home—in addition to reducing the risk of mold. Those are very important objectives; I'm focusing on mold prevention in particular, not just because I cannot live with it, but because it is unhealthy for anyone to live with it.

Mold is a major sick home issue, resulting from excess moisture in the home. According to a mold expert, "Exposure to mold can cause cold-like symptoms, respiratory problems, nasal and sinus congestion, watery eyes, sore throat, coughing and skin irritations, and can trigger asthma attacks. Children, the elderly, pregnant women and people with existing respiratory sensitivities are at higher risk for adverse health effects of mold. If you can smell or see mold, you have a mold problem. Since people react to mold whether it is living or dead, the mold must be removed."[29]

To control moisture and prevent mold, LEED requires that we install dehumidification equipment with sufficient latent capacity to maintain relative humidity at or below 60 percent. We can accomplish this by either adding additional systems or equipping a central HVAC system with additional controls to operate in dehumidification mode. Minneapolis gets very dry in the win-

---

29 Kenneth Hellevang, PhD, *Keep Your Home Healthy*, North Dakota State University Extension Service, 2003.

ter and very humid in the summer, so our builder was definitely paying attention to controlling indoor humidity levels. We have a VMB-HW Series Variable Speed 4-Pipe Hydronic Fan Coil air handler made by First Co. That title alone should qualify! One of its features is better humidity control. The product literature reads: "The VMB-HW is designed to extract much more moisture from the air than a conventional system by slowing the airflow over the cooling coil. The result is an improved summer comfort level at higher indoor temperatures."

We also have a Honeywell VisionPRO IAQ programmable thermostat that allows us to control the humidity levels in the home. While not required to achieve this point, the programmable thermostat allows for additional efficiency, because we can program it to run less while we are not at home, thereby saving energy.

The best information from the *LEED for Homes Reference Guide* comes from the table that shows the maximum comfortable humidity at summer temperatures, which helps us set our fancy programmable thermostat:

Indoor Temperature (degrees F)	Relative Humidity (%) (maximum for comfort)
70	76
74	66
78	58
82	50

In the winter, best practices are to keep relative humidity levels between 25 and 45 percent. This is difficult to do in Minnesota, as severe condensation builds up on our door handles and windowsills during those polar vortex days. Nevertheless, it's excellent guid-

ance for a comfortable home. We paid more for this point, but having a comfortable, mold-free, durable home was a priority for us, regardless of the LEED point available.

Contaminant Control

Controlling contaminants is like source control for clean air, but it applies to actual dirt rather than invisible air pollution. The LEED credit entitled "Contaminant Control" awards points if you do the following:

- Design and install permanent walk-off mats at each entry that are at least four feet in length and allow accessibility for cleaning.
- Design a shoe removal and storage space near the primary entryway, separated from living areas. This space may not have wall-to-wall carpeting, and it must be large enough to accommodate a bench and at least two pairs of shoes per bedroom.
- Install a central vacuum system with exhaust to the outdoors. Ensure that the exhaust is not near any ventilation air intake.[30]

Why are these important? According to the *LEED for Homes Reference Guide*, "A majority of the dirt and dust in homes is tracked in by occupants. Debris carried into the house from shoes often contains lead, asbestos, pesticides, and other hazardous materials. Shoes also track moisture into the home, leading to mold growth in carpeting near entry-ways.

_____

30 *LEED for Homes Reference Guide,* 315.

Mudroom.

. . . One of the most effective approaches to reducing indoor contaminants is removing shoes upon entry."[31]

The great thing about this credit is that it encourages mudrooms in the design. Our architect's very first proposal for our house did not include a mudroom. Once we added it by the garage, with a short enclosed breezeway connecting it to the house, it became a nice, workable design.

---

31 *LEED for Homes Reference Guide,* 318.

For the first bullet: we do have mats at every entryway, but they are not permanent and not four feet long. We met the requirements for the second bullet as shown in the photo, as it was part of our overall program. Having a shoe removal space with a bench is also what makes the mudroom functional.

As for the third strategy, we did not install a central vacuum system. We had it in the initial plan for the home, because of this credit, but removed it during a cost-cutting exercise. Turns out, we barely had enough room for the ductwork and wiring inside the walls, much less for vacuum pipes. The extra cost of putting in all those pipes within the walls was not worth it to us. Additionally, I grew up in a home with a central vacuum cleaner, and my mom was always complaining about how it required so much work hauling around those long hoses. Bending around the corners, the hose would always dirty up or chip off the paint. The only fun part was opening up the vacuum holes in the wall and letting it suck my sister's ponytail holders into never-never land. I'm only sorry I deprived my daughters of that same joy.

Overall, we earned one LEED point for controlling indoor contaminants. Like other credits, though, much of our success depends on how we live in the home: do we enforce the shoe removal policy? We try. No shoes are allowed upstairs, where we have wall-to-wall carpeting, and it is more difficult to clean than flooring. The main level is enforced for our immediate family, but we are more lenient for guests. It seems that some people are insulted if asked to remove their shoes. To encourage people to take off their shoes, we have a basket of very soft, comfy, clean, one-size-fits-all fuzzy socks near the front door. I offer them up in the winter. Everyone actually appreciates that, except for my parents, who still will not take off their shoes.

The garage is also a source of contaminants due to cars that leak fluids, bring in all sorts of dirt from the streets, and are a source of unhealthy emissions like carbon monoxide. LEED requires that there be no HVAC (heating, ventilation, air conditioning) system in the garage connected to the home as part of an indoor air quality measure. We easily complied. (In some regions, apparently, it is common to install the HVAC equipment in the garage, so this prerequisite can require significant design changes.)

Basket of fuzzy socks to encourage guests to take off their shoes.

LEED also provides three points for having *no garage* or a *detached garage*. Not having a garage was not an option, as our winters in Minneapolis are just too harsh. Our architect, in his initial designs, sketched out a detached garage because he prefers the scale of the home without a garage. I concur from an aesthetic standpoint. However, I think anyone who lives in a cold climate would agree that from a comfort, convenience, and livability standpoint, an attached garage makes a huge difference. For homeowners like us with an attached garage, then, keeping contaminants and car exhaust out of the house requires that all shared surfaces between the garage and the home be tightly sealed, doors next to the garage be weather-stripped, and carbon monoxide detectors be placed in rooms adjacent to the garage. We earned two LEED points for ensuring these measures were met.

Cleaning Products for a Healthy Home

Nobody actually goes into a store and asks for the most toxic cleaning product on the shelf—we just want to get the job done. Tough chemicals do the job of cleaning pretty well; that is how they are marketed. So, what is wrong with household cleaners? The big picture answer is that there are at least 83,000 chemicals on the market today, and they are not well regulated. Exposure to chemicals is linked to health problems such as cancer, birth defects, asthma, allergies, skin reactions, and reproductive disorders. Sometimes illnesses stem from overexposure (acute), which is an immediate one-time reaction that can trigger chronic illness; sometimes illnesses come from long-term exposure that builds up over time. The problem is, we do not know!

Why? First, ingredients often are not disclosed. Unlike makers of packaged food, cosmetics, and personal care products, manufacturers of cleaning supplies are not required to list the chemical ingredients on consumer product labels (though many do). Second, even if we do know the ingredients, it would be very difficult to conduct a controlled experiment, because there are too many uncontrolled variables (we aren't just exposed to one chemical in our lifetime), and we do not typically conduct experiments on humans.

The US Congress enacted legislation to regulate the safety of chemicals with the passage of the Toxic Substances Control Act in 1976, which has been governing chemical policy since then through the EPA. The EPA itself recognizes that current chemicals management law needs to be strengthened.[32] In a nutshell, the EPA can only restrict chemical usage if it is *proven to be unsafe*—and that takes time, money, and data that is difficult to obtain.

Many people argue that the EPA should *not* allow chemicals to be included in household products *unless and until* they are *proven to be safe*. That's an example of the precautionary

---

32 US Environmental Protection Agency, "Essential Principles for Reform of Chemicals Management Legislation."

Too many cleaning products choices!

principle, and how the European Union manages chemicals. But that's not how it is in our country. So, we need to take it upon ourselves to understand what products are safe and which ones to avoid. With the overwhelming number of choices on the shelf, how?

One resource I have relied upon in the past is the Environmental Working Group's (EWG) online Guide to Healthy Cleaning. Their guide provides information and safety assessments for over 2,500 products, 197 brands, and more than 1,000 ingredients across the categories of all-purpose cleaners, laundry detergents, dishwashing, floor care, and bathroom, kitchen, and furniture cleaners.

EWG translates final product scores into letter grades familiar to most readers. An "A" indicates very low toxicity to health and the environment and extensive ingredient disclosure. An "F" means the product is highly toxic or makes little to no ingredient disclosure. A "C" indicates an average cleaner that poses no overt hazards and provides some disclosure of ingredients.

The EWG Guide to Healthy Cleaning published the results of their tests on 513 all-purpose cleaners. What is disturbing is that over 60 percent scored a D or F, and only 22 percent scored a B or A. (Note that EWG does not test or score for the effectiveness of the cleaners.)

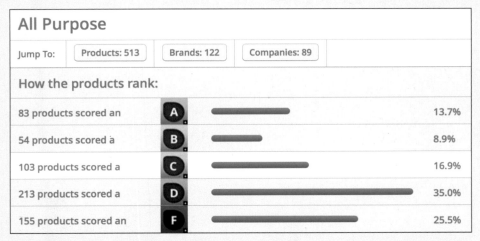

Environmental Working Group scores of all purpose cleaners. Source: EWG.org.

So, what can we do? One solution is to make our own cleaners. The all-purpose cleaner I like to make and use at home requires the following:

- A clean 16-oz. trigger spray bottle (or 32-oz. and double the recipe)
- 1 teaspoon of borax
- 2 tablespoons of vinegar

- ¼ cup of home soap or Dr. Bronner's soap
- Essential oil of lemon, tea tree, or lavender (optional)
- Hot water (enough to fill bottle)

Instructions:

1. Mix the vinegar and borax in the spray bottle.
2. Fill the bottle about half full with water and shake to dissolve the borax.
3. Add soap.
4. Optional: add 5–10 drops of essential oil (I like lavender).
5. Fill bottle with water and gently shake.

Making your own cleaner ensures you know what ingredients went into it, but another benefit is that it will save you money. While the up-front purchase of all the ingredients can cost in the $20 range, you will not need to buy another $4.99 bottle of multipurpose cleaner for years. Here's my math:

- Spray bottle = $1.83 online
- Borax = $3.99 for 12 oz. at Target
- Vinegar = $1.64 for 32 oz. of Heinz vinegar at Walmart
- Soap = $11.99 for 32 oz. of Dr. Bronner's soap at Whole Foods

With these ingredients, you can make sixteen spray bottles full and still have a lot of leftover borax and vinegar! That's only $1.21 per bottle, and the cost will continue to go down as you reuse the same bottle, helping to reduce waste as well.

For other types of cleaners, the American Lung Association Health House suggestions include the following:

- Make your own furniture and floor polish by mixing one part lemon juice with two parts vegetable oil.
- Clean your oven in a healthy way by using a solution of baking soda dissolved in water.
- Use baking soda for rug and carpet odor removal.
- For a toilet bowl cleaner, pour in one cup of vinegar and leave overnight. Brush the next day.

But let's face it: many of us do not really have the time or inclination to make our own cleaners. So now what can we do? Many cleaning products have "green" label certifications. Green Seal and the Environmental Choice program's Ecologo are two of the more well-known certifications in the commercial cleaning industry and have the most stringent requirements for our health and the environment. Green Seal is robust with its product certification: it only certifies products that fully comply with their standards, covering all environmental and health attributes of a product. In addition to its high standards for health, Green Seal looks at energy and water efficiency of the manufacturing process, the recycled content of the packaging materials, product marketing and labeling, and—this is key—demonstration that the product performs equally or better than a comparable non-green product in the same category. Unfortunately, not many household products carry the Green Seal.

Label for safe cleaning products.

For both household and industrial cleaners, the EPA developed a certification program in the mid-2000s based on its own Standard for Safe Products. Formerly referred to as Design for the Environment (DfE), this labeling program became the Safer Choice label in 2015. The Safer Choice label requires annual audits, so you can count on it being up to date.

While each of these is noteworthy and has its own online database to search for products, it is still time-consuming and difficult, and unfortunately, many household cleaning products do not have any certification. So, since the certifications are not that helpful in the aisles of Target and Walmart, the choices are overwhelming, and EWG's database might be tough to access, I've done a little of my own research on brands that typically get As and Bs (to buy) as well as those that get Ds and Fs (to avoid) for most of their products.

EWG's best scoring all-purpose cleaner brands (mostly As and Bs) include Biokleen, Bon Ami, Ecover, Green Shield, Ballard Organics, Dr. Bronner's, Whole Foods, Arm & Hammer, and Seventh Generation. EWG's worst scoring all-purpose cleaner brands (mostly Ds and Fs) include Clorox/Formula 409, Method, Green Works, Mr. Clean, Windex, Up & Up, Fabuloso, Pine Sol (which received top ratings from Consumer Reports for effectiveness), Soft Scrub, Scrubbing Bubbles, and Spic and Span.

What about Simple Green, a name that implies a safe product? Simple Green's All Purpose Cleaner scored an F, while at the same time earning the EPA's Safer Choice label. How could this be? Digging a little deeper, I found that EWG gave Simple Green's All Purpose Cleaner such a low score due to its ingredients—primarily 2-butoxyethanol, a harmful chemical. But, Simple Green's website did not list 2-butoxyethanol as an ingredient, nor was it listed as an ingredient on its Safety Data Sheet (SDS). I contacted Simple Green directly, and Carol Chapin, the Vice President of Research and Development, confirmed that their formulation changed in 2012. Due to California law, they have not used 2-butoxyehtanol for six years, and Simple Green earned the EPA Safer Choice label in 2016. So, I contacted EWG to let them know their database has been incorrect since 2012. Their response was that while they do their best to update products, I should defer to the company website for the most recent list of ingredients. This leads me to believe that there may be more inaccuracies in the EWG database—formulations often change as companies improve their products to meet consumer demand and comply with legislation. Who can stay on top of all of this? Not being able to rely on what you read on the Internet, we have to be our own self-advocates.

This is a confusing subject, so I'll try to bottom-line it. First, read the label. If it is has an EPA number, then it is classified as a pesticide, so be cautious. Be careful if it says "hazard" or "danger!" Second, try to avoid chemically dangerous products. About 80 to 90 percent of household cleaning chores can be done without chemicals. Sometimes we need a tough cleaner for really dirty jobs. When we do, only buy and use what you need, store it where children cannot access it, do not use it around our pets, and follow the guidelines for proper disposal. Finally, trust your nose, and try to go for fragrance-free. If it smells bad, it probably is bad. If sniffing it makes your eyes water or your skin itch, do yourself a favor and do not bring it into your home.

Thankfully, California enacted the Cleaning Product Right to Know Act in October 2017, making California the first state to require ingredient labeling (online by 2020 and on product labels by 2021) for all cleaning products. Because California is such a populous state, this law will drive changes in manufacturing and ingredient disclosure across the entire United States. Will this make it easier for consumers to choose healthier household cleaners? We can only hope.

GREENER CHOICE	DOLLARS	SENSE
Whole-house water filtration system and RO/DI filter system	$1,500–$3,000, plus annual filter changes; save money on not purchasing bottled water MEDIUM-HIGH COST	Most important healthy home strategy DO AS MUCH AS YOU CAN AFFORD
Filter your air beyond MERV 8 filtration, to at least MERV 11	About $10 more per filter (HEPA filter is higher cost) LOW COST	Improves indoor air quality A LOT OF SENSE
HRV (heat recovery ventilator)	Unit is between $500–$1,500, plus installation HIGH COST	For cold climates, energy savings can make it worth it. For warmer climates, get a standard ventilation system DEPENDS ON CLIMATE
Specify cabinetry that is NAUF or TSCA Title VI compliant	Was high cost for us; should be no different now NO INCREMENTAL COST	Ensures no exposure to urea formaldehyde DO IT!
Specify no- and low-VOC paints, finishes, sealants	NO INCREMENTAL COST	Reduces exposure to unhealthy VOCs DO IT!
CRI Green Label Plus carpets and carpet pads, FloorScore certified flooring	NO INCREMENTAL COST (depends on comparison)	DO IT!
Test for radon	$40 for kit and lab results (radon mitigation can be more costly: ~$1,500) LOW COST	Radon is a poisonous gas DO IT!
Require shoe removal	NO COST	DO IT!
Central vacuum cleaner	Minimum $1,000 HIGHER COST	NOT ENOUGH SENSE
Make your own all-purpose cleaner	$20 for all the equipment; makes 16 bottles; saves money LOW COST	DO IT IF YOU HAVE TIME!

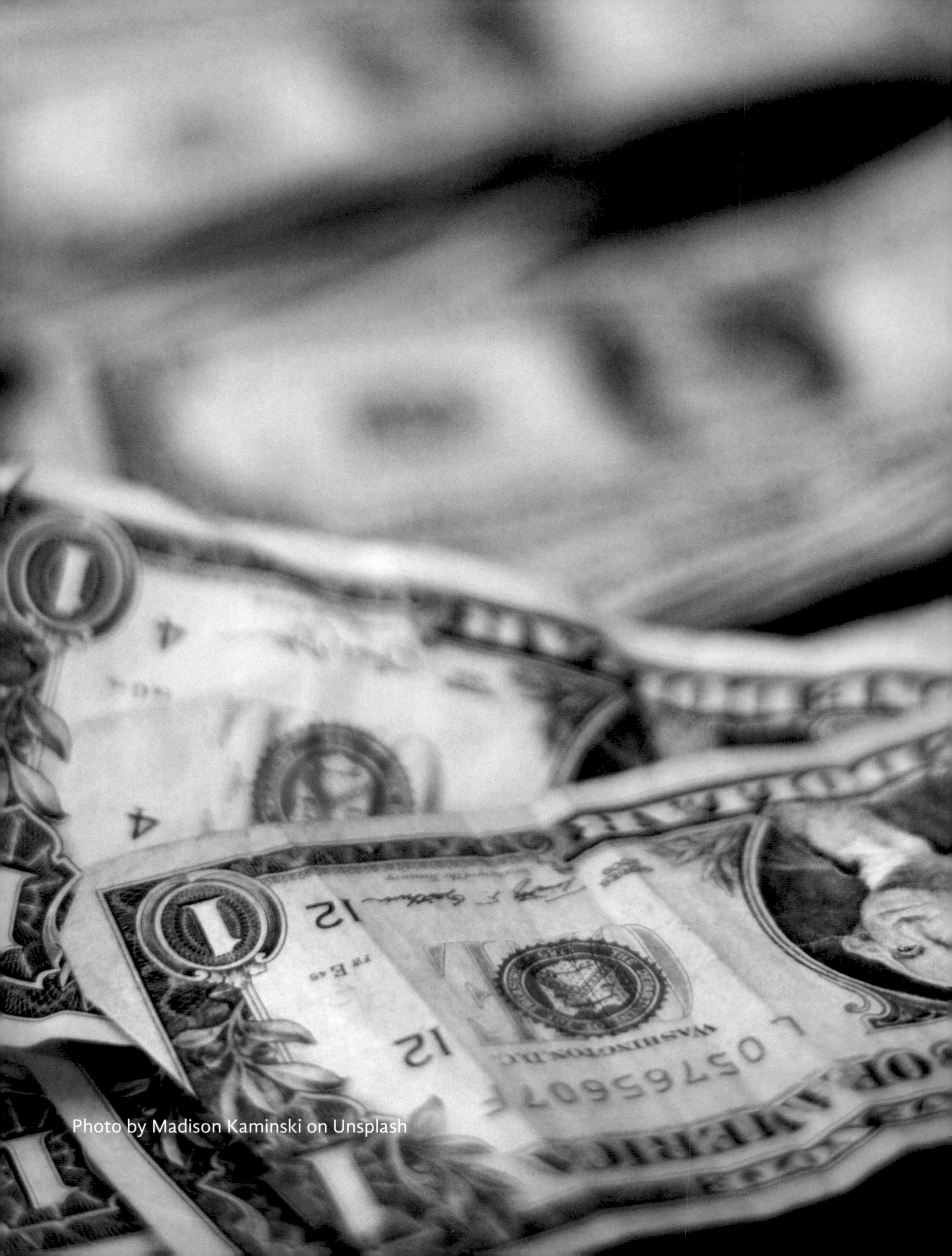

Photo by Madison Kaminski on Unsplash

PART II
FOR OUR WEALTH

There is an interesting dichotomy in people's values around doing the right thing *and* profiting from it. It is often the case that those who invest in sustainable technologies like solar panels, drive a Prius, shop at Whole Foods, etc.—often referred to as "cultural creatives"—do not do it to save money; they are almost offended when the financial benefits are pointed out. When I asked Steve Glenn of Living Homes[33] if he had any interesting financial payback stories about how the homes he has developed cost less money to operate, he replied, "No—it is never about that. It's based on values. We do have an extremely low energy bills, but our sell is not economic. It's a values-based sell." That led me to question whether I should eighty-six this entire part of my book. But I am sticking with it, because money savings do matter.

Anyone who doubts that sustainable investments result in substantial financial savings only has to read *Force of Nature: The Unlikely Story of Walmart's Green Revolution,* by Edward Humes and Michael Quinlan. Walmart's very mission is to be the low-cost provider of consumer goods, so they care deeply about saving money. This is an entire book devoted to convincing readers that making a bigger profit while becoming more sustainable are *not* mutually exclusive.[34]

Walmart has been criticized for its sustainability efforts, citing the fact that the company is *only* doing it to save money. I think that's unfair. Why not embrace the double benefit with full force? Save natural resources and reduce pollution, *and* save money. Walmart's efforts are having ripple effects up and down their supply chain. Other companies are beginning to follow suit, because they see the benefits as well.

In my consulting work, I have analyzed clients' expenses before and after they have gone through LEED for Existing Buildings certification, and they have always seen a financial return that shows the investment was well worth the money. Having conducted the analyses myself, in addition to reading a multitude of studies that show positive returns on sustainable investments, I thought I would be able to sell LEED certification to chief financial officers all

---

33 Steve Glenn built and lives in one of the first LEED platinum homes in the world. He is founder of Living Homes, a Los Angeles–based company that designs and builds modern, LEED certified, prefab homes. See LivingHomes.net.

34 For additional success stories, see also Daniel C. Esty and P. J. Simmons, *The Green to Gold Business Playbook: How to Implement Sustainability Practices for Bottom-Line Results in Every Business Function* (Hoboken, NJ: John Wiley & Sons, 2011).

day long. The icing on the cake would be that they could report, market, and promote their commitment to sustainability. Yet I still saw an unwillingness to believe in the financials. Clients were not doing it for the savings; they were doing it either because they *had* to for marketing or permitting purposes, to engage their employees, or because it was the "right thing to do." The reverse was true: the financial benefits were the icing on the cake, not the reason to pursue the investment in the first place. That's all well and good, but without a deeper understanding of the financials, "sustainability initiatives" are often the first line items to get cut when it comes time to trim budgets.

For our own home, I wanted to understand how, and to what extent, investing in sustainable technologies would pay off through a reduction in energy bills (electricity and gas usage), water bills (indoor and outdoor usage), and maintenance and repair bills (which fall under "durability"). Because we do not have a before and after for comparison purposes, we will never know for sure what our bills *would* have been had we *not* invested. But there are other ways to determine savings, as shown in these next three chapters: *Energy*, *Water Efficiency*, and *Durability*.

Often homeowners view building green as just an added expense, but when you look at costs over time, you almost cannot afford *not* to build green. In fact, you don't have to care one iota about the environment to benefit from this part of the book—because I'd imagine you do care about your bank account. Having said that, the costs and benefits will vary due to the nature of our economy, costs of fuel, geographical and climate differences, etc. Because there are so many variables, I provide the tools necessary to conduct your own analysis, so you can come to your own conclusions.

How to Conduct a Cost/Benefits Analysis

The first rule of thumb in any cost/benefit analysis is to compare the costs and benefits to what would be viewed as "standard" construction practice. For our home, we requested alternate bids on our green priorities so that we could understand these costs. You have to know what you are comparing it to, otherwise you can't figure out anything.

The next rule, and this is key, is to only pay attention to *incremental* costs and benefits in each category. And note that I am only referring to *financial* costs and benefits—those that are quantifiable. So, if you are building a new home, and you have to purchase a full HVAC system, you only want to know how much *more* it would be to purchase a more efficient system. That's the initial cost. Any additional costs, like maintenance or replacement parts, need to be included as well—but again, only incremental to your comparison choice.

On the benefit side, your contractor should be able to tell you a percentage or an amount you might save on electricity or gas (or both), water, repair, and/or replacement. For this, you'll need to look at your utility and maintenance bills and get an average yearly cost (if you just look at one month, it will be skewed due to weather variations). So, for example, if you think you might save 30 percent on your energy bills, and you pay $2,000 per year on gas and electric, then your incremental annual benefit will be $600.

Here's the simple payback analysis for this example: if the up-front investment costs an additional $6,000, your payback period will be ten years, because you save $600 per year. If you finance your investment, you could be cash flow positive in the first year if the principal and interest on the loan payments are less than the energy savings. Payback analyses are weak, though, because you cannot really compare projects with each other. A payback of three years may not always be better than a payback of ten years, for example, if the benefits of the latter continue to improve while the benefits of the former decrease or disappear.

What about the other hard-to-quantify benefits, like less pollution or a quieter home? There will always be benefits that cannot be directly measured, and these are usually tied with our emotions—which ultimately push us toward a decision one way or another. What's wonderful about many green investments is that they actually do work out to be a good decision financially, which helps justify what our heart tells us we want to do anyway, whether it's about being less wasteful or reducing our dependence on fossil fuels. In this way, these types of investments feed our bank accounts as well as our souls.

Conversely, one of the obstacles to green home investments is that people think they *have to be* financially justified, when many other items we buy for our home are *never* financially justified. What's the payback of a light, airy kitchen? What's the financial justification for a soft, comfortable couch? There isn't one—we just like it more. And that natural, human emotion should be enough justification. (See Part III: *For Our Souls*.)

Photo by Nagy Arnold on Unsplash

CHAPTER 6:
ENERGY

It's all just so technically difficult! Starting with what a kilowatt hour is.

—My mom

US households use up to 30 percent more energy than necessary to achieve the desired level of performance and comfort, according to the EPA. That's a lot of waste—wasted money and wasted resources that add to pollution.

So how do you begin to tackle this? Most homes have both an electric bill and a gas bill. Typically, gas is for heating the home and the water; electricity is for air conditioning, ventilating, and powering appliances, lighting, and electronics. When was the last time you looked at your electric bill (other than at the amount due)? Is it comprehensible? Do you know how much you spend on electricity? While there are all kinds of fees and charges, for the most part you are charged based on the kilowatt hours (kWh) used. The average home consumes about 700 kWh per month and spends about $2,000 per year on energy bills.[35] What do you consume?

Why do we care? When we use natural gas, we are burning a fossil fuel in the house. When we use electricity, we are indirectly burning fossil fuels, depending on where you live and what utility services your home. In Minnesota, through Xcel Energy, about 60 to 70 percent of the electricity used to come from burning coal. That percentage dropped to about 39 percent by 2017 (the remainder is a mix of nuclear, hydro, solar, and wind), thanks to a concerted effort on the part of Xcel Energy to meet its renewable energy goals.

What's wrong with burning fossil fuels? After all, coal and natural gas are abundant resources here in the United States. Here is what is released in the air when fossil fuels are burned:

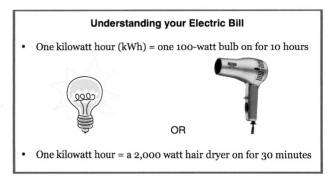

Understanding your Electric Bill

- One kilowatt hour (kWh) = one 100-watt bulb on for 10 hours

OR

- One kilowatt hour = a 2,000 watt hair dryer on for 30 minutes

What is a kilowatt hour?

---

35 US Department of Energy's Residential Program Solution Center, "Energy Data Facts," https://rpsc.energy.gov/energy-data-facts.

- Fine particulate matter, particularly from coal. This causes respiratory illnesses, asthma, and smog, which can make it just plain unhealthy to go outside.
- Heavy metals—including mercury. You know the phrase "mad as a hatter"? People who worked on felt hats used mercury, and it affected their brains. They went crazy. That's the story, anyway. But there is real scientific evidence that mercury causes neurological damage.
- Carbon dioxide (CO_2) emissions—accounting for 83 percent of total greenhouse gases and a significant contributor to global climate change.

Electricity generation is the single largest source of CO_2 emissions from fossil fuel combustion. (Check out the EPA's report on Inventory of US Greenhouse Gas Emissions and Sinks for more of this wonky data.)

You may have seen the ads: natural gas is clean, right? Not exactly. According to the EPA, compared to the average air emissions from coal-fired generation, natural gas produces half as much carbon dioxide, less than a third as much nitrogen oxides (a contributor to smog, respiratory illness, acid rain), and 1 percent as much sulfur oxides (also a contributor to smog, respiratory illness, and acid rain) at the power plant. Also, the process of

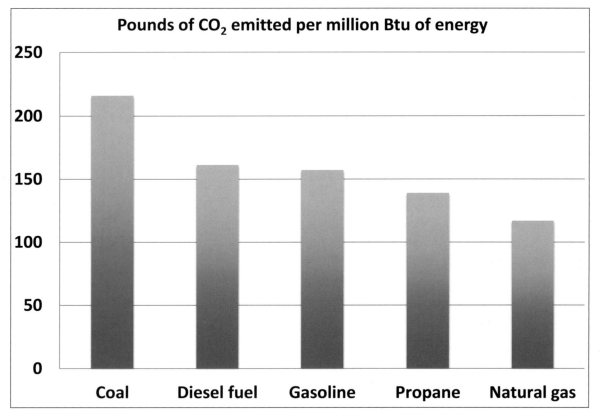

Pounds of CO_2 emitted per million Btu of energy

Data source: US Energy Information Administration.

Fossil fuel comparison: natural gas is not so clean.

extraction, treatment, and transport of the natural gas to the power plant generates additional emissions. So, while natural gas emissions are currently a little cleaner than power plant emissions that rely on coal, burning natural gas is still burning a fossil fuel, whereas electricity can get cleaner and cleaner through the growth renewable technologies like solar and wind.

One thing to point out is that even if you are uncertain about climate change,[36] burning fossil fuels still pollutes the air. I hope most of us care about reducing air pollution so kids (and grown-ups) can play outside. But the other reason to care about lowering your energy consumption is simple: you will save money.

Generally, when people talk about green homes, the first thing that comes to mind is energy reduction. LEED's Energy and Atmosphere category is the largest section in the LEED for Homes Rating System, accounting for 28 percent of the total possible points. The average LEED certified home uses 30 to 40 percent less electricity and saves more than 100 metric tons of CO_2 emissions over its lifetime.[37]

Energy consumption of a home can best be understood when it is divided in three basic categories: choices that *affect* our energy consumption, equipment choices that *consume* energy themselves, and design and equipment choices that can *produce* renewable energy on-site.

First, the four strategies that most *affect* energy consumption but do not *consume* energy themselves are driven by how the home is initially constructed through the choices of design (size and orientation), windows, insulation, and the overall tightness or leakiness of the home (referred to as air infiltration). These are the first four sections, and the primary variables for designing what is known as a "Passive House." According to the *LEED for Homes Reference Guide*, approximately one quarter of a home's heat losses and gains is due to windows. Another quarter is due to heat flow in and out of the insulated building envelope, and another quarter due to air leakage through the building envelope. So these components account for 75 percent of the heat loss and gain of a home—pretty important to make the right decisions!

Second, the four categories that *consume* energy during normal household operations revolve around equipment choices: HVAC (heating, ventilation, and air conditioning) equipment, hot water systems, appliances, and lighting—these are the next four sections. For homes, energy bills can quickly eat up a paycheck, especially in more extreme climates like Minnesota. What makes up the average household energy consumption? By far the largest is space heating, cooling, and ventilating, at

---

36 Ben Santer, the renowned, award-winning climate scientist (and a fellow advisory board member of the nonprofit Climate Generation: A Will Steger Legacy), wrote these twelve words in the 1995 IPPC report on Climate Change: "The balance of evidence suggests a discernible human influence on global climate." The science is real; climate change is happening.

37 *LEED for Homes Reference Guide*, 165.

39 percent. The typical makeup of a home's energy usage is shown in the chart below.

Third, whether the home *produces* energy on-site using renewable energy technologies: solar electric, solar thermal, and wind are the last three sections. (Geothermal is not included as a renewable, because it is technically not renewable energy—but it is an energy efficiency option and is discussed under the HVAC Equipment section.)

LEED certification requires that the home meet or exceed the performance of Energy Star–Homes. Energy Star is most commonly known by the rating of appliances—an Energy Star–labeled refrigerator, for example, ensures that it is designed to save money and protect the environment through reduced energy consumption. Run by the US Department of Energy, a home can also earn the Energy Star, which means it is at least 15 percent more efficient than a typical home. In colder climates, LEED's prerequisite is to be at least 20 percent more efficient than the standard home built to energy code.

How did we figure out if we met that requirement? We had to get a HERS index score. HERS is an acronym for Home Energy Rating System, which quantifies the energy performance of a home so that people can make sense out of it. The score is zero to one hundred: zero is a net zero energy home, and 100 corresponds to a "reference home" established as a baseline, based on the International Energy Conservation Code (which evolves

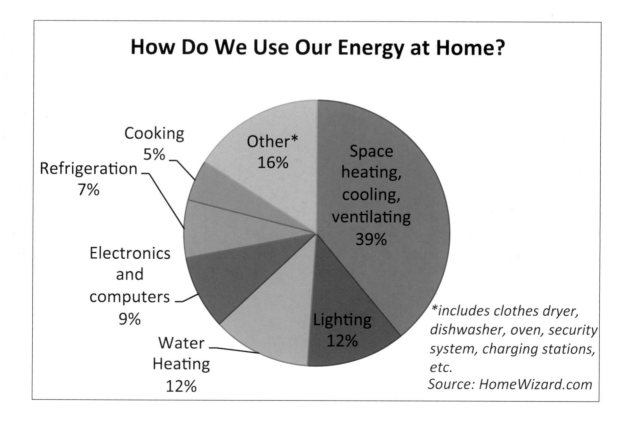

Our Green Rater, Jimmie Sparks, performing tests.

and is updated over time). Each one-point decrease in the HERS Index corresponds to a 1 percent reduction in energy consumption compared to the HERS Reference Home.

To get our HERS rating, we had to hire a LEED-approved Green Rater (that's Jimmie, in the photo, testing out our stove hood) who came to inspect our house as it was being built. He reviewed our home's orientation, insulation, number and size of windows, type of windows, HVAC system, appliances, and lights. Then, once we moved in, he conducted a blower door test to test the tightness of the house (testing leaks through doors, windows, etc.), as well as a duct-leakiness test. He

plugged a bunch of numbers into his energy model software, including square footages, ratio of windows to floor area, and all the components mentioned above, and voilà—out pops our home's energy efficiency rating based on its design and construction.

To meet LEED's prerequisite, our home had to have a maximum HERS rating of 80. We received a HERS score of 35, easily beating the requirement of 80, and earning twenty-five and a half LEED points in this category (over one quarter of the points needed to get to LEED gold). A HERS rating of 35 means that our house uses 35 percent of the energy it would take to run a "reference" home of similar size. This was intentional—we looked primarily at energy-efficiency investments that would save us in utility fees in the long run, as discussed in this chapter. But this is just energy modeling; it's impossible to really know, unless we built a reference home just like our home and operated it the exact same way. So, on a newly constructed home, we just had to trust the energy modeling, and assume our energy bills will be 65 percent lower than they would have otherwise been.

For remodeling an existing home, you *can* actually compare. For example, in 2011, after some cajoling from me, my parents replaced their old refrigerator from the mid-1970s with a new Energy Star–labeled refrigerator. Let's do the financials on this. The old refrigerator required 3,054 kilowatt hours (kWh) per year to run. The new refrigerator runs with 474 kWh per year, as rated by the US Department of Energy. (Refrigerator usage is pretty easy to calculate, because it is *always on*, compared to other equipment, which has variable and sometimes non-controllable operations.) That

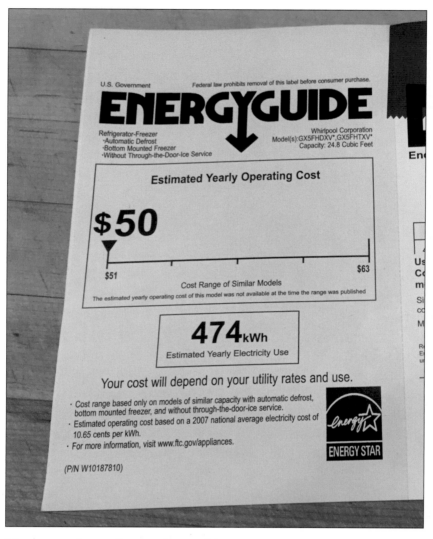

My parents' new Energy Star refrigerator rating.

means my parents are saving 2,580 kWh per year with the new refrigerator. At nine cents per kWh, that's a savings of $232 per year that they do not have to pay to Xcel Energy, their supplier of electricity. Their new refrigerator cost $800. If you divide $800 by $232, you get 3.45. So, after a little less than three and a half years, their refrigerator has been paid for through their annual electricity savings. And as electricity rates go up, savings go up.[38] Many utility companies will also provide an extra financial incentive and haul the old one away.

All of the strategies discussed in the next nine sections work together to give us just

---

38 A refrigerator calculator online calculates the savings of replacing an old refrigerator. See Energy Star Refrigerator calculator at www.energystar.gov/index.cfm?fuseaction=refrig.calculator.

one benefit: a home that uses 65 percent less energy than a same-size typical home. It is almost impossible to isolate windows from insulation, for example, to perform a cost/benefit analysis, because they are not independently controlled variables. (Similarly, the LEED for Homes Rating System provides a bundle of points for one HERS rating—termed the "Performance Pathway." The other option, for projects that do not have the ability or desire to do energy modeling, is the "Prescriptive Path," where a project can earn individual LEED points for each of the individual decisions around insulation, windows, lighting, appliances, etc.) So, rather than providing a cost/benefit analysis for every strategy discussed, I address it in one conclusion—with three exceptions. A ground-source heat pump, LED lighting, and solar electricity are each strategies that have their own identifiable costs and benefits.

Design

Design is the first signal of human intention.
—William McDonough

The design of the home, primarily its size and orientation to the sun, has the greatest impact on energy consumption. The LEED rating system addresses this by adjusting the point threshold required for certification based on the size of the home and awarding points for a home's orientation toward the sun.

HOME SIZE

Determining the appropriate size of a home is an iterative process with the architect, based upon your needs and wants, the size of the

lot, the neighborhood context, and of course, your budget. So, how did we decide how large a home we needed, wanted, or could afford?

Flash back to July 2006, when we sat down with David Salmela, our architect, and presented a program to him: three bedrooms plus a guest bedroom that can be multifunctional, a large open kitchen, a place for the piano, a home office that was away from bedrooms and common rooms, etc. The initial plan came back at over 5,000 square feet. It met all of our requirements. But I couldn't sleep at night. I kept picturing the rest of my life just trying to furnish, clean, and maintain a house that big. Then I thought about the potential mockery of a "green" house that is that large, and the judgments of others. So we made it smaller; it was easy. We took off the third floor office and decided the guest bedroom would go in the basement. We shortened the length of the house and put the powder room by the mudroom. Better.

At the time, I was taking a class at the University of Minnesota as part of the Masters in Sustainable Design program (as the only non-architect). I had the opportunity to present the initial design to some faculty and students (there were just nine of us in the program), thinking it would be great to get some feedback, and maybe even some more out-of-the-box thinking of how it could be improved. I laid out the plans and started talking about the great energy, water, and material savings the house would have—but I didn't get very far. The professor jumped down my throat at having a large home. "The average size of a home used to be 1,500 square feet for a family of four. Now it's something like 2,100 square feet. What is wrong with everyone?!" She continued her rant for the next twenty minutes, and my allotted time was over. What she didn't get to hear is that some of the square footage was my home office (no commute), some was an unfinished basement (easy extra space for an art studio or extended family), and that the livable portion of the house was, while spacious, nowhere near excessive or extravagant.

It seems that some people have a hard time grasping how a larger-than-average home can be considered "green." True, a smaller home uses less material and energy—both of which save homeowners money on up-front investment, utility bills, maintenance, furnishing, cleaning, etc. It also saves the homeowner time—time spent furnishing and cleaning a larger home. So, we have critics: many people don't believe a home the size of ours should be allowed to be LEED certified.

The USGBC does not play on this judgmental field; it simply designed the LEED for Homes Rating System with adjustable thresholds based upon what they define as a "neutral" sized home. The *LEED for Homes Reference Guide* explains: "As home size doubles, energy consumption increases by roughly one quarter, and material consumption increases by roughly one half; combined, this amounts to an increase in impact of roughly one third with each doubling in home size."[39] By LEED's definition, a "neutral" size four-bedroom home is allowed 2,600 square feet. Our home is about 4,800 square feet and has four bedrooms, so we had to add 16.5 points to each threshold level, making it more difficult to achieve LEED certification. Fair enough.

---

39 *LEED for Homes Reference Guide*, 9.

My view is that *any* size home can incorporate green features, even if it is big, and that is better for our world than that same home without green features. The LEED rating system does not arbitrarily say, "any home larger than 2,600 square feet is not green." What good would that do? It would, in fact, do bad: it would alienate those people who can afford larger homes—the same ones who can afford new green technologies. And that's what we need: more people who can afford it, doing it—so that demand goes up, cost comes down, and more and more people have access to affordable green technologies.

ORIENTATION

The next major consideration is orientation of the home, which means the direction the home faces with respect to the sun, and how much window and shading designs help reduce the need for cooling in the summer and heating in the winter. Many older homes that predate air conditioning are oriented and designed to take advantage of the natural laws of physics—meaning they were designed to bring in light and warmth from the sun during cooler seasons, and have shade during hot seasons.

To get a LEED point, you would have to orient the house along an east-west axis to make the best use of the sun, from both a passive and active solar perspective. Windows would have to be mostly on the north and south sides of the home, and at least 90 percent of the south-facing windows need to be completely shaded in the at summer solstice (June 21) and un-shaded at winter solstice (December 21).

Since we are across the street from a lake, we obviously want to face that way to take advantage of the view. (The former house on the lot was oddly diagonally situated.) The lake is directly east, so our home wants to be on a north/south axis. This is *not* the advised orientation for passive solar. If we did want to do a passive solar home, our views would mostly be of our neighbor's faux Italian Renaissance home. We decided that forgoing the view of the lake for that of our neighbor's home was not worth one LEED point, or the other passive solar advantages.

We did integrate other strategies, though, that are worth mentioning, despite being worth no LEED points. Regarding sun shading, our second floor is six feet wider than the first floor—which was designed mostly to meet space/bedroom/laundry room requirements. But it turned out that the six-foot cantilever to the east not only shades the sun from our living room (while letting in plenty of natural light), but also allows us to have a covered patio the entire length of the house. This does two things: makes for a great outdoor room, and keeps water/snow away from the foundation of the house. Had we *not* had the cantilever, we would not have been able to have *any* hardscape on the front side of the house, as that violates city code. So, this was a double bonus. On the west side of the house, we have a trellis that partially shades the entire length of the house, while letting light in, and balances out the cantilever. These elements turned out to be key attributes in keeping our air conditioning usage low.

Another design element that is both artistic and utilitarian: a Corbusian-influenced clerestory box and skylight that hangs in the top of the foyer above the stairwell in the center of our home. It is tilted slightly to the south,

Our clerestory under construction.

a character trait that prompts passers-by to stop, look, and tilt their head to their left, wondering what it could be.

It is an operable skylight. The skylight opens, acting as a chimney in the summer months. When we first opened the skylight in the late spring of 2009, the hot air moved up and out, limiting our need for air conditioning. We laughed later about the fact that we were surprised that it worked: wow—hot air actually *does* rise! It also brings in additional light, flooding our stairwell of slatted white wood with light—a signature Salmela design.

So the operable skylight is wonderful in the summer, but what about in the winter? Of

Operable skylight acts like a chimney.

View of our skylight from foyer below. Photo credit: Paul Crosby.

course we do not open the skylight, but I do find myself staring up there, almost seeing the warmer air stuck in that space, not circulating back down where we occupy the house. We should have put a fan up there.

Windows

With windows, there is always a tradeoff: the more windows, the more daylight, so the less you have to rely on artificial light (saving money and resources), and arguably the more pleasant it is to live in the home.[40] But, the more windows, the worse the house is insulated. This leads to the decision of double pane versus triple pane, how many layers of

low-E glazing, etc. Virtually all new windows are much more efficient than old windows, as building codes have required it.

One of the things we did not realize early on was how much the windows dictated the structure and layout of the house. I think our architect may have started with the windows and worked his way around them. We have a lot of windows! In fact, the entire east and west sides of our main level have hardly any wall space at all. This is great for reducing the need for lighting during the day, as well as for feeling an overall connectedness to the outdoors—which we love, and is a key component of biophilic design. It is not great for

Winter.

---

40 Many scientific studies, primarily those studying worker health and productivity, conclude in one way or another that exposure to natural light is vitally important to our physical and mental health. Anyone that works in a windowless office can attest to that!

energy use. So, we needed to make sure we invested in really good windows.

And that we did; or we should say, our architect did. David Salmela loves, and typically specifies, windows and doors from H Window Company, out of Ashland, Wisconsin. Our first major decision was whether to go with double pane or triple pane. The cost difference was not that substantial—about 8 percent more for triple pane. How did we know which is better?

Window efficiency is rated by the National Fenestration Rating Council. Like the R-factor of insulation, windows get a "U-factor" rating, which is the inverse of the R-factor. The rate of heat loss is indicated in terms of the U-value of a window assembly—not just the glass itself. That means it takes into account the window, the glazing, the spacers, and the frame. The lower the value, the greater the resistance to heat flow. The benefits of low-U value windows are not only reduced energy use, but also improved comfort and performance. Better windows can reduce the risk of condensation and improve the overall durability of the house. The LEED requirement for colder climates is that the U-factor is less than or equal to 0.35; you can get additional points for going lower than that. (The International Energy Conservation Code of 2009 also requires a U-factor of 0.35 or less; newer versions of LEED become more stringent as building codes improve.)

Windows have another metric: their solar heat gain coefficient (SHGC). Expressed as a value between zero and one, the SHGC of a window is a measurement of how much heat it transmits (the lower the number, the less heat it transmits). LEED only uses this metric for homes in warmer climates (which did not apply to us): the U factor can be up to 0.55, but the SHGC must be less than 0.35.

I learned that triple pane windows provide a substantially better U value than double pane: 25 percent better efficiency for our larger, non-operable windows, and 13 percent better efficiency for our smaller operable windows and doors. That seemed like a pretty good bump in performance for only 8 percent more in costs, and since our home is made of mostly windows, we figured that would pay off the most. Another added benefit of the triple panes, which we had not thought about, was the extra noise insulation—making our home very quiet.

The second decision was how many "low-E" coats to have on our windows. What is low-E? The "E" stands for emissivity, which is the ability of a material to radiate energy. Reducing the emissivity of a glass surface improves the window's insulating properties. Apparently, our windows already came with one low-E coating. (The way you can tell is by holding a match or candle up to the window. The reflection off the glass will show how many panes there are, and if there is low-E glass, one of the flames will be a slightly different color than the others; see photo—the farthest left flame is slightly pink, indicating low-E.) A second coating of low-E basically doubles the improvement in energy efficiency, but with a bigger price tag: that second coating was 29 percent more expensive. Visually, the second low-E coating would add a reflective look that darkens the interior and makes the exterior look like an office building. That was an easy decision: triple pane with one low-E coating provides significant energy savings for only 8 percent more. The additional energy sav-

Triple pane window with one low-E coating (at left).

ings, combined with an aesthetic I think we would have regretted (darker, more reflective windows), was not worth another 29 percent more in cost.

Our choice of triple pane, single low-E coating absolutely provides superior insulating performance and was one of the best decisions we made. We did not do it for LEED points—we did it for durability, comfort, and lower utility bills.

Insulation

The primary goal of insulation is to minimize heat transfer and thermal bridging between inside and outside of the house, so we are pri-marily referring to insulation along exterior walls and roofs. Insulation is typically one of the best bang-for-the-buck investments, particularly in colder climates: spend a little money on insulation, and save a lot of money on your heating and cooling bills. Though nobody will be able to see it once it is in, this is one of the most important decisions we can make.

Insulation is measured in terms of R-values, which gives a number to its thermal effectiveness. The higher the R-value, the higher the resistance to heat flow through the insulation.

LEED requires that insulation meet or exceed the R-value requirements listed in Chapter Four of the 2004 International Energy

Conservation Code (IECC). This is a complicated topic, so we had to assume our builder was familiar with both the IECC as well as the State Residential Code.[41] We had Jimmie, our Green Rater, conduct a pre-drywall thermal bypass inspection as part of his LEED duties. This was another value-add of LEED, because we had a third party coming in to verify how our insulation was installed.

Choosing insulation was one of the toughest decisions for me. Getting up the learning curve on all the different types of insulation and making an educated guess was a long process. We also had a deadline—once the house was framed and wired, we needed to make the decision, or further delay the building process and suffer the consequences.

We had many discussions about insulation. I visited different booths at the Building Green Expo in Chicago. Here's what I learned: Open-cell spray foam is the best because it assumes there will be water, and it allows absorption and drying. Closed-cell spray foam is the best because it completely fills the wall cavities and does not allow water anywhere. Open-cell foam can collapse behind the walls. Soy-based spray foam has soy in it (so that makes it green)! Fiberglass has been used forever and is the least expensive—and it now comes in the new and improved formaldehyde-free, so it's green! Cotton denim is the only natural product, and it's recycled, so it's really green. Cellulose works well too, and it's made from recycled newspapers—so it's green! Everyone

was selling, and their product was the best and greenest. I was confused.

Adding to the confusion was trying to figure out how to meet the LEED requirements: what in the world did all this mean? What is Chapter Four of the 2004 IECC? I had a hard time even finding this. The *LEED for Homes Reference Guide* suggests using RESCHECK, a free web model developed by the US Department of Energy that helps determine whether a home's insulation levels meet the IECC requirements. I checked out this model, and it required many inputs: square footage of walls, ceilings, windows, doors, plus the U-values of the windows and doors and the R-values of the insulation. Some of these things I knew, some I had to estimate. The reality is that there is not just one R-value for insulation. You have to take into account what the structure is made of (wood or metal, e.g.) and how many inches of insulation are installed, and that varies depending on whether you are talking about a roof or a wall.

Flash back to 2008: The house is framed and wired. It's time to insulate. To keep on schedule, the decision has to be made today. Our builder recommends closed-cell spray foam, a spray-on foam that expands as it is applied to the walls of the home, because it has the best insulating qualities per square inch. I have been assured it will meet the LEED requirements. Now that the house is framed, we cannot increase the depth of the

---

41 This was updated to the 2012 IECC in the newer version of LEED for Homes, v4, and will continue to be updated as building code evolves. The IECC is developed and published by the International Code Council (ICC) and is revised every three years through the ICC's governmental consensus process. The most recent IECC can be found and purchased through codes.iccsafe.org.

walls, so we are somewhat limited in that respect. But I can't help but wonder . . . what is spray foam?

I am thinking that the fact that foam is a petroleum-based product, and installers have to be fully masked to install it—presumably due to the health risks—makes it *not* a viable option.

What are our other options? Fiberglass, even formaldehyde-free, can shed fibers and off-gas long after it is installed, making it *not* a healthy choice. The insulating qualities of fiberglass for the exterior walls are also not compelling, particularly for areas around electrical outlets. Cotton denim interests me because it is an entirely natural product, is made out of recycled material, and is also biodegradable, but it is quite expensive, and if it gets wet, we are at risk of getting mold behind our walls. Even if we did want to use it, it turns out that the space in between the studs in our walls is *not big enough* to get enough cotton denim to attain the R-value we need to pass the building code (much less to get LEED certified). Whether it was fiberglass, denim, or cellulose—each of those three has a significantly lower R-value, so just to reach code level, we would have had to drop our ceilings and lose square footage along our walls, because we would have had to add many more inches of insulation. From a design standpoint, that simply would not work. Besides, anything but foam will not insulate around electrical outlets and other wall penetrations very well, which is always where the biggest leaks occur. Open cell lets water penetrate (like a sponge) and has R-value of only 3.5 per inch of foam. Closed cell spray foam will not let water penetrate it, has an R-value of 6 per inch of foam, and can help improve the home's structural strength. All signs point to closed-cell spray foam.

But the decision is not over, because there are different options for closed-cell spray foam—like soy. Is soy-based better? I find out that all spray foams have some sort of agricultural component, like soy or corn. But the component derived from natural materials is less than 5 percent, so it does not make much of a difference. The performance difference is negligible, our subcontractor does not carry it, and what's the difference to me if it is part soy or part corn? They are all some weird processed derivative of a crop that was once grown for food.

The builders recommended closed-cell spray foam for insulation called BASF Comfort Foam 178 Series. So, I get my hands on the Material Safety and Data Sheet (MSDS, now called Safety Data Sheets, or SDS). The US Occupational Safety and Health Administration (OSHA) has been requiring MSDSs for hazardous materials since May 26, 1986. I discover that spray foams used to have blowing agents that harmed the ozone layer (CFCs and HCFCs, which have been banned). But the BASF Comfort Foam 178 Series utilizes "an EPA-approved Zero Ozone-Depleting (Zero-ODP) blowing agent"—probably because it would be banned otherwise. So we are good there. But the MSDS reveals the following hazards:

- Causes serious eye damage.
- Causes skin irritation.
- Suspected of damaging the unborn child.

This pictogram is required by the US Department of Labor's Occupational Safety and Health Administration (OSHA) for chemicals that are considered a health hazzard. Closed-cell spray foam's Safety Data Sheet contains this warning.

- May cause damage to organs (kidney) through prolonged or repeated exposure (oral).[42]

Then I read through what the stuff is made of and their corresponding health effects. To name just a few:

- 75 percent polyol: Contact with the eyes and skin may result in irritation.
- 15 percent fluorocarbons (flame retardant): At levels above the recommended exposure limit, the fluorocarbon acts as a weak narcotic. Acute overexposure causes tremors, confusion, irritation, suffocation, and may result in cardiac sensitization.
- 5 percent dimethylaminoethanol: Contact with dimethylaminoethanol may result in severe irritation. Burns and permanent injury may result. Dimethylaminoethanol is extremely irritating to the skin and eyes. Direct contact with the liquid is corrosive. Acute inhalation exposures at high concentrations have been known to produce respiratory difficulties, loss of coordination, and decreased motor activity in rats.
- 2 percent ethylene glycol: Acute inhalation overexposure to ethylene glycol may produce irritation to the nose, throat, and upper respiratory tract. Acute ingestion overexposure is extremely harmful and may produce central nervous system effects, followed by depression, vomiting, drowsiness, coma, respiratory failure, convulsions and

---

42 BASF, Safety Data Sheet, COMFORT FOAM 178-XF B-Resin.

Spray foam installed in our garage, with fully protective garb.

damage to the kidneys, which may lead to death.[43]

Enough! It sounds horrible! How can we choose this stuff for our home? How was this hazardous substance ever concocted in the first place? Feeling like we have no other option, I take a few deep breaths. My primary question is whether we were exposed to any toxins once it is installed. I call my new friend, Jeremy, the insulator subcontractor. His answer? No, once the foam is sprayed,

it becomes completely inert and harmless within a few seconds.

My next concern is for the workers/installers of this product. Jeremy says that they require their workers to wear masks. (Although this does not entirely do the trick: I spoke with the worker who was taping around the windows, preparing for insulation, and he no longer blows the insulation because he had respiratory issues. He was twenty-five years old.)

Then I have an idea: what does the American Lung Association recommend for its healthy home? After all, a healthy home is our number one priority; energy efficiency was number two. It turns out that the American Lung Association actually recommends closed-cell spray foam for homes. Why? It is the least likely to allow mold in the house. Mold is a very serious allergen to everyone, but particularly to those of us who are especially sensitive to it (see chapter 5, Clean House). Ultimately, the conclusion is this: closed-cell spray foam not only has the highest R-value per inch (about 6.0), it also has the added benefit of finding its way around outlet holes and can cozy right up to any openings—a vast improvement over fiberglass insulation—least likely to have mold, and the American Lung Association recommends it. I am sold. We choose closed-cell spray foam.

Spray foam insulation can cost about three to four times more than blown cellulose or fiberglass, but their R-values are in the three to four per inch range, significantly lower than the rating of six per inch you get with spray foam. Additional benefits of closed-cell

43 BASF, Safety Data Sheet, COMFORT FOAM® 178-XF B-Resin.

Closed-cell spray foam installed around skylight.

spray foam include resilience to pests and additional structural soundness. For a home that you plan to live in for a long time, which we do, this seemed like the only way to go.

As with everything, it's a tradeoff. When I look at this guy who worked on our house, I am sad. When I look at our gas and electric bills, I am glad we did it. I have since referred many friends to Jeremy to add insulation to their roofs and attics, and they have noticed a huge difference in improved comfort and reduced draftiness of their homes—and lower gas bills.

With respect to insulation on interior walls, there is no need to go to the expense of closed cell spray foam. The only real reason for insulation on interior walls is to add a noise barrier. Recycled cotton denim is superior in its noise reduction qualities. It costs about twice as much as fiberglass or cellulose, which is why we picked it for only a few strategic spots: around our laundry room and mechanical room.

For remodeling, insulation can often have a strong return on investment. If you want to

Cotton denim insulation installed around the laundry room.

geek out, get a FLIR thermal imaging camera and point it at your walls and ceilings. It illustrates in rainbow colors the hot areas (red) and the cold areas (blue). When it is cold outside, you can very easily find the places where whoever built your home might have accidentally missed something—like entire areas of your wall or ceiling. I have an old FLIR camera, but now you can get them to work with a smartphone. It's really fun to aim that at people and pets. I brought my FLIR camera to my daughter's fifth grade class, where I was guest speaking on energy, and that was the kids' favorite part.

Air Infiltration

There are two LEED credits that address the tightness of the home: sealing up the house, and minimizing duct leakage. I put them in the same category because they both require a Green Rater to test the leakage rates, and they both have to do with air infiltration and leakiness, either within the house or between the house and the outdoors. The tighter the home, particularly in more extreme climates, the less energy it uses for heating and cooling. Typically tighter houses are also more comfortable because they are less drafty. The tradeoff, though, is that a very well sealed home can lead to poor indoor air quality and mold growth, so you have to pay a lot of attention to the mechanical ventilation.

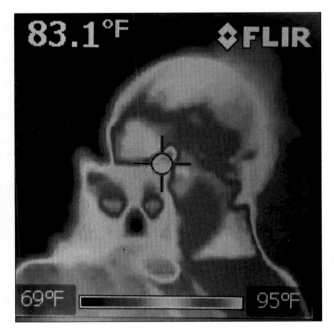

Infrared camera shows warm and cold spots.

Blower door test to determine leakiness of the house.

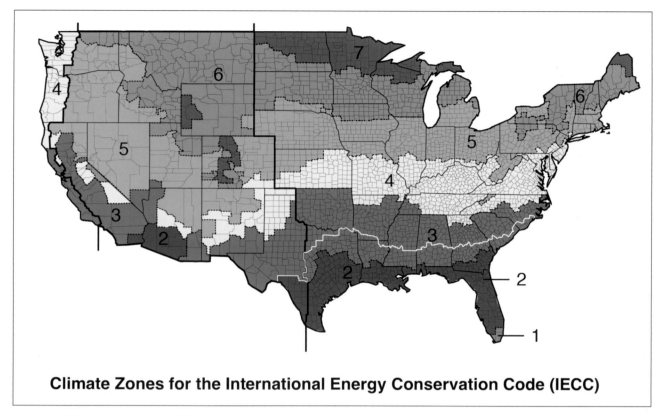

Climate Zones for the International Energy Conservation Code (IECC)

Source: US Department of Energy.

Going through LEED provides the quality assurance that your home is built tightly, because it requires the "blower door test," which is pretty cool, because it can actually test the leakiness of the house. A blower door test uses a powerful fan, mounted in the frame of an exterior door, to pull air out of the house, lowering the air pressure inside. The higher outdoor air pressure then flows through the home's cracks and openings, so the energy auditor can determine how tightly the home is sealed—that's the air infiltration rate. The measurement standard is referred to as "air changes per hour" (ACH) at the standard pressure differential, indoor to outdoor, of fifty pascals (equivalent to about a twenty-mile-per-hour wind buffeting the home). The performance require-

ments depend on your climate zone. Minneapolis is in climate zone six, so the maximum air leakage requirement was 5 ACH at 50 pascals (building codes have since become more stringent, so the LEED threshold requirements have decreased as well)—which only an energy rater can determine (and understand). Through Xcel Energy, you can get a home energy audit for $30, or an enhanced audit with a blower door test for $60—which puts the cost of our blower door test at $30. I've seen other quotes as high as $500 to $600. Since about quarter of a home's heat can be gained or lost through the home's walls, floors, and roof, it is worth the effort to have the test performed, and to check into utility-sponsored offerings that may dramatically reduce the price tag.

Just as a home's envelope should be tight to save energy, so should the air duct system—the system that distributes hot and cold air throughout the house, usually hidden behind walls. According to the *LEED for Homes Reference Guide*, duct leakage may account for 15 to 25 percent of total heating and cooling energy use. There is also a health and comfort issue: leaky ducts can draw moisture, dust, and other contaminants into the house; they also may distribute air unevenly throughout the house, so some rooms are hot and some are cold. While it never occurred to me to ask our subcontractor if the duct system they were installing would have minimal leaks, now that I understand this credit, it makes perfect sense.

The requirements for this credit are divided into two types: one for forced-air systems, and one for non-ducted HVAC systems (also called hydronic systems, because they use hot water to run through radiators or in-floor pipes to heat the house). We have a hydronic system to heat the house through in-floor heating—it is very comfortable, quiet heat. But we decided to have an air duct system as well, for two reasons: it's the only way to have air conditioning and dehumidification, and well-designed air systems are necessary for ventilation to keep the indoor air quality clean and healthy.

The LEED credit also goes on to require that no ducts be installed in exterior walls unless extra insulation is added to maintain the overall insulation level quality for an exterior wall without ducts. Ducts may be run inside interior wall cavities, but must be fully ducted—i.e., you cannot use the wall cavity as the duct (do people do that?). And, the insulation around ducts in unconditioned[44] spaces must have an R-value of at least six.

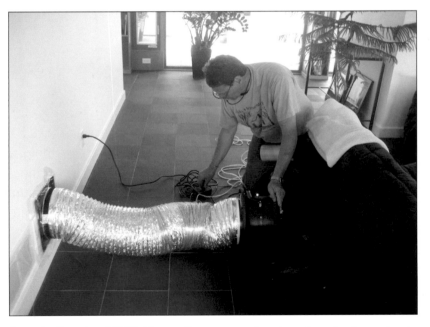

Jimmie Sparks, LEED Green Rater, conducting duct leakage test.

44 Unconditioned spaces are basically any spaces that are not "conditioned" for human occupancy, such as crawl spaces, spaces between walls, etc.

So, how do we know if we meet the performance standards? Again, Jimmie, our Green Rater, had to come and test the leakiness of the duct system, just as he tested the leakiness of the building itself through a blower door test. The duct leakage test took the longest, because all air supplies and returns had to be sealed before Jimmie could run the test. He covered them all with a plastic-wrap–type product, and then ran the test through an air return, as shown in the photo.

Another option LEED suggests is to locate the air-handler unit and all ductwork visibly within conditioned spaces—that is, no ductwork can be hidden in walls, chases, floors, or ceilings. This would be a very interesting design element and probably help us all better understand how the air is distributed throughout the house. Our builder actually has this in his house; it looks pretty cool but has a very industrial aesthetic. Most people would not consider this, however, unless they view ductwork as artwork (we didn't).

Both tests proved we met the LEED requirements. There were not really any options for us to think through here, other than considering *not* hiding ductwork behind walls. The extra cost was part of the Green Rater's overall fee of $1,800 for all of his tests. It's yet another added quality assurance process, for which I am thankful.

We have gone through the four major pieces of home design and construction that affect a home's energy efficiency: design, windows, insulation, and air infiltration. The next section addresses decisions around the major energy-consuming equipment in a home: HVAC systems, water heaters, appliances, and lighting—all of which started out as luxuries in the last century and have become necessities

today. The choices can be overwhelming, so I am hoping to simplify this process. It is important to remember that these *are* in order of priority—the first four have by far the largest impact in hot and cold climates, so those deserve primary attention. If you cannot change windows or have already insulated and sealed up your home, addressing these next four sections will have the biggest impact on your energy bill.

HVAC Systems

HVAC (heating, ventilation, and air conditioning) equipment can account for about 40 percent of a home's energy use. While ventilation is primarily addressed under *Clean Air* chapter 4, if you have ducted air conditioning, most of the equipment also serves to ventilate, so they are commonly combined into one scintillating discussion of HVAC equipment.

Heating and cooling equipment is not a decision that should be left solely up to the subcontractors, because it has an enormous impact on the comfort level and indoor air quality of your home. After a fair amount of research and discussions with the HVAC subcontractor, our plan was to install a ground-source heat pump, which many people refer to as geothermal. ("Geothermal" can be confusing because it refers also to geothermal energy, which works only in specific geographical places where underground reservoirs of steam and hot water can be tapped to generate electricity or to heat and cool buildings directly. In that case, geothermal *can* be considered "renewable" energy.) Ground-source heat pumps, also known as geo-exchange systems, take the relative heat and cooling from the earth to heat and cool the home. While some

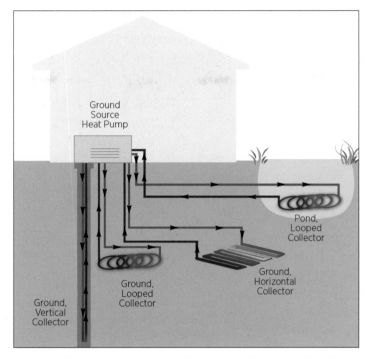

Ground Source Heat Pump Options. Photo credit: U.S. Department of Energy.

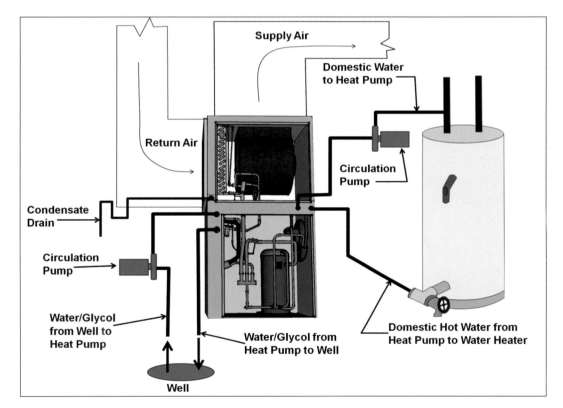

Ground Source Heat Pump Illustrated. Photo credit: U.S. Department of Energy.

might consider it "renewable" energy technology, it really is just super efficient technology.

The easiest way to think about it is as a heat exchange system that uses the earth's constant 50–55 degree Fahrenheit temperature to help you get to your desired home temperature, which is usually between 68 and 72 degrees. In the hot summer months, think about how hard that outdoor air-conditioning compressor has to work to bring in 90–100 degree air and cool it down. Instead, the ground-source heat pump relies on the 50-degree temperature of the earth for heat transfer—as a heat source in winter and a heat sink in summer, rather than outside air. With this type of system, there is no outdoor air-conditioning compressor. Those things are loud, ugly, take up valuable outdoor space, and need to be cleaned out at least annually. Not having an outdoor air conditioning compressor may even be reason enough to recommend this type of system, but its real worth is in its efficiency.

The system itself involves drilling holes either vertically deep into the ground or horizontally underground. (Ponds can also be used, but that was not an option for us.) Horizontal installation is usually less expensive, but requires more land where no tree roots could interfere with the pipes. In our case, we have ten vertical loops under the driveway that descend 120 feet.

Geo-exchange systems can cost an incremental 20 to 30 percent on a whole-house system. Through 2016, there was a federal tax credit that gave a 30 percent rebate off the total cost, including labor and installation.

That assumed specific models, though, and our particular model did not qualify us for the 30 percent federal tax credit (which I did not learn until after it was installed). That led me to believe that we do not have the most efficient heat pump on the market. Indeed, I believe our system was oversized. I believe we overpaid for that size, and we will continue to overpay as we use it (not to mention forgoing the tax credit that would have been in the $12,000 range had we gone down one model in size). If you are counting on a tax credit, be sure to read the fine print ahead of time and make sure your model is covered.[45] I now believe most homes have oversized HVAC systems, because the subcontractor does not want to hear complaints on that rare twenty-five-below night, that happens less than 1 percent of the time, that your system was not designed to handle.

The efficiency ratio of ground-source heat pumps is 3:1—which means you should be using about one third of the energy to heat and cool your home. (Nothing else can have more than a 1:1 efficiency ratio.) That does not necessarily translate into a utility bill that is one third the cost, because your home uses energy for other things like lighting and appliances. If heating and cooling your home is 39 percent of your utility bill, which is about average, then you can expect to save two thirds of that cost on an annual basis—thereby reducing your total utility bills (gas and electric) by 26 percent. So, if your utility bills are $5,000 per year, you can expect that to go down to $3,700, saving $1,300 per year.

45 The tax credit expired; check the website www.dsireusag.org for updated information on rebates and incentives.

For a newly constructed house, assume a geothermal system costs an incremental $15,000. The 30 percent federal tax credit brings it down to $10,500. If you save $1,300 per year, the system basically pays for itself within eight years. Is that a quick enough payback? That depends on your time horizon, but I would venture to guess that it is enough—and it should increase the value of the home. The cost to operate the heat pump is just the cost of the electricity it takes to run it; there is no natural gas. Granted, our electricity bill is higher than average, but our natural gas bill is much lower.

From an environmental standpoint, if you get all of your electricity from coal, that's *not* ideal. But it depends on the comparison. Most new homes in our area would be using natural gas for heating the home and electricity for cooling the home. Though cleaner than coal, natural gas is still a fossil fuel, still pollutes, and will never be clean or renewable. Electricity generation can keep getting cleaner and cleaner from renewable sources. When I did my analysis for our home, the geo-exchange system was so much more efficient, that even when assuming our electricity was 70 percent generated by coal, the net effect was significantly less pollution.

For us, we planned on being in our home longer than eight years (it has already been longer), and the annual reduction in energy use and corresponding pollution makes it an investment well worth consideration. For remodels, it might not make sense financially unless you are planning on replacing your furnace anyway and have an appetite for a messy yard for a while!

On the maintenance side, it was predicted to be slightly less than a standard system, because there is no outdoor air conditioning compressor to clean. In our experience, however, the maintenance and repair costs have been significantly higher than expected. I have our HVAC subcontractors' mobile phone numbers and text them all too often. The boiler has had to be replaced twice in six years, valves and sensors go out unexpectedly, a gasket was installed incorrectly, etc.—it's always a fun game to find out what's wrong. The maintenance and repair bills have, by now, offset some of our financial savings (but at least the environmental savings are still there). I have spoken at length to our HVAC contractor about our problems, and the crux of the issue is this: most high efficiency equipment is just more complicated because it has more variables. The way he explains it, more variables, parts, sensors, and valves naturally lead to more maintenance. So, there is a balance point between the level of efficiency and the level of complication. That tradeoff needs to be communicated and discussed, ideally early in the process, between the homeowner and the design team, inclusive of the HVAC contractor, in order to find the sweet spot—and in order to manage expectations. So, in hindsight, we deliberately chose more efficiency, but that came with more complications.

In addition to a closed loop ground-source heat pump, our system consists of a backup boiler powered by natural gas, a side-arm tank that preheats our hot water whenever the pump is running (sold to us as "free hot water"), a heat recovery ventilator, and an air source heat pump for air conditioning. We also decided on in-floor radiant heat as the primary method of heating our home. Radiant heat is very comfortable and quiet, and is an excellent way to distribute heat throughout the home. Ground-source heat pumps, since they are hydronic (water-based) systems, work particularly well with in-floor heating systems, because a closed-loop, water-to-water transfer of heat is simply more efficient.

There are different methods of installing in-floor heat. We used Warmboard (as shown in the photo), which is made with grooves in which the pipes snugly fit, so the flooring can go directly over the Warmboard. Warmboard also has layers of aluminum, which help dis-tribute the heat more evenly across the floor, thereby decreasing energy bills, relative to other types of installations. Warmboard can itself be a structural layer of flooring, typically used in new construction, or it can be a thinner layer used in remodeling.

Ecowarm, a newer product competing with Warmboard, touts its sustainability certifications, ease of installation, and 30–40 percent lower cost than Warmboard. While I have no experience with Ecowarm (it was not available when we built our home), it is worth

Warmboard for in-floor heating.

checking out as an alternative, high-performance product for in-floor heating.

LEED does not specify which type of system you get; it only requires that equipment be efficient—the more highly efficient, the more points you earn. (This is where it gets pretty technical and boring, so feel free to skip or skim this next part.)

LEED's prerequisites are that you have to (a) design and size HVAC equipment properly using ACCA Manual J, the ASHRAE 2001 Handbook of Fundamentals, or an equivalent computation procedure, (b) use Energy Star–labeled programmable thermostats, and (c) install HVAC equipment that meets the requirements of the Energy Star for Homes national Builder Option.[46] What's that? ACCA is the Air Conditioning Contractors of America association that writes the standards for design, maintenance, and performance of "indoor environment" systems. It is supposed to help contractors model expected heating and cooling loads, and then design and size the system to handle those loads, with a 15 percent cushion account for "extraordinary loads."

For (a), our subcontractors did use Manual J to size our system. The term "properly" is open to debate, though, as I believe the 15 percent cushion may have been a bit higher. They told us we needed two heat pumps. Did we really, though? We also have Energy Star programmable thermostats, meeting part (b).

Then, for part (c), there is a table of incomprehensible numbers that we needed to exceed to meet the prerequisite or earn any

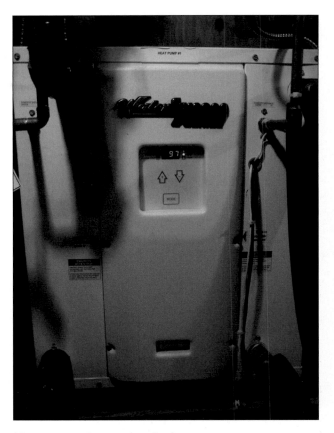

Heat pump in mechanical room.

points. There are minimums for central air conditioners and air source heat pumps; gas, oil, or propane furnaces; gas, oil, or propane boilers; and ground-source heat pumps. For our climate zone and our system, central air conditioning and air source heat pumps must be ≥ 13 SEER for the prerequisite, ≥ 14 for two points, and ≥ 15 for three points. SEER, I learn, is the Seasonal Energy Efficiency Ratio. It is the cooling output (in BTUs) divided by the total electric energy input (in watt-hours); the higher the rating, the more efficient the system. Since 2006, the United States has required that all new air conditioners have a minimum SEER rating of 13—so we knew we at least met the prerequisite.

46 *LEED for Homes Reference Guide,* 201.

Moving on to our natural gas boiler: since we have a ground-source heat pump that heats our house and preheats our domestic hot water, the boiler is relatively small and only serves as a backup. As a result, our gas bill is minimal. The boiler needs to be ≥ 85 AFUE for the prerequisite; ≥ 87 AFUE for two points; and ≥ 90 AFUE for three points. What is AFUE? The acronym stands for the Annual Fuel Utilization Efficiency. According to Furnace Compare, "the AFUE is the most widely used measure of a furnace's heating efficiency. It measures the amount of heat actually delivered to your house compared to the amount of fuel that you must supply to the furnace. Thus, a furnace that has an 80 percent AFUE rating converts 80 percent of the fuel that you supply to heat—the other 20 percent is lost out of the chimney." Our boiler is a Buderus Logamax plus GB142, with an AFUE of 96 percent—so only 4 percent is wasted, easily exceeding the highest LEED threshold.

But we are not yet done with this agonizing credit. We also have a closed loop ground-source heat pump. It needs to be ≥ 14.1 EER and ≥ 3.3 COP for the prerequisite; ≥ 15.5 EER and ≥ 3.6 COP for two points; and ≥ 17 EER and ≥ 4.0 COP for four points. COP—oh boy, another acronym—is the Coefficient of Performance, or the ratio of heat output to the unit of supplied input. In general, ground-source heat pumps are 300 to 350 percent efficient, as opposed to even the most efficient furnaces, which can never exceed 100 percent. We have a Water Furnace E-Series heat pump. The specifications that came with operating instructions give COPs ranging from a low of 2.93 to a high of 8.98, depending on the temperature of the loop field (underground) and the temperature required by me, the owner. So while there is not one COP rating for this system, Jimmie Sparks affirmed that we met the prerequisite. Phew.

Water Heaters

According to the Water Research Foundation, hot water usage is one third of total indoor water usage. Water usage is addressed in *Water Efficiency,* chapter 7; this section addresses the energy needed to heat water for showering, laundry, dishes, hand washing, etc.

The goal is pretty obvious: reduce energy consumption associated with the domestic hot water system, including improving the efficiency of the hot water system design as well as the layout of the fixtures in the home. According to the USGBC, as much as one third of a home's total energy bill is spent on heating water—not only for the end use, but also in the heat lost through the piping system and storage tank. Three strategies work together to achieve this goal: the hot water distribution system, pipe insulation, and the efficiency of the equipment.

Hot Water Distribution System

About 10 to 15 percent of energy use in hot water systems is wasted in distribution losses, so this LEED credit encourages locating fixtures as close as possible to the central water heater. I have been in many development and architect meetings, and the location of the hot water tank has never been under discussion: it is always located in the mechanical room, which is typically the farthest away from all household activity. That seems logical: in day-to-day living, why would anyone want it closer?

First, we needed to choose one of three designs for the distribution system: a structured plumbing system, a central manifold system, or a compact design of conventional system. We have a structured plumbing system, because it allows for a recirculation loop. For two points, the system must meet all of the following:

- The system must have a demand-controlled circulation loop that is insulated to at least R-4. The total length of the circulation loop must be less than forty linear feet of plumbing in one-story homes. (Add twice the ceiling height for two-story homes, add four times the ceiling height for three- or four-story homes.)
- Branch lines from the loop to each fixture must be less than ten feet long and a maximum of one half inch nominal diameter.
- The system must be designed with a push-button control in each full bathroom and the kitchen and an automatic pump shutoff.[47]

The plumbing system is probably the thing with which I am least familiar. I had to ask our plumbing contractor several times which type of distribution system we were installing. The one thing I did know was that I wanted a recirculation loop, because in our previous home, it would take at least three minutes of

the water running in our shower for it to get hot, which drove us crazy. It was a waste of water, a waste of energy, and a waste of time. Having a recirculating loop fixes this problem, because it slowly and constantly pumps hot water through the pipes. Now, our wait time for hot water in the shower is about three seconds. I love the recirculating loop! It does take energy to run the pump, but it can be turned off on a timer, and overall it is a net energy saver—in addition to a huge water saver.

The issue in this credit for us was the length of the recirculation loop, and I think this is where design and functionality of the house won out over energy efficiency of our hot water distribution system. Our ceilings are nine feet on the main level, and we are three stories, so that allowed us seventy-six feet for the entire recirculation loop. That seems like a lot, but our house is very long and thin. Our water heater is located in the mechanical room in the south end of the basement; our master shower is located in the north end of the second floor. Since the length of our house is sixty-two feet, I don't need a measuring tape to know that the full loop has to be longer than seventy-six feet. We also do not have a push-button control in each full bathroom and kitchen to turn off the pump. We considered that, but it was more expensive (and more complicated) than just installing one central timer on pump.

While we spent more money for the recirculation pump, I'm not sure how we could have even gotten the points, given the maximum branch length requirement. I suppose we could have installed a tankless water heater for our master shower and not attached it to the recirculation loop; the

---

47 *LEED for Homes Reference Guide*, 208.

rest of the hot water demand fixtures would have fallen within the linear foot limit. But doing that would not have allowed us to utilize the hot water tank that is preheated by our ground-source heat pump system, and in the end would probably have cost us more in energy bills. So, no points here, and I have no regrets.

PIPE INSULATION

To meet the LEED performance requirement of pipe insulation, all domestic hot water piping needs to have a minimum of R-4 insulation. As discussed under "Insulation," the R-value gives a number to its thermal effectiveness. The higher the R-value, the higher the resistance to heat flow. Insulation needs to be properly installed on all piping to elbows to adequately insulate the 90-degree bend. This helps reduce energy use and keep the water temperature as high as possible.

To start, what types of pipes are out there? Copper has been the metal of choice for plumbing fixtures because it is a relatively soft metal, so it can bend easily and requires fewer metal fasteners. It is also resistant to bacteria, contains no lead, and resists corrosion—so it is very durable. Our central manifold uses copper for those reasons; they are shown with foam insulation sleeves around them—complying with LEED. In 2006, the price of copper rose dramatically, and though it peaked then, it still is expensive; many plumbers have switched to plastic pipes for cost as well as ease of installation.

Plastic pipes can be made of PVC, CPVC, or PEX. PVC is polyvinyl chloride—one of the most widely used plastics in the world and

PEX piping.

one of the most toxic, from cradle to grave. I was clear with our builders I wanted absolutely *nothing* made from PVC in our house. (There is one air pipe that vents to the outside that simply could not be found in anything other than PVC, so we got 99.9 percent there. But then, there were the toys.) PVC piping is meant to be used for cold water applications only. For hot water applications, CPVC, or chlorinated polyvinyl chloride, is often used. It's the same thing, to me—so, no CPVC either.

We ended up using PEX for all of the plumbing beyond the copper central manifold for our in-floor heating. PEX, which is cross-linked polyethylene, has been used in Europe for decades and in the United States since about 1980, according to the PEXinfo website. Its benefits are that it resists buildup of chlorine and scale (though our water should be chlorine-free!) and it will not develop pinholes. Since it is flexible, it is much easier to install and requires fewer fittings. From my research, PEX does not leach any chemicals into the water, but I've seen mixed reviews on the toxicity of PEX. Unlike copper, it cannot be recycled.

Manifold plumbing system with foam insulation around copper pipes.

Back to the point . . . our hot water piping needed to have R-4 insulation. This point caused me some grief in getting the correct information. If you look up "PEX R Value" on the web, you get all sorts of comments that its R-value is better than copper's. But what is the R-value? Our plumber did not know. I called the technical service department of Uponor, the company that supplies PEX tubing. They emailed me a chart of the R-values of the piping, because of course it varies with the size of the pipes. The half-inch pipe has an R-value of 0.199; the one-inch pipe has an R-value of 0.193. Not even close to four—the minimum required value. How would we even get there? We would have to wrap all pipes in pretty thick insulation, which would no doubt cost a lot in materials and labor. Would it have been worth the energy savings due to heat loss from the pipes? I really don't think so, since the PEX lines are all in interior walls, and the home is heated. So, no LEED point here.

For homes with copper pipes, adding foam insulation on the outside of the pipes is an easy addition that does make a lot of sense. Foam insulation comes in many sizes, pre-slit, and can be placed around metal pipes simply and inexpensively.

R-Value Equation for Tubing:
R-Value = (Ln(O.D.ft/I.D.ft))/(2*pi*K)

Wirsbo AquaPEX	R-Value
1/4"	0.3199
3/8"	0.258029911
1/2"	0.198536275
5/8"	0.193477293
3/4"	0.192038343
1"	0.192637558
1 1/4"	0.192332441
1 1/2"	0.193283421
2"	0.192292068

PEX piping R-values.

This section prescribes minimum efficiency standards for gas water heaters, electric water heaters, or solar water heaters. The measure is EF, or energy factor, and there are different requirements for different size water heaters (ranging from forty to eighty gallons). According to the US Department of Energy, the EF indicates a water heater's overall energy efficiency based on the amount of hot water produced per unit of fuel consumed over a typical day. This includes the following:

- Recovery efficiency—how efficiently the heat from the energy source is transferred to the water.
- Standby losses—the percentage of heat loss per hour from the stored water compared to the heat content of the water (water heaters with storage tanks).
- Cycling losses—the loss of heat as the water circulates through a water heater tank, and/or inlet and outlet pipes.

A higher energy factor means a more efficient water heater. You might think: great, all I have to do is buy the water heater with the highest EF factor. Not true. Higher energy factor values do not always translate into lower annual operating costs—you have to compare fuel sources. It is also important to consider the size, overall cost, and first hour rating. Natural gas water heaters tend to be much less expensive than electric, partially due to the fact that currently, natural gas is cheap.

We have two hot water tanks in our mechanical room: one that stores hot water that is preheated by the ground-source heat pump, whenever the pump is running (meaning, whenever we are either heating or cooling the house, which is more than half the time). We have a natural gas boiler that serves as a backup heat source that heats the domestic hot water when the pump is not running. In this case, our gas bill goes up marginally, and our electric bill goes down. The first tank, the pre-heat tank, feeds the second tank—an eighty-gallon Boilermate tank by Amtrol. This, I learned, is called an "indirect-fired water heater." So it is not actually a water heater, it is a "side-arm" tank, and it does not have an EF rating. So, we are left not knowing whether we would have met the LEED requirements of hot water equipment, except that intuitively, we know that a pre-heat tank that captures and stores excess heat is pretty darn efficient.

The *LEED for Homes Reference Guide* clarifies that homes using alternative water heating designs, such as a small-tank, combination

Domestic hot water pre-heat tank.

tankless/tank systems, or heat-pump preheat systems (ours), should submit what is called a "Credit Interpretation Request" or use the "performance pathway." The performance pathway is the energy modeling route, which we did use.

Our HVAC and ground-source heat pump contractors designed this entire system. Thankfully, they knew about the side-arm pre-heat tank, because that is something I would not have figured out on my own.

We did briefly consider tankless water heaters, because at the time tankless water heaters were becoming trendy due to their efficiencies, and natural gas was twice as expensive. Tankless water heaters are supposed to save you a lot of money, because you do not have to heat a fifty to eighty gallon tank of hot water continuously. Wanting to cover all my bases, I did a little more research on tankless water heaters. *Consumer Reports* had come out with some interesting conclusions:

> Tank-less water heaters, which use high-powered burners to quickly heat water as it runs through a heat exchanger, were 22 percent more energy efficient on average than the gas-fired storage-tank models in our tests. That translates into a savings of around $70 to $80 per year, based on 2008 national energy costs. But because they cost much more than storage water heaters, it can take up to 22 years to break even—longer than the 20-year life of many models. Moreover, our online poll of 1,200 readers revealed wide variations in installation costs, energy savings, and satisfaction. . . . Here's what else we found: Tank-less water heaters do not deliver hot water instantaneously. It takes time to heat the water to the target temperature, and just like storage water heaters, any cold water in the pipes needs to be pushed out. And tank-less models' electric controls mean you'll also lose hot water during a power outage.

This review, combined with the high up-front costs, made me question their viability. Then, I learned that tank-less models need electrical outlets for their fan and electronics, upgraded gas pipes, and their own ventilation system—vastly complicating the installation when you think about having to have these near every showerhead and appliance that needs hot water. All of this adds up to my one conclusion: do not install tankless water heaters.

There are several other types of water heaters, including solar thermal (discussed later). Because technologies continue to change, it's best to visit websites like Consumer Reports for more recent unbiased views. In any case, you need to think about overall goals (do you want to eliminate natural gas and go electric?), the size of the system you need (depends on the size of your household), what you can fit in your mechanical room (or behind your shower), and what you can afford. Just remember to only include the *incremental* up-front costs and savings in any analysis.

Appliances

Household appliances are responsible for 20 to 30 percent of a home's energy use and about 25 percent of its indoor water use. Thankfully, the Department of Energy has the Energy Star program, which independently certifies products that save energy without sacrificing features or functionality. The Energy Star label ensures the appliance is more energy-efficient than its alternative, so I did not have to look up every different standard of energy efficiency measure for each type of appliance. I just had to look up our appliances in the list of Energy Star products on the energystar.gov website. LEED only cares about the biggest appliances: refrigerators, dishwashers, and clothes washers. Energy Star–labeled ceiling fans are also included, not because they are big energy hogs, but because ceiling fans themselves are encouraged, as they reduce the demand for heating and cooling.

Energy Star logo. Source: US Department of Energy.

Because models and technologies are constantly changing, I won't go into detail about every brand we considered for every appliance; just a few. We like our Bosch refrigerator. We like our Miele dishwasher primarily due to the cutlery tray and its quietness, but they have valve issues that require replacement every two years, so we do not like that. We do not love our Miele clothes washer, even though it gave us a lot of LEED points for efficiency, because the cycles are long and loud—but it still does the job well. That's about it. It's simple enough to just look for the Energy Star label when choosing appliances, and you know you are saving energy compared to the alternative. Energy Star–labeled appliances do not cost more, but they absolutely cost less to operate. Many utilities offer rebates for

Energy Star–labeled appliances as an incentive to purchase them. I honestly do not know why anyone would buy something *not* Energy Star–labeled.

I should add, though, that Energy Star does not label *all* types of appliances. Small refrigerators, ovens, and stoves, for example, are not yet rated. Many other product categories are rated—including lighting, heating and cooling equipment, electronics, commercial food service equipment, water heaters, and computers—so it is worth checking out. Everything is listed on the website, as long as the Department of Energy still exists and continues to be funded by Congress.

Speaking of stoves, the stovetop decision was difficult for us. Even though LEED does not address this appliance, I am including it here because we have a stovetop with two electrical induction burners and four natural gas burners. We were accustomed to natural gas burners, so moving to induction was a big deal. Induction only works with pans that are magnetic, so they do not work with our nonstick pans that we use to fry eggs every morning. Other than that, we *always* use our induction cooktop. It heats up water much faster, it melts chocolate without a double boiler, and it is much safer—we are not burning a fossil fuel in our home. When you think about it, it's pretty crazy how easily and safely we just turn a knob, and fire is burning and polluting the inside of your home. Without proper ventilation, that can be a health hazard. Had we to do it all over again, I would go with only induction stovetops and no gas burners. I would also switch our gas dryer to an electric dryer, even though gas dryers are more efficient.

The idea of not burning fossil fuels in our home is growing on me, even as I inhale the fumes of the gas-powered lawn mower from outside. (I know—dream big.)

While these appliances are all important, there are many more electronic items that can significantly add to a home's energy use: microwaves, sump pumps (ours runs *all* the time), televisions, extra bar-size fridges and freezers (which are not Energy Star–rated at all, so you cannot look it up), computers, etc. Like lighting and air conditioning, it ends up being the homeowner's responsibility for how much energy is really saved. Starting out with more efficient appliances is definitely important, but the daily operations can have a huge impact.

Lighting

Lighting can account for 5 to 15 percent of a home's total energy use. That may not be a huge portion, but it is typically one of the easiest things to address and has the best return on investment.

Switch Your Light Bulbs to LEDs ASAP

The winters are dark and cold here in Minneapolis, and I was not happy with our outdoor lights. They got my attention because we were advised by the police to keep them on all night after a recent burglary. So, in the winter, they are on from about 4:30 p.m. until 6:30 a.m.—fourteen hours per day. The fixtures themselves are okay, but the bulbs that came with them were 50-watt halogen spotlights. With CFLs (compact fluorescent lights) and LEDs (light emitting diodes) offering lower wattage options, and their color and quality continuing to improve, I decided to do a little comparison-shopping.

Light bulb comparison can be tricky—you have to understand the concept of "lumens" (the amount of light they emit) as well as the "K factor" (color) of each light to be able to compare apples to apples. People tend to think that wattage represents how bright a bulb is (as in, a 100-watt bulb is much brighter than a 50-watt bulb), but that is no longer the case since CFLs and LEDs were introduced to the market. The brightness of the bulb is represented by "lumens"—so when you shop, that's what to compare. The K factor is the "color" of the light. LEDs used to have more of a bluish tint, but their color has become softer and warmer, more like the older incandescent bulbs.

CFLs have mercury in them and have to be disposed of properly as a hazardous material. LEDs do not have mercury, are lower wattage than CFLs, and last longer. (Green building guides published in 2008 or earlier will recommend replacing bulbs with CFLs, but since around 2009, LEDs have become a much better way to go.)

I was pleased to have found some LED EcoSmart bulbs at the Home Depot. These 8.6 watt bulbs cost $9.97 each, provide 429 lumens (similar to our existing bulbs), and last 50,000 hours. I compared them to three different options:

1. 50-watt halogen bulb (what I am replacing): This 50-watt bulb is $7.47 at Home Depot, provides 520 lumens, and lasts 3,000 hours. According to the box, 3,000 hours is equivalent to 2.7 years—which means they assume the bulb is turned on three hours per day. Realistically, though, they are on about fourteen hours per night in the winter and maybe seven in the summer, for an average of ten hours per day, so if you use that as the assumption, they would last less than ten months.

2. 40- to 60-watt traditional incandescent bulbs[48] (the cheapest bulb): The 40-watt and 60-watt bulbs have lumens of 360 and 630, respectively (so about in the mid-

---

48 Note: The Energy Independence and Security Act of 2007 included light bulb provisions that require light bulbs to be more efficient. They did not ban incandescent bulbs, as much of the press reported. I've included incandescent bulbs here because you can still buy them, and they are still the least expensive—in terms of up-front cost only.

dle of the LED's 429 lumens). A six-pack of these incandescent bulbs goes for $7.97 ($1.33 each), and they last 1,000 hours.

3. Compact fluorescent bulb (CFL) bulb: A necessary comparison, because of its low wattage, these 14-watt compact fluorescent lights have an output of 450 lumens, last 8,000 hours, and cost $10.97 for a two-pack ($5.49 each).

How do the LEDs compare to these three different options? Other than the initial purchase price, two other costs need to be factored in: the replacement costs of the bulbs over the life of one LED, and the annual operating costs of the bulbs. These three variables combine to form the true cost of the light bulbs over their lifetime.

Replacement costs of the lights. Since I am comparing the LED bulb to the others, that is my base case. The LED lasts 50,000 hours. So, the proper comparison is how many times I will need to buy another light bulb over that timeframe. I'll assume the costs of the various bulbs stay constant over time. Assuming they are turned on an average of ten hours per day, I first calculate how many years the bulbs will last. Then, in comparison to the LED bulb, I need to figure out how many times I would need to purchase the bulb, and multiply that by the cost of the bulb.

LED: life of 13.7 years. $0 lifetime replacement cost.

Halogen: life of 0.8 years—so you'd have to buy a replacement bulb seventeen times over the life of one LED bulb = 17 x $7.47 = $127 lifetime replacement cost.

Incandescent: life of 0.3 years—so you'd have to buy a replacement bulb forty-six times over the life of one LED bulb = 46 x $1.33 = $61 lifetime replacement cost.

CFL: life of 2.2 years–so you'd have to buy a replacement bulb six times over the life of one LED bulb = 6 x $5.49 = $33 lifetime replacement cost.

Annual operating costs of the lights. To get to this, you have to look at your electric bill and find out how much you are charged per kilowatt-hour (kWh). One kilowatt hour = a 100 watt bulb turned on for ten hours (which equals 1,000 watt hours, which is the same thing as one kilowatt hour). In Minnesota, our utility rate is about nine or ten cents per kWh. I'll assume that rate stays at nine cents over the years, though it is likely to go up.

The formula for the annual operating cost of the bulb is as follows:

Cost of electricity per kWh x 10 hours per day x 365 days per year x bulb wattage rating / 1000.

(You have to divide it by 1,000 because we have the cost per kilowatt-hour, not the cost per watt-hour, and one kilowatt-hour = 1000 watt-hours.)

- Annual cost to operate one LED bulb: $0.09 x 10 x 365 x 8.6/1000 = $2.83
- Annual cost to operate one halogen bulb: 0.09 x 10 x 365 x 50/1000 = $16.43

- Annual cost to operate one incandescent bulb: 0.09 x 10 x 365 x 50/1000 = $16.43
- Annual cost to operate one CFL bulb: 0.09 x 10 x 365 x 14/1000 = $4.61

So, while the initial cost of the LED bulb is higher, the ongoing operating costs of electricity are lower, and you avoid the replacement costs of the other bulbs. Comparing the incremental costs of the other three bulbs to the LED bulb for a life cycle analysis:

LED versus halogen: You pay $2.00 more for the LED bulb, but save $13.60 in electricity costs each year (from above, $16.43 - $2.83 = $13.60). That more than pays for the incremental cost of the bulb within a few months' time. Plus, you avoid an additional $127 for not having to purchase replacement bulbs. Over the life of the LED bulb, you save over $300—and that's just for one bulb! Multiply that by five outdoor light fixtures, and that's a savings of $1,500. This is clearly a financial no-brainer, not even including the avoidance of labor time to replace the bulb. (Note: the lifetime savings is calculated by taking the difference in lifetime energy costs + lifetime replacement costs, less the initial cost of the LED bulb.)

LED versus incandescent: You pay $8.14 more for the LED bulb, but also save $13.60 in electricity costs each year. So, just on operating costs alone, the LED bulb pays for itself in less than two years. Plus, you save an additional $61 by avoiding having to purchase replacement bulbs. Over the life of the LED bulb, you would save $243—again just for one bulb!

LED versus CFL: You pay only $3.98 more for the bulb, and save only $1.77 in electricity costs per year; this has a payback of two and a quarter years. Plus, you save $33 by avoiding replacement costs, not to mention the hassle of having to properly dispose of the CFLs due their mercury content (a hazardous waste). Over the life of the bulb, you would save a little over $49.

So, compared to any of these bulbs, the LED comes out a clear winner, even above the CFL. Compared to a CFL, I would save almost $50 per bulb; if I have six bulbs, that equates to $300—and worth the trip to Home Depot!

What does the analysis look like if the bulbs are used for less than ten hours per day? The lifetime cost comparison remains the same. The only thing that changes is how quickly the LED bulb pays for itself. If the bulb is turned on only one hour per day or less, the energy and replacement costs barely make it worth it.

In our case, since we do average ten hours per day, and we replaced halogen bulbs, we save $13.60 in energy costs per year, *and avoid* $127 in replacement costs over the next decade. Our payback in energy savings alone is a little less than two months. If we had the lights on for only three hours per day, it would take a little more than seven months for the energy savings to pay for the incremental cost of the LED bulb. Still a great deal! It's surprising that Home Depot can keep these bulbs in stock!

Another note: Nowhere do I quantify the benefit of the time and energy needed to go buy more bulbs and replace them every year. Surely this is worth something!

Many people decide they will wait to replace their current bulbs until they burn out. It does seem like a waste to get rid of a perfectly good bulb before it wears out, but I disagree with that approach. It is a waste—a waste of energy and money—for every day you have incandescent bulbs in your home, even if they are still working. If LEDs add value, why not start adding value *today*? I hereby give you permission and relieve the guilt to get rid of your old incandescent bulbs (and if they are CFLs, they have mercury, so they must be disposed of as hazardous materials), and replace them with LEDs immediately! You cannot afford not to.

While lighting typically accounts for a small percent of a home's energy use, it is hands-down the easiest, quickest way to save energy. And financially, switching to LED bulbs is a slam dunk.

Being one of the first to install the new LED (light-emitting diode) recessed can fixtures made by CREE, we were among the early adopters in this area. The fixtures we chose, LR6 recessed down lights, had just come on the market. They were rated at 12 watts for 673 lumens and were projected to last 35,000 hours (though the website says 50,000, I am going with the Energy Star rating of 35,000 hours). When I plugged the fixture into my watt meter, the reading was only 6 watts. The reason for this low relative wattage is that *all* the electricity goes into producing light instead of heat. Older light bulb technology is so inefficient because of heat waste. While the extra heat might not be exactly wasted in the winter in our climate, the heat is unwelcome in the summer and in warmer climates.

The light output of the LEDs we chose compares to a 60-watt incandescent (regular)

LED lights under the cantilever.

bulb, or a 14-watt CFL bulb, which have life-times of up to 1,000 hours and 15,000 hours, respectively. The LED recessed can light is more diffused than spot lighting, but I like that; it is also dimmable. Another benefit is that they do not give off any heat, thereby reducing the risk of snow melt and ice dams in between the roof and the ceiling. And, unlike CFLs, they do not contain any mercury.

Did the LED cans cost more? Of course they did. While the large price tag of $143.75 cost per can was about 25 percent more than our choice of incandescent cans, the price has been going down steadily since we purchased them. And, if they do last 35,000 hours, that's really about twenty years (assuming they are on five hours per day, every day). The energy savings amounts to about $10 per year per can; so if we paid $30 more per can, that's a three-year payback, not including any bulb replacement costs. It was well worth it, regardless of the LEED points.

Yes . . . getting back to the point—LEED points. The prerequisite for lighting requires that you install at least four Energy Star–labeled light fixtures or Energy Star–labeled compact fluorescent light bulbs in high-use rooms (kitchen, dining room, living room, family room, hallways).

This seemed odd to me. We could have had an entirely inefficient lighting package, then go for LEED, and all we would have to do would be to *add* four more fixtures or CFL bulbs in a common area. What if you lived in a small little studio and you only needed two fixtures? It seems like the overall percentage would be more important than the number. Anyway, all of our LED lights are Energy Star–labeled, we have way more than four,

and they are all in our high-use rooms, so we met the prerequisite.

For additional points, you need to install at least 60 percent Energy Star–qualified hard-wired fixtures and 100 percent Energy Star–qualified ceiling fans (if any). I counted all of our LED cans and the rest of our fixtures, which are mostly FLOS Glo-Balls that dim down to look like moons floating in the sky (but are not Energy Star–qualified). By my calculations, 82 percent of all of our indoor fixtures are the LED lights, so we would have earned three LEED points here.

LEED also rewards you for having all outdoor lights either on motion sensor controls or integrated photovoltaic cells, because that obviously saves energy (some of ours comply). Commercial building codes now require much more in terms of occupancy and vacancy sensors, as this technology is pretty inexpensive and another easy way to be more energy-efficient.

After living in our home for eight years, we have not had to replace one LED recessed can. Not true for our halogen, electricity-sucking, expensive FLOS Glo-Balls—those bulbs need replacement at least once per year. As for the quality of the LEDs, I'd say, "Meh." The overall output of light is not that high, and their dimming functionality is mediocre at best—they start to slightly flicker when they are dimmed, driving everyone in the house a little batty. And while no lights have gone out, some of them have turned a little pink. We got a quote to replace them with improved LED technology, but then the pink ones turned back to normal again, so the originals remain. (You can't just unscrew these like a normal bulb; it's the entire fixture, and somewhat

FLOS Glo-Balls in main living area.

of an inconvenience in terms of having to replace them.) So from a financial standpoint, they rock. And I'm confident the newer fixtures and light bulbs, which have better light quality and lower costs, rock even more.

Producing Renewable Energy

Up to ten LEED points can be earned for generating electricity on-site through renewable energy sources. Solar photovoltaic (PV), wind, micro-hydro, and biofuel-based systems are the types of renewable energy that are eligible for this credit. We invested in a solar electric system, as wind, micro-hydro, and biofuel-based systems were not viable options when we built our home, nor are they very typical (yet).

The relevant metric here is the *percent of total energy that is produced by renewable energy.* The goal is to make that percentage as high as possible. What is powerful about this metric is that it encourages energy efficiency first, to decrease the denominator (the total energy consumed by the home), while adding as much

renewable energy as possible, to increase the numerator (total energy produced). Renewable energy providers will often recommend many of the eight strategies discussed above before installing solar, because if a home starts out as inefficient, solar panels are just a bandage on a wound.

SOLAR ELECTRIC

The first thing to understand about solar energy is that there are two very different types of solar technologies: those that provide electricity (called photovoltaic, or PV), and those that provide heat (called solar thermal). They work in entirely different ways, with different equipment, costs, and benefits. So when someone says: "I want solar," I always clarify which kind first. ("Passive" solar is another type, but that does not involve energy production.)

Solar panels are by far the biggest poster child of green building. In my sustainability consulting work, often solar panels are the first (and only) thing people ask me about when they are interested in becoming more sustainable. I love solar electricity, because once the panels are installed, they just sit there and produce electricity, with no moving parts and virtually no maintenance. What I also love about solar is that it is a kind of distributed generation: you produce power where you consume it. According to the US Energy Information Administration, 5 percent of electricity is lost in transmission—so it's just a more efficient model.

The economics of solar electricity are highly variable. It can be a tremendous investment if there are rebates and if electricity costs are high. In Minnesota at the time, electricity was too cheap to make great financial sense, but rebates and tax incentives made solar a compelling purchase for us.

Determining whether solar panels are right for your location requires thinking through several potential issues. First, solar panels require a fair amount of un-shaded space, typically on a roof. If there are trees nearby that shade them, they will not produce effectively—and I would *not* recommend cutting down trees for solar electricity. Second, not all roofs are oriented appropriately for solar panels. They work best when tilted at a 30- to 45-degree angle toward the south (in the northern hemisphere). Third, not all roofs are built to support the weight of solar panels. Depending on the brand, solar panels weigh about two to three pounds per square foot. If they are tilted in any way, they may carry a bigger snow load, so that has to be factored into the equation. It is wise to have a structural engineer sign off on any solar panel installation.

Then, there is the battery issue. Many people look to solar panels as a backup power supply. That means they need batteries to store that extra power, and batteries are not beneficial to the environment. If you live in a developed area with easy connection to the power grid, most solar installers will recommend that you just "grid-tie" your solar panels and forgo the batteries, so that you consume what you produce in real time. If you produce more than you consume, it just feeds back into the power grid, again in real time. If you produce more than you consume over a given time period, like a month, many utilities have "net-metering" rules, where they pay you for that excess power produced.[49] A grid-tied system is the cleanest and easiest type of system, but does not always meet people's expectations of what "going solar" should be. For those who want to be "off-grid," batteries are a necessity.

My plan was to design our house as efficiently as possible, and then make it "solar ready" for a grid-tied system. Like most architects, ours did not like the aesthetics of solar; he was not particularly excited about integrating them into the design of our house (this was before Tesla came out with roof shingles). We pushed, however, and settled on a plan to put solar panels on the flat roof of my office above the garage.

The system was installed almost two years after we moved in, and I wrote a "Solar Saga"

---

49 Xcel Energy's territory, for example, has net metering rules, with certain constraints. A customer cannot produce more than 120 percent of the energy used by the customer's home, as determined by the total electricity usage from the previous year. See energysage.com.

Solar panels on top of the office.

blog post about my issues and frustrations with the insane and inane process. Highlights of the solar saga: I received three different quotes, all of which proposed that we would be able to fit sixteen panels on our roof. When it came time to install them, only twelve panels fit. Since we paid for sixteen, and our rebates from the State of Minnesota and our utility were based on sixteen, we had to install sixteen. That meant finding another spot to install four more panels. After many frantic calls to our architect and project architect, we settled on using them for double-duty: west-facing awnings that would serve to keep my office cool in late summer afternoons. Since those four awnings are flat, at no angle to the sun, they lost about 28 percent of their productivity compared to having panels angled toward the sun. They also slightly reduced our rebate from the State of Minnesota.

Our system was rated at 3.68 kilowatts, with Enphase micro-inverters, which help the system produce electricity even when parts of it are shaded or covered in snow. (Without micro-inverters, if any part of a solar panel is covered or shaded, the whole array will not produce electricity.) This system size was estimated to produce about 2,000 kilowatt hours per year. How did that pan out? The first

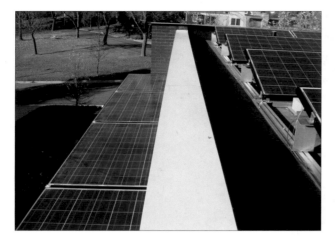

Four solar panels also function as west-facing shade awnings.

View from underneath the solar awnings. Photo credit: Karen Melvin.

two years, production was about as expected, a little over 2,000 kilowatt hours each year. Over time, though, the production decreases, as they lose a bit of efficiency every year. During the past seven years, our system has produced a total of sixteen megawatt hours of electricity. The graphs show total production and the percent of our electricity covered by solar. On average, our solar panels produce 10 percent of our electricity, ranging from a high of 31 percent in the peak summer months to 0 percent when they are covered in snow.[50]

According to EPA's greenhouse gas equivalencies calculator, producing sixteen megawatt hours of solar electricity equates to *not* burning over 13,000 pounds of coal or *not* driving over 29,000 miles in an average passenger vehicle. It is also equivalent to the carbon sequestered by fourteen acres of trees—which is pretty cool.

Was it worth it economically? We had a unique situation with discounts and rebates, so for us, it was worth it financially, but barely. The problem is, electricity is so inexpensive here that the economics do not always work. At about nine cents per kilowatt hour, we save less than $200 per year on our electric bill. If someone were to ask me about it now, I'd have to perform

---

50 This does not translate directly into LEED points. LEED awards one point for every 3 percent of the annual *reference* electrical load met by the renewable energy system. The reference load is the amount of electricity that a *typical* home (i.e., the HERS reference home) would consume in a typical year. Solar is one of the many inputs in the HERS index model, so some of the 25.5 points we earned for having a low HERS rating is attributable to these solar panels, but it is not broken down.

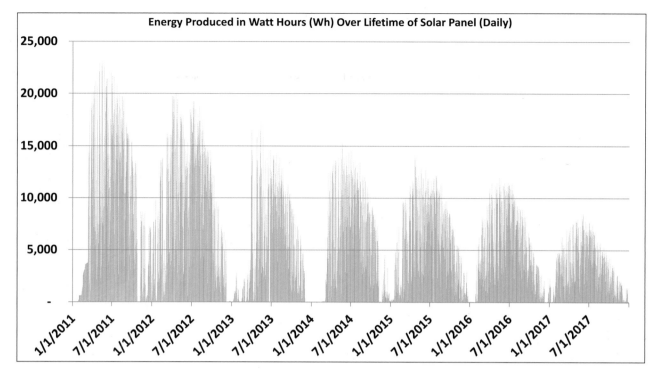

Solar power production over the past seven years. Production shows degradation over time.

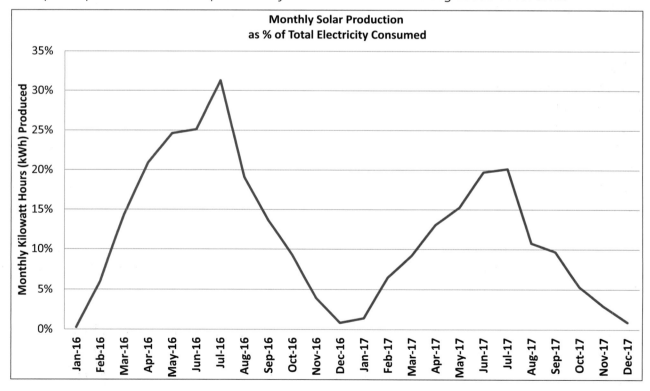

Solar production over the past two years, and as a percent of total electricity.

a new analysis, which depends on three variables (assuming enough un-shaded space facing south, and a roof that can support the panels):

1. The up-front cost,
2. The rebates and tax incentives available, and
3. What you pay for electricity.

The up-front cost is typically in the $17,000–$30,000 range, depending on how much space you have and the size of the system. Residential projects are usually sized between 1.5 and 3.5 kilowatts. The rebates vary across every state. In Minnesota, for us, Xcel Energy had a $2.75 per watt rebate; the State of Minnesota had a $2.00 per watt rebate, and the federal government had a 30 percent federal tax credit on the cost of the entire system. So for a $20,000 system, the federal tax credit would be $6,000 and the rebates would be in the $4,000–$8,000 range.[51] There are often neighborhood grants as well. Taking all of these things together, it's possible to get your total up-front cost down to between $6,000 and $10,000. (New solar financing companies have been selling "no money down" leasing options, but they are making money on the financing.)

Once you figure out your system size in terms of kilowatts, you need to figure out how many kilowatt hours (kWh) your system is expected to produce over the course of the year. You can do this by going to the Department of Energy's online PV Watt calculator at pvwatts.nrel.gov, and plug in all the variables (you'll need location, system size, basic module type, tilt and angle toward the sun). This should provide a good estimate of how many kWhs your panels will produce (though your installer should tell you).

Then, find on your electric bill what you are charged per kWh. (This is no easy task. There are so many different prices and fees wrapped up in the bill, it can be incomprehensible.) If you can figure that out, multiply the cost of electricity by the number of kWhs your system will generate, and the result is your expected savings on your electric bill.

The pros of solar panels are that once the system is installed, there is hardly any maintenance—especially if you have a grid-tied system and no battery backup. You will get some of your electricity for free, forever. As utility prices increase, which they probably will, your savings increase. Had we to do it all over again, I would pay more attention to the accessibility of the roof—like installing a ladder along the side the house by the office windows. It would be beneficial to climb up there once or twice per year to push the snow off, as they do not produce electricity when covered in snow. It would also be nice to be able to check on them, especially after a hailstorm, to see if they suffered any damage.

The cons, unfortunately, are the up-front cost and the possibility that they may not look cool. The costs are the real barrier, but prices continue to decrease. As far as looking cool, beauty is in the eye of the beholder.

Solar Thermal

Full disclosure: we did not install solar thermal in our home, so I know less about it—but

---

51 Check the Database of State Incentives for Renewable Energy at www.dsireusa.org.

we did consider it, and I used to work for a company that sold these systems, so I know enough about it to provide a good overview.

Solar thermal basically takes the sun's heat and transfers it to the home to heat domestic hot water and/or the home itself. To do this, it needs to store the heat—usually in the form of a fifty- to eighty-gallon water tank.

Solar thermal systems vary widely in their complexity and construction. In Israel, for example, most residences have black water tanks on the roofs for their domestic hot water—they simply absorb the sun's heat for free. These could be considered solar thermal systems, but they are very basic and really only a passive solar design. More complex systems can have vacuum tubes, reflectors, drain-back systems to prevent overheating, antifreeze liquid to prevent freezing, pumps, and an extra hot water storage tank sitting in the mechanical room.

Solar thermal is one of my favorite technologies because it is so efficient and simple, taking the sun's heat and using it for heat. The problem is that heat is difficult to store, and many people don't have space in their mechanical rooms for another large hot water tank.

Swimming pools, however, are built-in storage tanks—the heat goes directly to where you want it: in the pool. Why aren't there more solar thermally heated swimming pools? At this point, it's a combination of economics and awareness. According to the Department of Energy, a solar pool heating system usually costs between $3,000 and $4,000 and provides a payback of one and a half to seven years, depending on local fuel costs. In 2008,

it looked like solar thermal was going take off because of high natural gas prices. Now, with natural gas prices low, it's difficult to even find a solar thermal installer in the Twin Cities.

A general problem with solar thermal collectors is that they are much less aesthetically pleasing than solar electric panels (and that's not saying much). On the financial side, there is still a 30 percent federal tax credit, and the State of Minnesota introduced a 25 percent rebate (up to $2,500) in January 2014. In any case, it is worth checking out the costs and benefits of solar thermal—particularly if you have a pool!

Alex Wilson, the founder of *Environmental Building News* and a trusted source on everything related to green building, prefers solar electric (PV) systems to solar thermal. His reasoning: If you are considering whether to put PV panels or solar thermal panels somewhere on your roof, PV panels can be located farther away from where the energy is being used than can solar thermal panels, because electrons can be easily moved fairly long distances through electrical cables, while piping runs for solar-thermal systems have to be much shorter. PV systems do not have any moving parts to wear out or that require maintenance; freeze protection isn't a concern; and pressure build-up from stagnation in full sun (if a pump fails or during a power outage) can't occur. So, PV systems are more attractive from a long-term durability standpoint.[52]

For LEED, solar thermal technology is not classified as a renewable technology and is

52 Alex Wilson, *Environmental Building News*, "Picking a Water Heater: Solar vs. Electric or Gas Is Just the Beginning," February 26, 2014.

addressed under efficient hot water equipment. I would argue it is, indeed, a renewable technology, since the warmth from the sun is endlessly clean, free, and renewable, and it does replace burning natural gas for heating.

Wind

Wind energy continues to grow in this country, accounting for 5.5 percent of total electricity generation in 2016, up from 4.7 percent in 2015, according to the US Energy Information Administration. But wind turbines need a lot of space, and they are typically installed only in open, nonresidential rural locations—primarily in big windy states right in the middle of the country. Small residential wind turbines exist, but have not gained much traction.

Many utilities, such as Xcel Energy's Windsource, offer a program for customers to subscribe to 100 percent wind energy. The LEED rating system does not recognize this for homeowners, since you as the homeowner are not *producing* renewable energy, and the utility gets to keep the renewable energy credits. Enrolling in Xcel's Windsource program costs a little more than one cent more per kilowatt hour and can be purchased in blocks of one hundred. So, for a home that uses 1,000 kilowatt hours per month (slightly higher than average), it would cost $10 more per month to subscribe to 100 percent wind energy. Where does the money go? Xcel's customer service representative says it supports renewable energy infrastructure and helps meet their goal of 41 percent renewable energy by 2021. Xcel would work toward that goal anyway, but with more and more people subscribing to Windsource, they might just get to their goal sooner. That seems like a pretty good reason, but I am trying to help people *save* money, not spend more money, and Windsource only costs you more. At some point—like if the negative externalities of fossil fuels ever have a real price tag—it is possible that the fuel cost credit on the electric bill *could* increase over and above the cost of wind; in that case, Windsource could be a slight money-saver.

Energy Conclusions

While it is not possible to conduct a before/after analysis for our home (that's what I love about remodels), it is comforting to receive

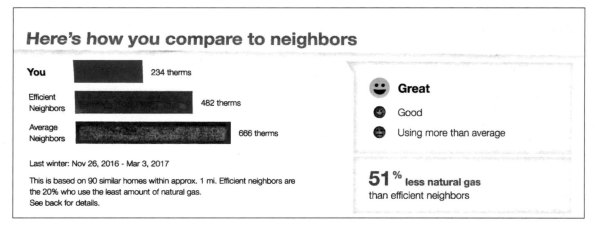

CenterPoint Energy scorecard shows low gas consumption.

CenterPoint Energy's scorecard on how we compare during the winter. From November through March, we were 51 percent more efficient than our "efficient" neighbors, and those are the 20 percent of neighbors that use the least amount of gas. We more than make up for that on the electricity side, using a great deal more than our neighbors, but our electricity is partially generated by solar and is getting cleaner every year.[53]

What is our true return on investment? In the HERS rating model, Jimmie estimated our annual energy costs of gas and electric bills to be $2,272. Had we *not* done all of these things described above, we would have been more like a typical "reference" home. To understand the magnitude of that, we can look at our HERS rating score, which was thirty-five—meaning our bills would be 35 percent of a reference home. Doing the math, a typical similar-sized home would have energy bills at almost $6,500 per year, meaning we should save about $4,200 per year for the actions we took. We did pay incremental costs for the triple pane windows, spray foam insulation, ground-source heat pump, heat recovery ventilator, and LED lights (our Energy Star appliances did not cost more)—all of which contribute greatly to the lower energy bills. My estimate is that we paid about $30,000 to $40,000 more for all of these things, which would mean the investments pay off in seven to ten years, more quickly as utility prices increase.

We were taught in business school that the payback form of analysis is weak, so staying true to my training, I like to look at investments in terms of the net present value of expected future cash flows. This analysis requires a time period for those cash flows: how long will we live in the home? Our plan was a minimum of fifteen years. The net present value of $35,000 in incremental costs, with annual savings of $4,200, is over $25,000 (using a 3 percent discount rate and 3 percent inflation rate), with an internal rate of return of 11.2 percent. To me, given that we get to live in the house, that's a very good investment. If you finance or mortgage that incremental amount, which we did, the return is immediate.

The bigger question is whether the HERS energy model accurately predicted our energy costs, and the answer is no. Our actual energy costs (electricity and gas) have averaged just under $5,000 annually over the past eight years, still 24 percent below the LEED reference home, but not 65 percent lower, as predicted. But that does not necessarily mean we did not still realize a significant savings. Why? The reference home can suffer from some of the same inaccuracies as the energy model. Indeed, research conducted by design engineers on how accurate home energy rating systems have been in predicting actual energy costs in homes has found wide variability, with large margins of error. The most significant determinant of actual energy usage is occupant behavior, as it is very difficult to predict that. How was our energy modeler to know that my husband and I would both work

---

53 In fact, in 2018, Minnesota met the goal it set for itself for 2025: 25 percent of its electricity generated by renewables. Minnesota was able to accomplish this seven years ahead of schedule because the economics are working: wind energy in particular has proven to be a lower cost alternative, even without subsidies.

from home, running two businesses out of our office above the garage? That certainly affects energy consumption. Other variables include weather, unit cost increases, and simply incorrect assumptions. We will never know what our energy costs *might* have been had we not made the investments we did. At a minimum, we are saving $1,500 per year, in addition to reducing our carbon emissions by about 8,000 pounds per year.

Financing Energy Efficiency

If it's a financial no-brainer to *invest* in energy efficiency projects, then it should be a no-brainer to be able to *get financing* for energy-efficient projects. Unfortunately, that's not always the case. Recognizing that people do not always have the cash to pay for energy-efficient investments, here are some options.

First, try to get the cost down. There are many rebates, incentives, and tax credits available through utilities as well as at the state and federal level. Check the Database of State Incentives for Renewables and Efficiency, at dsireusa.org. Utilities are often "program sponsors" who work with lenders to offer special financing to homeowners that participate in their energy efficiency programs. Customers of Xcel Energy, for example, can get their old refrigerator hauled away for free and get a $35 check. Rebates are available for insulation, weather stripping, lighting, and more. Low-income customers are eligible for additional free materials and labor. While some federal tax credits have expired, solar and electric car tax credits still exist, and more could be coming (write to your Congressional representatives!).

Property Assessed Clean Energy (PACE) financing is becoming more available as a tool to help finance the up-front costs of energy efficiency and renewable energy. The project is paid for through an assessment added to your property tax bill. According to the US Department of Energy, between 2009 and 2016, more than 100,000 homeowners have made energy efficiency and renewable energy improvements to their homes through residential PACE programs, totaling nearly $2 billion upgrades to their homes. While many states have PACE financing available for commercial buildings, it's not always available to homeowners (yet); check the website pacenation.us. Additionally, many utilities offer "on bill financing" in which they become the lender; it may be worthwhile to check that out as well.

Finally, check with your bank. A Home Equity Line of Credit (HELOC) can provide flexibility and fast access to funds. HELOCs have variable interest rates, but you can pay off the balance whenever you want, as long as you make regular interest payments.

To illustrate an immediate payback from financing these investments, I turn back to my parents, who changed out all of their recessed can lighting fixtures from basic regular 65-watt incandescent bulbs to the CREE LED LR6, which involved not just light bulb replacement, but complete fixture replacement. The new lights are 11 watts. That means they save 54 watts per bulb, but that figure alone is meaningless without the number of fixtures and how many hours per day they are turned on (the lights, not my parents). They have sixty-five canisters all over the house, and they are

LED recessed lighting fixture.

all on five hours per day, on average. So, annual savings are 54 watts multiplied by sixty-five lights times 5 hours per day times 365 days per year, divided by 1,000 (to get from watt-hours to kilowatt-hours), times nine cents per kilowatt-hour, which equals $577 per year. That's a monthly savings of $48. The total cost of the new canisters was $8,000, including installation labor. (Note: it costs much more to replace the entire fixtures than just the bulbs, so this financial return on investment is way worse than a typical bulb replacement—but it still works financially. And, typically you would only be looking at the incremental cost compared to the standard fixture alternative, not the full replacement cost, so that $8,000 would be much less. Additionally, LED prices continue to drop over time, so the financial benefit only improves.) If you wrap that $8,000 into a 30-year mortgage, with an interest rate of 3.92 percent, your monthly payments would be $38 on that portion. With monthly electric bill savings of $48, you are still saving $10 per month. So, while this payback is fourteen years, if you finance it, you are better off from day one!

Why Homeowners Invest in Energy Efficiency

In a study by Steven Nadel, the executive director for the American Council for an Energy Efficient Economy (ACEEE), households have multiple reasons for making energy efficiency investments. When asked to rank the top three reasons to "participate in energy conservation activities or buy an energy-efficient product/make home improvements," saving money was most important, followed by comfort and health.[54]

To save money	61%
To make my home more comfortable	35%
To make my home healthier	27%
To be responsible and not waste	26%
To get more control over personal energy consumption	25%
To protect our environment	23%
To make my home more valuable for resale	20%
To have a high-quality home	19%
To have a higher-performance home	17%
To preserve the quality of life for future generations	15%
To be a good citizen	11%
To protect our nation's economy and reduce our dependence on other countries	9%
To be a good example	9%
To keep up with my neighbors	4%

54 Steven Nadel, "Who Invests in Energy Efficiency and Why?" July 24, 2017, http://aceee.org/blog/2017/07/who-invests-energy-efficiency-and-why; Source: Shelton Group 2016 Pulse Survey.

Energy Dollars and Sense

GREENER CHOICE	DOLLARS	SENSE
Triple pane, low-E windows	5–15 percent more (ours was 8 percent more) HIGH COST	Wonderful for very cold climates CONSIDER IT!
Closed-cell spray foam insulation	At least two to three times more expensive than conventional pink fiberglass HIGH COST	Worth every penny in reduced energy costs and improved comfort FOR COLD CLIMATES: DO IT!
Ground-source heat pump	About 30 percent more HIGH COST	Most efficient system; better for new homes than remodels; pays for itself in about seven years FOR NEW CONSTRUCTION: DO IT!
Tankless water heater	Varies; about $1,000–$2,500 MEDIUM COST	NO SENSE
Solar water heater	Varies; $8,000–$12,000 HIGH COST	Currently does not make economic sense when compared to natural gas, but it does make sense from an efficiency standpoint CONSIDER IT
Energy Star appliances	NO INCREMENTAL COST	DO IT!
LED lighting	More expensive; depends on comparison and size of project LOW-MEDIUM COST	Best return on investment DO IT!
Photovoltaic panels	$1,000–$25,000, or $0 if financed through solar company HIGH COST	If home is already efficient and there is space with no shade CONSIDER IT

CHAPTER 7: WATER EFFICIENCY

The operation of our water supplies is, to most of us, invisible. Invisibility encourages complacency.
—Dr. Robert D. Morris, author and expert in field of drinking water

At home, we use water for everything: washing dishes, washing clothes, bathing, brushing teeth, cleaning, cooking, and irrigating outdoor plants. While the *Clean Water* chapter addresses the *quality* of water coming in to our homes, this chapter addresses the *quantity* of water we use.

In the United States, approximately 340 billion gallons of fresh water is withdrawn per day from rivers and reservoirs to support residential, commercial, industrial, agricultural, and recreational activities. Personally, I have no idea if that is too much or too little. But the scary piece is the "water deficit": it is estimated that Americans extract 3,700 billion gallons per year *more* than they return to the natural water system to recharge aquifers and other water resources. That does not sound very sustainable.

But we are talking about homes here, and the residential component of total water use is less than 10 percent. According to the Water Research Foundation's 2016 report on Residential End Uses of Water, homes use an average of 88,000 gallons of water per year for indoor uses. The good news is that this has decreased by 22 percent since 1999 (the last time it was studied), due to more efficient toilets and clothes washers. Here in Minnesota, the Land of 10,000 Lakes, many people do not view water

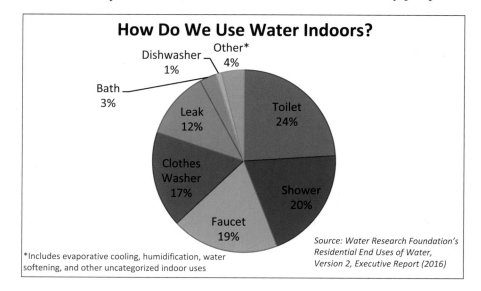

How Do We Use Water Indoors?

Other* 4%
Dishwasher 1%
Bath 3%
Leak 12%
Toilet 24%
Clothes Washer 17%
Shower 20%
Faucet 19%

*Includes evaporative cooling, humidification, water softening, and other uncategorized indoor uses

Source: Water Research Foundation's Residential End Uses of Water, Version 2, Executive Report (2016)

availability as an issue. On top of that, Minnesota has relatively low per capita water use in the nation. Many places, like Tucson and San Francisco, have more stringent regulations on water usage than LEED prescribes.

So why would we care? At a minimum, for financial reasons: water costs money, so why not try to be more efficient with it and save money every month? And it's not just the water bill that can be reduced. Heating water for showers, dishes, and laundry takes a lot of energy—about 10 to 15 percent of a home's total energy use. So saving hot water also reduces your energy bill.

The relevant LEED for Homes Rating System section, Water Efficiency, helps homeowners reduce water usage through three strategies: water reuse, efficient irrigation, and efficient indoor water use. LEED requires a minimum of three points out of fifteen possible points; we earned nine points relatively easily and inexpensively.

Water Reuse

"Water Reuse" requires that water be captured somehow. A home can implement a water reuse program in the following three ways:

1. Rainwater harvesting,
2. Graywater reuse, or
3. Use of the municipal recycled water system.

Rainwater Harvesting

Rainwater harvesting involves capturing rainwater to use either for irrigation or for indoor use—like toilets. From a practical standpoint, though, rainwater harvesting is really only used for outdoor irrigation. Why? Our indoor plumbing systems in the United States do not tie into outdoor water collection systems.

For this component of the credit, worth three points of the total, it does not matter if the rainwater that is captured and stored is *used* at all. All that matters is that you have a system installed that can *hold* all the water from a one-inch rainfall event, which is equivalent to 0.62 gallons per square foot of roof area used for capture.

Rainwater harvesting systems are prevalent in many areas of the world and are basically just storage tanks that accumulate water from rain running off the roof. They can range from complicated underground cisterns to basic rain barrels. Public policies around rainwater capture vary widely. Some cities, such as Los Angeles, advocate for rainwater capture—not for irrigation, but as a stormwater management measure to reduce runoff into the streams and rivers. Santa Fe, New Mexico, mandates rainwater catchment systems for all new commercial and residential development.[55] Colorado, however, has gone so far as to *outlaw* rainwater capture because of legal water rights: rain must be allowed to flow downstream to those who have a legal right to use it. It has only been since 2009 that Colorado allows homeowners to have rain barrels.[56]

In Minneapolis, stormwater runoff is a major concern, so the city encourages rainwater harvesting. The city's website reads, "Imagine the number of rooftops in your community and you can quickly see how much runoff is headed toward the storm drains, picking up pollutants along the way, discharging into

---

55 Santa Fe County Ordinance No. 2003–6.
56 Colorado Senate Bill 09–080.

our lakes, rivers and creeks. Rain barrels are one way of trapping some of this runoff. They are not only ecologically responsible, but they also help conserve water."

To me, capturing rain seemed to just be common sense, so I was excited about exploring this option. I had brought up the idea of a rainwater harvesting system to our architect and landscape architect, and three issues right off the bat were illuminated:

1. Cost. We have a really wet lot, and in order to hold a large storage tank or cistern, we would have to put pilings in to support its weight—which is very expensive. Architects do not like you to spend money on things that go underground and unseen, because that takes money away from the budget that could be spent on cool design features or neat, pricey materials. And, whatever form the storage tank is, each system requires a catchment area, a conveyance system (like gutters), and a distribution system (piping and pumps) requiring electricity. These are not standard components of a home, so there was some reluctance on the part of our builders.

2. Maintenance. I was guilty of that reluctance too, because the maintenance of these things scared me. What about the filter? What if it gets clogged with gunk (or a frog or chipmunk)? What kind of winterizing would we have to do? What happens when it freezes? Combined with the added expense

of pilings to support the weight of a water storage system, cisterns did not seem practical for our home. So, that left us with rain barrels as an option, which led to the third issue.

3. Design aesthetic. Our design team did not want to even consider rain barrels, because frankly, they can be pretty ugly.

I have to say this initially was an area of disappointment for me. We achieved zero LEED points for Water Reuse; here's why.

We considered rain barrels at the base of each of our two gutters that run off the roof (despite our design team's protests), figuring we could find some that fit architecturally. Compared to city water, rainwater is better for landscaping because it has higher nitrogen and lower salt content than city water, so I thought that would be beneficial for our garden.

Rain barrels can typically hold as much as fifty gallons of water. How big is a fifty-gallon cistern? Look at your hot water tank—those are typically fifty to eighty gallons—pretty big! But the real question is: would two fifty-gallon rain barrels at the end of our two roof gutters actually be sufficient for irrigation, reduce our water bill, *and* meet the LEED credit requirement, which requires at least 50 percent of the roof area's water to be harvested?

Let's do the math. Our flat roof is 1,800 square feet, and 0.62 gallons of rainwater falls on one square foot of roof. So, if we are aiming for 100 percent of the roof area, then one inch of rain produces 1,116 gallons of water runoff—all of which would need to be stored. That means we would need twenty-two rain fifty-gallon barrels to meet this credit. If we

Rain barrels are pretty common in our neighborhood.

were going for just 50 percent rainwater capture, we would need eleven rain barrels. We only have two roof gutters, so how would that even work? It wouldn't, because they would just take up too much space.

Other potential problems with rain barrels include them becoming mosquito (and other critter) breeding grounds, growing algae from sitting water, and overflow issues (a fifty-gallon tank can fill up pretty quickly).

How would it have played out from a cost/benefit standpoint? There are many variables that factor into this analysis. On the cost side, a typical rain barrel is about $100, plus a little extra if you want spigots and hoses that attach. The cost can often be lower, due to lower quality, or because some cities subsidize the cost to motivate people to buy them.

On the benefit side, you can figure out the value of the water that will be stored in whatever catchment apparatus you choose, assuming you size it big enough to meet the LEED credit requirements. Variables you will need are:

Variable	Our home in Minnesota as an example
Average annual rainfall in your climate zone (during irrigation months)	20 inches (May–September)
Square footage of harvest area (100 percent)	1,800
Number of gallons a 1-inch rainfall produces per square foot of roof	0.62 (fixed number)
Cost of water per gallon	$0.005

Equation:

20 inches average annual rainfall x 1,800 square feet of roof x 0.62 gallons per inch of rainfall = 22,320 gallons x $0.005 cost per gallon of water = $112 worth of water stored.

The other big variable is how much rain you get at a time and whether the rain barrels will hold it all, or just overflow. But remember: storing just one inch of rainwater would require twenty-two rain barrels. The least expensive fifty-gallon rain barrel I can find is a collapsible polyester one for $40. According to the EPA, a typical fifty-gallon rain barrel can only store 1,300 gallons during the summer months. Water is seriously cheap: 1,300 gallons is only $6.50 worth of water, which means that a $100 rain barrel has a fifteen-year payback. Even a $40 rain barrel would not recoup the investment for six years.

Plus, is that the real savings? Probably not, because you may not even *use* that much water for your irrigation needs. That is a much trickier calculation, but still can be done. If the main goal is to water flower beds, then one or two rain barrels would suffice, but again, it's just not that much water, so savings are low. And, it's not nearly enough to earn LEED points. Even if you were to figure out exactly how much irrigation you need, the pitfalls with *that* analysis are twofold:

- There may not be enough rain in your climate to actually capture and store what you will need to irrigate, and thereby offset your irrigation costs, or
- There may more than enough rain to keep your plants happy, so you would not have spent that much

money on irrigation in the first place.

Until water gets more expensive, rain barrels do not make sense from an economic perspective. That, plus the complexities, aesthetics, and maintenance issues led us to *not* pursue this choice. The bottom line is that rain barrels are a drop in the bucket (so to speak) in terms of making a difference for your wealth or a difference in your overall ecological footprint.

GRAYWATER REUSE

Graywater? Sounds gross. Graywater is wash water—basically all the water that goes down the drain from the clothes washer, showers, bathtubs, faucets, or some combination of these. It does not include wastewater from toilets (this is called "blackwater"). For LEED points, the system would have to include a tank that can be used as part of the irrigation system, and it has to collect at least 5,000 gallons of water per year. Graywater can be used for toilets or irrigation.

The LEED rating system awards just one point for what I would consider to be a huge plumbing endeavor. We did look into this, and were told by our builder that no governing body in Minnesota regulates the use of graywater for irrigation, and that it would be difficult to get a permit. While initially surprised by this issue, when you think about it, it makes sense. What goes down our drains, anyway? Common items include hair, chemicals, and bacteria. Should people be allowed to take what they put down their drains, even if it is filtered, and spray it all over their yard? From a health perspective, there are warnings for those who do use graywater: "If someone in your family develops a communicable disease, such as the flu, measles, or chicken pox, stop using your graywater system until the person has recovered."[57] From an environmental perspective, it could turn into a nightmare when the groundwater seeps into nearby lakes and rivers. Finally, from a logistics perspective, what would we do with graywater in the winter, when there is no demand for irrigation?

We then looked into the possibility of storing graywater and using for indoor use—which would only be for toilets. There are systems out there, and it seems like a good idea, in theory. When we had our plumber price it out, it would have required almost double the number of pipes *to and from* all of the sinks, showers, and toilets, because the graywater requires two separate waste and water supply systems. That was the first strike.

Then I saw a YouTube video about how "easy" these systems were to operate and maintain—except that the tanks needed to be completely rinsed out and cleaned two times per year, which uses a lot of water and thus negates much of the savings. The maintenance issues were strike two. We did not need a third strike; the price and inconvenience of this system rendered it a no-go, a decision we do not regret.

Having said that, we were only looking at whole-house graywater systems, and there are smaller, individual systems that might be

---

57 Eric Corey Freed, *Green Building and Remodeling for Dummies* (Hoboken, NJ: Wiley Publishing, 2008), 268.

feasible, especially in areas where a shortage of water is of greater concern. A sink/toilet combination, where the used sink water flows directly into the toilet bowl, can save water and save space. It may save a small amount of money on the water bill as well—but it is not big enough to earn a LEED point.

MUNICIPAL RECYCLED WATER SYSTEM

This credit is an either/or with the first two in Water Efficiency (you cannot get points in the first two and claim the points here). It grants three points to homeowners who design the plumbing such that irrigation water is supplied by the city's municipal recycled water. Obviously, this can only happen if you live in a community with a municipal recycled water program. Minneapolis does not have this.

California and Florida are leaders in developing reclaimed water systems in the United States. It's good that the LEED rating system gives points here, because if I lived in a town with municipal recycled water for irrigation, I would definitely use it. It may cost more for the city to treat it and distribute it, but cities that do have reclaimed water for irrigation may sell it a lower rate than freshwater to encourage people to use it.

Outdoor Water Use

Like the Water Reuse section, the idea is to reduce the demand for city-supplied water—but in this section, through the irrigation system itself.

The first question I had: what if we did not have an irrigation system? Many people do not! No points, unless we accounted for a landscape design that reduced overall irriga-

tion demand through specific plantings and shading (and that's part of a different LEED category, called Sustainable Sites).

We figured we would have some sort of irrigation system, so my next question: what if we install a well for irrigation? My idea for a well generated from our discussion about the possibility of building a cistern to hold rainwater, and decided against it because our lot is already so wet. The City of Minneapolis was open to it. I then consulted the *LEED for Homes Reference Guide*, assuming we would be awarded a plethora of points for that, because we would be saving municipally-supplied freshwater resources.

Not so. The LEED rating system does not care that we utilize the groundwater to water our grass and trees. We ended up installing one anyway, because I liked the idea of not using fresh, treated water solely for irrigation purposes. It also would save money on the cost of irrigation—which is often a large component of water bills. And since much of what we were trying to do was invest up front to lower the ongoing operating costs of our home, this was another investment that initially made sense. (To learn how this played out in reality, see chapter 12, The Worst Green Decisions We Made.)

So, LEED's assumption is that you have an irrigation system, and it does not matter where the water comes from. You can earn up to four points by installing a high-efficiency irrigation system and having a third party inspect it—which we did. What constitutes a "high-efficiency" irrigation system? Any of the following ten criteria contribute to the definition of high-efficiency. What we did is *written in italics:*

1. Install an irrigation system designed by an EPA WaterSense certified professional. (WaterSense is an EPA program that partners with industry to label water-efficiency products.) *No—we did not want to pay for one and could not find one.*

2. Design and install an irrigation system with head-to-head coverage. *Yes—this means the sprinkler heads are spaced so the water overlaps slightly with the adjacent ones.*

3. Install a central shutoff valve. *Yes—we can shut off just our outdoor irrigation, which is what we do every fall to "winterize" or system. We let the water run out of the spigots to protect the pipes from freezing and bursting when the temperature drops below thirty-two degrees. This is very important for a durable home in cold climates.*

4. Install a sub-meter for the irrigation system. *No—this is not standard practice for homes. A sub-meter would allow you to measure the water usage for irrigation separately from indoor water usage. It is important for many commercial projects, and many of my clients have installed them, but the reality is that most homeowners do not use them. In climates where irrigation is used only during the summer months, it is pretty easy to figure out how much water you use for irrigation by comparing your water bill usage to the months with no irrigation. The sub-meter itself is around $300, but* the labor costs would have put it above $500.

5. Use drip irrigation for at least 50 percent of landscape planting beds to minimize evaporation. *No— the sprinkler heads for turf grass accounted for a larger share than drip irrigation for trees.*

6. Create separate zones for each type of bedding area based on watering needs. *Yes—this is part of basic irrigation design and should always be done. Trees and flower beds should have drip irrigation, not sprinklers. Different types of plantings need different water frequencies and duration.*

7. Install a timer or controller that activates the valves for each watering zone at the best time of day to minimize evaporative losses while maintaining healthy plants and obeying local regulations and water use guidance. *Yes—that's what the irrigation controller does, and this is how water use is reduced.*

8. Install pressure-regulating devices to maintain optimal pressure and prevent misting. *Yes—that is the system we bought.*

9. Utilize high-efficiency nozzles with an average distribution uniformity of at least 0.70. *Yes—the system we bought does this.*

10. Check valves in heads. *Yes—this means the water only flows one-way.*

11. Install a moisture sensor controller or rain delay controller. *Yes—this is a selling point of an irrigation control system, though*

it only senses current and recent rain, not future rain. Newer models with built in wireless capability connect to weather forecasts, so if it is going to rain soon, the sprinklers will not turn on. I think our rain sensor has not worked anyway, so we just manually turn it off when it rains a lot.

Our primary consideration was whether to have an irrigation system or not (we did), and then to invest in an irrigation controller. Our system was designed to water the lawn with spray heads and to have drip line irrigation for the arborvitaes lining the property. We did not install irrigation for the areas we had native prairie grasses and wildflowers, as they were designed to be drought-tolerant. The total cost to install the system was $4,600 from the subcontractor we selected. (Our builder's subcontractor's initial bid was twice that, so the real learning here was making sure the system was designed appropriately. So many times subcontractors over-design a system, which means you are getting more than what you need, and paying for it too.)

On the cost and benefit side, assuming an initial investment in an irrigation system, the Smartline irrigation controller we purchased did cost more—but the incremental cost was only $361, and that price has come down considerably. On Smartline's website, it shows the payback for the system based on how much water is saved, and it usually pays for itself in less than one year. But since we were not paying for any of our irrigation water because we dug a well, we did not get the financial bene-

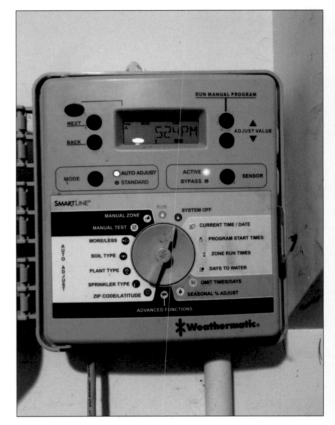

Irrigation controller.

fit. (Again, see chapter 12, The Worst Green Decisions We Made.)

We wanted the controller anyway, though—not for the LEED points, but because of its functionality. It takes the guesswork out of setting up a watering schedule, and maintains moisture in the lawn appropriately.

We were able to meet the LEED requirements and rack up six points (four for the credit, plus two for exemplary performance[58]), because we purchased a Smartline by Weathermatic controller system, had a well-designed system, and had third-party verification.

---

58 LEED rating systems award extra points for going above and beyond certain credits' performance standards; these are called "exemplary performance" points.

Jimmie Sparks inspected the irrigation system during operation, ensuring that:

- All spray heads were operating and delivering water only to intended zones.
- Any switches or shutoff valves were working properly.
- Any timers or controllers were set properly.
- Any irrigation systems were located at least two feet from the home.
- Irrigation spray did not hit the home.

Any time you can get a third party in to verify that something was installed correctly and operating as designed, it is worthwhile. You can design and build the most efficient, environmentally friendly home, but if you are not operating it correctly, the benefits go away.

Indoor Water Use

This last component of Water Efficiency focuses on water-efficient fixtures: toilets, sink faucets, and showerheads—which typically account for two thirds of a home's indoor water use. Installing high-efficiency fixtures is an easy, low-cost strategy for reducing indoor water use, as the most efficient fixtures use less than half the water of conventional alternatives.

Choosing fixtures is an interesting exercise, because there are so many options, and you have to decide what you really care about: look, feel, function, placement, etc. (While dishwashers and clothes washers are notably absent from this section, they are addressed in chapter 6, Energy, under "Appliances.") A home can reduce its indoor water usage by installing efficient bathroom sink faucets, showerheads, and toilets. We achieved a total of three LEED points out of six possible points (so we could have done better).

Installing "low-flow" or "efficient" fixtures is always close to the top of the list of "eco-friendly tips." What does low-flow mean, exactly? The relevant metrics to understand are gallons per minute ("gpm") for sinks and showers, and gallons per flush ("gpf") for toilets and urinals.

Toilets

Toilets use about 30 percent of total indoor water consumption, so as far as priorities go, the flow rates of toilets should be considered above that of sinks and showers. Since 1992, the federal standard for toilet flush rates (gallons per flush, or "gpf") has been 1.6 gpf. If you think about it, it's crazy: over a gallon and a half of fresh, drinkable water is wasted every time every person goes to the bathroom! But conversely, before indoor plumbing inventions like this, life was quite stinky. So, we take the good with bad, and try to do a little *less* bad with the lifestyle to which we have become accustomed.

For a LEED point, the average flow rate for all toilets must be a maximum of 1.3 gpf; a gallons-per-flush rate of 1.1 gpf or less would get you two LEED points. Many toilets now have a 1.28 gpf rate, saving 20 percent on water consumption.

For us, choosing a dual-flush toilet was another no-brainer: there were several models available at about the same cost as the non-dual-flush models. Toto and Kohler both had models available, and we chose the Toto

Toto dual-flush toilet.

saves about 2,000 gallons of water per year, or $10. I like the sound of saving 2,000 gallons of water per year; the extra $10 per year, while small, is still better than no savings.

SINKS

With reading glasses, you can usually see the flow rate written in tiny little letters right above where the water comes out of the faucet. Most conventional sink faucets have a flow rate of 2.2 gpm. That means that if you run the faucet for one minute, it would fill up a tank with 2.2 gallons of water. This is important for teeth brushing, face washing, shaving, etc., because people tend to run the water more than what they need—every day, so it adds up. An "efficient" sink, according to LEED, has a maximum flow rate 2.0 gpm, and a "highly efficient" sink has a maximum flow rate of 1.5 gpm.

It should be noted that kitchen faucets are excluded from this credit, because most water consumption in the kitchen is based on volume: filling up glasses of water and pots. I would argue they still should be included, because there is still a lot of water wasted—particularly hot water—for washing hands and rinsing dishes, and lower flow kitchen sinks would also save water, energy, and money. Generally kitchen sinks do not advertise that they have low flow rates, however, because nobody seems to care. So, we focus on the bathroom sinks.

For sink fixtures, this should have been an easy way to rack up two more points. I had wanted to buy the Kohler Purist single-control lavatory faucet, which has a maximum flow rate of 1.5 gallons per minute. Many commer-

because we liked the looks of it better. The dual-flush toilets have two buttons on top: one for the "big" flush, which is 1.6 gpf, and one for the "little" flush, which is 0.9 gpf. LEED views dual-flush toilets as having an average flush rate of 1.25 gpf, so we got one point and save about 22 percent on water. Assuming four flushes per day each, a family of four

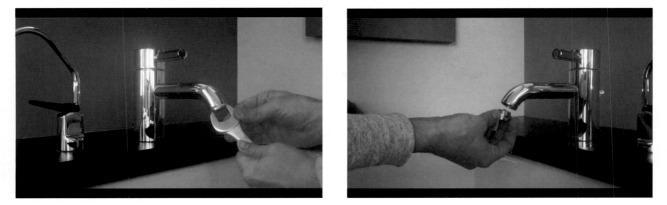

Installing faucet aerators.

cial buildings have faucets with flow rates are as low as 0.5 gpm, which is the LEED standard for public lavatories. I wanted to go that low, which would have been possible if we had installed a low-flow aerator on the faucet head.

My husband, and our architect, however, much preferred the Dornbracht line of faucets and showerheads. It is hard to argue that they are more beautiful, more durable—and more expensive. Dornbracht is a German company, so I would have thought their flow rates would be even lower than American-made faucets, as Germany has been a leader in sustainable practices. But the faucets we chose for form and function all had flow rates of 2.2 gpm—too high for any LEED points, or any water savings for that matter.

I looked into finding standard aerators that could simply be installed on most faucets on an after-market basis. Aerators lower the gallons per minute flow rate by mixing the water with air, so while the pressure feels the same, you use less water. Aerators are sold at Home Depot (among other places) and are often provided for free by local utilities as an easy way to decrease energy bills (remember you are saving *hot* water, too, and therefore saving the energy to heat the water). But aerators have

to actually fit your "standard" faucet, and of course, the Dornbracht line is not standard. So, with no points here so far, I lost this battle.

But I did not give up! After we moved in, as I was going through the process of documenting all of our purchases for LEED certification, I was scrounging around for a few more LEED points to hit the gold threshold. I remembered this credit—in fact I had felt a little remorse that we had not achieved it. Two years had passed since our initial specifications, so I checked with the manufacturer again, and by this time, they had come up with aerators that fit the faucet and decreased the flow rate to 1.5 gallons per minute—the LEED threshold for two points.

While most aerators are free or in the $10–$15 range, the aerators we ordered were $20 each (these are Dornbracht!), and we have six sinks, so the total cost was $120. I installed all of them by myself in about ten minutes (it really was easy), so there was no incremental labor cost.

For the cost/benefit analysis, I assumed each of us uses the faucet for one minute per day for daily hand and face washing, brushing teeth, shaving—a very conservative estimate. Reducing the flow rate from 2.2 gpm to 1.5

gpm saves us 0.7 gallons per minute per person. Since there are four of us, that is 2.8 gallons per day, which is over 1,000 gallons per year. Right now, since water is ridiculously inexpensive (about a half a cent per gallon), that's a savings of only about $5 per year. If you factor in the energy savings from reducing our hot water consumption, I'd estimate that savings roughly doubling. But, if you can get the aerators for free, it's an immediate financial gain. Because of the low cost, ease of installation, ongoing water savings, and the two additional LEED points, choosing low-flow faucets is a good choice. And I do feel better knowing we are saving that much water, for just ten minutes of my time.

An easy way to find efficient fixtures is to look for the EPA's WaterSense labeled products. Not only does the label mean the fixtures are more efficient and will save you money, but they have also been tested for function, ensuring they provide ample flow of water. The faucet aerators did not change the look and feel of those oh-so-precious Dornbracht fixtures, and I have on video my husband admitting that he cannot tell the difference in flow rates.

SHOWERS

Showers typically use about 17 percent of a home's indoor water usage. Since 1992, standard showerheads use 2.5 gpm, but they used to use a lot more—between five and eight gpm. The EPA's WaterSense label ensures the maximum flow rate is 2.0 gpm or less. This would have given us one LEED point; going down to 1.5 gpm would have given us two points.

For shower fixtures, we compromised: Jim got his Dornbracht shower fixture in the master shower, and the kids' rooms and guest shower got the Kohler brand. This ended up being more of a compromise on expense than on water efficiency, because both brands had flow rates of 2.5 gallons per minute—over the minimum requirement of 2.0 gpm for even one point. The 2.5 gpm flow rate is actually the maximum flow rate that federal regulations allow. It is now much easier and more commonplace to find lower flow showerheads; you just have to ask.

In reality, regardless of flow rates, if we take twenty-minute long showers, or several showers per day, it will not be efficient water use. This is a problem for all green building rating systems, though: they can only prescribe how the building is designed and constructed, not how people use it. (The one exception is the LEED for Existing Buildings Rating System, which does monitor ongoing energy, water, and waste metrics. It's my favorite rating system, but there is not one yet available for homes.)

The savings for a low-flow showerhead depends on the comparison product. There is no incremental cost to specifying a low-flow showerhead if you are building new. So the financial savings is a pure win. The difference between 2.5 gpm (the current requirement) and 2.0 gpm is a 20 percent savings. Can that add up to any significant savings over time?

Let's do the math again—the best part. A family of four taking daily five-minute long showers uses 18,250 gallons of water in the shower per year with 2.5 gpm showerheads.

With the 2.0 gpm showerhead, we would use 14,600 gallons of water per year—a savings of 3,650 gallons of water. But remember, water is cheap—around a half a cent per gallon. So that's a savings of only $18.25 per year. The general rule of thumb is that is costs about one to two cents per gallon to heat water, so we would realized additional energy savings of between $36 and $72 per year. To Jim, that was not enough rationale to change our choice in showerheads. In general though, a $100 per year savings does financially justify a low-flow showerhead.

If you are remodeling an existing home, replacing an old showerhead is a different economic story. Low-flow showerheads are widely available and range between $10–$50, depending on the design and quality. For a family of four taking daily five-minute long showers, an older showerhead with 5.5 gpm flow rate would use over 40,150 gallons of water per year. Going down to a flow rate of 2.0 gpm would save 25,550 gallons of water per year—about as much as a large swimming pool holds. That translates into a water bill savings of $128 per year, plus another $225–$450 in energy savings, because showers use hot water. If you have two bathrooms, and showerheads cost $20 each, this pays for itself in about one month. As there is really no sacrifice in performance, I would call that another no-brainer.

Water Efficiency Dollars and Sense

GREENER CHOICE	DOLLARS	SENSE
Rain barrel	Cost of a rain barrel plus accessories: about $100 Savings per rain barrel: about $6 LOW COST	Poor economic investment unless your city subsidizes them; won't get you LEED points, unless your roof is tiny; can be aesthetically unpleasing NO SENSE
Graywater	Doubles the price of plumbing pipes HIGH COST	Requires extensive plumbing network; too much maintenance NO SENSE
Municipal recycled water system	Unlikely your city supplies it NO COST	If your city supplies it A LOT OF SENSE
High-efficiency irrigation system	Irrigation systems can run between $3,000–$7,000 depending on size and scope; assuming an irrigation system is installed, controller is only about $200 more; third-party inspection is $100 LOW COST	Saves a lot of water and corresponding costs; works better for your landscaping needs because it reduces over- and under-watering Verification that it works appropriately is one of the major benefits of going through the LEED process DO IT!
Low-flow/flush indoor fixtures	Faucet aerators are very low cost— between $0 and $20 each Low-flow showerheads and low-flush toilets are not more expensive than alternatives NO INCREMENTAL COST	Saves about 20 percent on water bill Very easy to specify up front to contractor Very easy to install aerators DO IT!

Chapter 8:
Durability

Before "green" became a pop catchword, I always believed things should be as simple, durable and local as they could be.

—Kevin Streeter, Owner of Streeter & Associates, as quoted in a *Star-Tribune* article, "Modern, Minimal, and at Home with Nature," June 17, 2008

This final chapter under "For Our Wealth" addresses one of the more concrete expressions of sustainability: durability, or building a home to last. How it can help your bank account is a little more abstract, but in general it decreases costs related to repairs and replacement. As a bonus: if you have less maintenance and repair, you save the time it takes to schedule the repair or do it yourself.

The LEED for Homes Rating System prescribes two prerequisites and three additional points under what is called "Durability Management Process." LEED does not tell you what types of equipment, windows, or materials to use on the exterior, etc., that might improve or hinder your home's durability. That is something we all have to learn for ourselves. It's like self-advocacy in health care. You have to ask as many questions as you can about every material that goes into your home. The best one is always, "What would you do if this were your

house?" (Just as I ask our pediatrician, "What would you do if this were your daughter?") That always reveals the most honest answers.

Building for Durability and Resiliency

The LEED for Homes Rating System does, however, prescribe the *process* of durability planning and management. I have added the term "resiliency," because resilient design is becoming more prevalent in the building community, as hurricanes, tornadoes, and severe storms wreak havoc on buildings, landscapes, and communities—and as we learn more about how buildings can withstand natural disasters.

To build a more durable and resilient home, LEED requires that prior to construction, the project team must: (a) complete the Durability Risk Evaluation Form to identify all moderate and high-risk durability issues for the building enclosure, (b) develop specific measures to respond to those issues, and (c) identify and incorporate all applicable indoor moisture control measures as follows: for tubs and showers: use non-paper-faced backer board on walls; for kitchen, bathroom, laundry rooms, as well as an entryway within three feet of an exterior door: use water-resistant flooring and do not install carpet; for tank water heaters and clothes washers in or over living space: install drain and drain pan; for conventional clothes dryers: exhaust directly to the outdoors; (d) incorporate those measures into the project documents; and (e) list all the durability measures in a durability checklist, for use in verification.[59]

Whew! Since this was a prerequisite, we obviously had to do all of it. Our builder's project manager filled out the risk evaluation form. That included things like risks of natural disasters, common regional pests, and the depth of groundwater below the home. It took him a few hours, at least (and more than a few requests by me). For me, I had to go through each item one by one and ask, "Do you guys do that?" They knew all of these things and did them as a matter of course; they just normally did not have to write them down. That's the beauty and power of a checklist. And, it allows for third-party verification—worth three LEED points.

More than the points, though, this is the quality assurance process that is key to any construction project. The *LEED for Homes Reference Guide* outlines the principal durability risks:

- Exterior water (*high risk for us, as we get major storms and are near a lake*)
- Interior moisture loads (*moderately high risk for us, as our house sits on top of an underground river*)
- Air infiltration (*low risk for us*)
- Interstitial condensation (*fancy words for when water vapor in between the inside wall and the exterior of a home hits dew point, due to temperature and humidity level differences, and moisture forms where we cannot see it—behind walls and ceilings—increasing the risk for mold and rot; high risk as our temperatures and humidity levels are extreme*)
- Heat loss (*high risk—we live in Minnesota*)
- Ultraviolet radiation (*low risk—we live in Minnesota*)
- Pests (*low risk—we have ants, Japanese beetles, and box elder bugs, but luckily we do not have termites*)
- Natural disasters, such as hurricane winds, earthquakes, wildfires[60] (*overall low risk, but we do get tornadoes and blizzards, and they are becoming more frequent*).

These things should always be taken into consideration for any building project, and are key components of resilient design planning as well. All homes eventually fail in some way. Building homes, furnishings, products, etc. in a shoddy way so that they fall apart represents irresponsible business practices. Homeowners and builders who address risks early in the design and construction process will more likely have homes with fewer failures, and this translates directly into saving money on repair costs down the road.

Building for resiliency can be taken a step further by undergoing a comprehensive hazard assessment and addressing two things:

---

59 *LEED for Homes Reference Guide*, 37.
60 *LEED for Homes Reference Guide*, 37–39.

1) how to build a stronger home, which may mean going beyond building code requirements on the strength of roofs, windows, and the home's connection to the foundation,[61] and 2) how to keep a building functioning after a natural disaster strikes. Because we are so dependent on energy for our homes, and as electrical grids can be brought down by storms, back-up power generation is one of the first things we addressed. Back-up power can be provided by batteries connected to solar photovoltaic panels (which we did not do, as discussed in chapter 6, but is worth considering), or, more commonly, by a generator. Stand-by generators (as opposed to portable generators) are permanently installed natural gas-powered combustion engines that turn on automatically in the event of a power outage. They are sized based on wattage to deliver a certain level of kilowatt-hours; the larger the size, the more electricity it will produce, balanced against higher cost and the more space it takes up in the yard.

To choose the appropriate size for our home, we had to determine our most critical electrical needs. This meant thinking about what we could live without and what we really wanted, again, balanced against size and cost. Knowing how much power our "needs" required was challenging, which is why we had to sit down with our electrician to figure it out. For example, if we wanted air-conditioning, would that put us in a much higher cost bracket (yes), and is that *really* critical (no)? We ended up deciding that if we lose power, we would need (want) electricity for the following: the sump pump in the basement, refrigerator and freezer, garage door opener, skylight closer, a few LED lights in the kitchen, bathroom, and basement, one outlet (for charging phones and laptops), and a heat pump to keep us from freezing. We figured we could forgo air conditioning, air ventilation, and many of the other things that require electricity, like the dishwasher, clothes washer, dryer, oven, television, and additional lighting. All of this meant we needed a 12,000 watt generator, costing $11,000—a relatively large generator, but since our heat comes from electric-powered heat pumps as opposed to natural gas, that's what it required.

Our generator is an ugly thing at the back of our home, measuring three feet wide by four feet long, and a little less than three feet high. An annual maintenance program is needed for oil and filter changes, which costs us $350–$400 per year. It also has to run itself once a week, for reliability. So every Sunday afternoon, for twenty minutes, we are greeted with loud noise and smelly gas fumes. I view the generator like insurance: you hate to pay for it, but when you really need it, you are very glad you bought it! (Had we to do it all over again, though, I might nix the gas-powered generator and figure out a solar-powered battery backup.)

Designing homes for resiliency is an emerging trend: new programs and rating systems are being developed, and newer versions of LEED are addressing this important topic. To be sure, almost all of the LEED credits, while their first aim might be water

---

61 The Insurance Institute for Business Home and Safety (IBHS) developed the FORTIFIED Home program for these purposes; more information can be found at www.disastersafety.org.

efficiency or energy efficiency, also serve to enhance the durability of the home. Two other LEED credits worth mentioning, because they will not come up in any other section but are totally worth the effort, are integrated project planning and homeowner education.

Integrated Project Planning

Integrated project planning means simply that the project team of designers, engineers, builders, and subcontractors—particularly mechanical, electrical, plumbing, and landscaping—work together from the beginning as a team. While it may seem like a waste of time for all of these team members to be sitting at the table during initial design reviews, that is absolutely not the case. As well intentioned as we were as a team, not everyone was always at the same meeting, and that hurt us. Our project architect was at one meeting where we met with the ground-source heat pump subcontractor, and we were discussing the merits of high-velocity ductwork, which requires much smaller but much more numerous ducts throughout the walls. Our project architect drew that into the design set. She was *not* at another meeting with the HVAC contractors, where we decided *against* high-velocity ductwork due to the loud noise and the difficulty in figuring out how it would fit in our limited wall space. Somehow the communication system broke down, and the builders were left wondering where the ductwork was going to go when the HVAC contractors showed up with large metal ducts. A portion of the ceiling in our foyer needed to be dropped, and one side wall in our basement had to be furred out to make room—which our architect did not appreciate. Whose fault was that? Nobody's

really, but it may have been prevented had everyone attended the same meeting.

LEED awards one point for having an integrated project team (which we had), plus another for the team to meet together for a full-day "design charrette"—a workshop to integrate green strategies across all areas of building design and construction. While we did not earn a point for holding a design charrette due to timing and schedules (and due to nobody really knowing what that was or how to run one back then), I have led these workshops for clients, and they are very worthwhile—particularly for projects that are complex or have unique requirements.

Homeowner Education

The final prerequisite of the entire LEED for Homes Rating System requires that the homeowner receive "basic operations training" on how to operate and maintain the home. Why? From the US Green Building's perspective, it is the first step in trying to help limit the resource consumption of the home *after* it is designed, built, and green-rater verified. After all, "without adequate training, the full benefits of the LEED measures likely will not be achieved."[62] This is because "some homebuyers may know very little about green home construction."[63] This is a generous statement. What happened to home economics? I'm not talking about sewing and cooking and balancing a checking account (though that would be beneficial, too). I'm talking about how to take care of a home. I have two master's

---

62 *LEED for Homes Reference Guide*, 333.
63 Ibid.

degrees and learned nothing on this subject. I would venture to say that hardly anyone my generation and younger knows much about home operations. We don't understand what preventive maintenance means until there is a problem looming that is no longer preventable. Then we learn, usually the hard way.

The prerequisite requires a minimum of a one-hour walk-through of the home, with the builder identifying all the equipment and giving instructions on how to operate and maintain the equipment. One hour? Is that a joke? I know it can be boring, but this is your house! I contend that all builders should provide at least three hours of training for all homeowners. If you want a sustainable home, the key piece is to build and *maintain* it so that that it lasts. Otherwise, all those upfront investments that are supposed to save money will end up costing more money.

PART III
FOR OUR SOUL

There is a moral dimension to environmental issues that informs, and in some cases trumps, a purely utilitarian or economic calculus.

—Frederic Rich, *Getting to Green*

Build a sustainable home for your soul? What can that possibly mean? If you picked up this book, you know that building a sustainable home is more than making your home healthier and more efficient. You know that every action you take can have a ripple effect on someone or something. You know that we can do better, as humans taking care of humans.

At first, I thought this was my catch-all category that would include sustainable choices that were more "nice to haves" rather than "must-haves." These would be the decisions that do not reduce the operating costs of your home, nor do they have an immediate impact on your health. Less utilitarian, I figured "For Our Soul" would be the least persuasive value. But I found this assumption to be wrong; this is an extremely compelling category. Why?

Feeling good about what we are doing is a huge part of why people have been going green. I know several homeowners who have simply dictated to their architect or designer that they want their home to be as "green" as possible—without knowing much about the actual costs and benefits. But they want to feel like they are doing something good for the environment and feel less guilty for consuming resources. I know that was, and still is, a huge motivator for me.

As I have spoken with schools and synagogues, and even for-profit businesses, about why they are going green, often their *primary* reason is that it is right thing to do. They consider it a moral imperative to not only bring sustainable practices to their organizations, but also teach it to their students or engage with their employees. It reflects their values of wanting to take care of our earth so that future generations can enjoy it as well. Being part of a movement that is working to improve people's lives can provide us with a sense of meaning, purpose, and belonging to something bigger than ourselves. That's what "For Our Soul" means.

As with the theme of this book (there are always *three things*—easier to remember), there are three chapters: Materials, Landscaping, and Location. These three topics are much more tangible and concrete than the previous categories like clean air and energy efficiency. You can see them and feel them; there is more of an aesthetic appeal to these choices—and that makes them more fun to discuss! But what they *all* have in common is that *all* of our choices around the three values of health, wealth, and soul have an effect on our overall ecological footprint, and because of that, ultimately, on our *collective* health and wealth—and souls.

CHAPTER 9: MATERIALS

I've often thought that the *greenest* material is *no* material, so forgoing materials like wall coverings can be considered an environmental benefit—saving us money and resources. But if you go down that path of trying to be greener, then really, the greenest home is no home. And if you keep going, then the conclusion has to be: the greenest human being is no human being. That's why you see books like *No Impact Man: The Adventures of a Guilty Liberal* and *Confessions of an Eco-Sinner.* Oh, the guilt of being human! The guilt of wanting stuff! But where does that leave us? I'd prefer to believe that we humans live in a symbiotic relationship with Earth. It's not a contest to see who can be the greenest. It's all of us figuring out together how to make choices that support life. If the environmental movement is trying to win by requiring austerity, shaming people for consuming, and telling us that capitalism is the enemy—we are not going to get very far.

I dream of a day when there is no such thing as "green" material, because all products are designed to be closed-loop, per William McDonough's *Cradle to Cradle* philosophy. Until then, we can still improve on what we do today by following the LEED criteria for purchasing and waste management. This chapter is thus divided in two: materials that are purchased for framing, cabinets, flooring, countertops, trim, etc., and the waste that is generated onsite.

Purchasing Materials

While choosing materials for our homes is often the fun part, it can also be the most overwhelming. These are the big decisions that will affect the look and feel of the home every day. And trying to run it through a green lens can be intimidating. We spent a majority of our time on these decisions, and most questions I get from friends revolve around materials choices. Well, I should clarify that: my female friends ask me about material choices. My male friends ask me about geothermal heat pumps, solar energy, and furnaces. (Think what you like, but that's been my experience!)

Materials are important from an ecological footprint perspective because the extraction, processing, and transportation they require may pollute the air and water, destroy natural habitats, and deplete natural resources.[64] In the *LEED for Homes Reference Guide,* an "environmentally

---

64 *LEED for Homes Reference Guide,* 233.

preferable" product is a material or product that causes *less* environmental damage than the *conventional* alternative. Let's be clear: we are still talking about purchasing new materials. New materials have to be grown or mined, processed, and freighted to our home, requiring a tremendous amount of energy and resources. LEED only encourages us to be *less* bad. The LEED rating system did not label this category "sustainable" materials, because there is not really a sustainable version of this. Or so I thought.

After we built our home, there was an article in the Minneapolis *Star Tribune* about a home that was built and furnished *entirely* with previously used materials. Reading the article, I was ashamed at ourselves for thinking that what we were doing was at all sustainable. I showed the article to Jim. "Look at this home. We should have done *that*!" He reviewed the photos of the hodge-podge design of a home, filled with antiques and a wide variety of different woods and metals, and handily dismissed my comment. "No way. I would never live in that home. It probably smells!" Okay, maybe *used* materials are not the same thing as *sustainable* materials—but they certainly should be considered first. If a reuse center or a Habitat for Humanity ReStore is nearby, using some of those items could save a lot of money and definitely reduce your environmental footprint.

The more sustainable, or *less bad* choices, are defined as materials that are made from recycled content (which differs from *recyclable* material), FSC-certified wood, and/ or materials that are locally grown or manufactured. For LEED, this really is the big kahuna of credits: we could earn up to eight points total. (This LEED credit also has criteria on low emissions, but I address that in "Clean Air," chapter 4.) As this is one of the more complicated credits, I first define each of these environmentally preferable criteria, then discuss our considerations for nine different building components.

RECYCLED MATERIALS

Simply stated, products that contain recycled content are less harmful to the environment and to people than the conventional alternative. Products that are "reclaimed" fall into this bucket as well. To earn the LEED point, or to make this worthwhile, at least 90 percent of a given component (by weight or volume) must meet the requirements. Many materials now make the claim they are made from recycled materials, so it is important to understand the definitions and thresholds.

Recycled content is material that includes at least 25 percent *post*-consumer *or* 50 percent *pre*-consumer recycled material. Pre-consumer recycled content, also known as post-industrial, is only counted at half the rate of post-consumer content. Why? *Post-consumer* recycled content is really much more critical when evaluating the recycled content of products, as this closes the loop with product manufacturing. *Pre-consumer* recycled content is a bit of a greenwashing claim, since it is just an efficient manufacturing process that decreases the manufacturer's raw material costs by using scraps or materials that may have been wasted. This is just good business practice, but it does not help us get any closer to a circular economy. By that I mean a closed-loop system where post-consumer waste is used as an input or raw material for another use. *Reclaimed* content is material that has been recovered from a demolition site, but only post-consumer reclaimed material can be counted—not construction leftovers.

We actively searched for products that were made out of recycled materials or wood that was reclaimed, because we like the aesthetic. More and more, these types of products are becoming available and affordable.

FSC-Certified Wood

Wood gets its own sustainability rating because it is such a ubiquitous building material. Developed in the first half of the nineteenth century, wood light frame construction is the least expensive, most versatile form of durable construction, and has thus become the common currency of small residential and commercial buildings in North America.[65] Wood is also a top choice for flooring and cabinetry. The downside of wood is that it burns quickly, can rot or decay when exposed to water, and expands and contracts in response to changes in humidity and temperature. Nevertheless, wood is a beautiful and renewable resource, so it continues to be a major component of home building.

So what's the problem? The primary issue is *tropical* wood, where poor forestry practices degrade tropical rain forests and cause irreversible harm to our climate and biological diversity.[66] According to the Rainforest Foundation, tropical forests comprise approximately 7 percent of the earth's dry land surface (2 percent of total surface) and sustain over 50 percent of all species. The current rate of destruction is about one acre each second, and we are losing one species each year to extinction.[67] For these reasons, the choice of wood matters. In the best case, the purchase could support a sustainable community rain forest initiative. In the worst case, it could contribute to the impoverishment of families, the clear-cutting of forests, or the endangerment of wildlife.[68]

To address the issue of forests that have not been managed in a sustainable fashion, several certification programs have emerged. The United States Green Building Council favors the Forest Stewardship Council's (FSC) certification, as it is a third-party chain-of-custody stamp of approval that the wood has been sustainably grown and harvested. There has been some controversy over this credit, to the point where some states (Maine and Georgia, for example) introduced legislation to ban LEED certification altogether. They viewed LEED as unfairly and exclusively recognizing FSC certification as the only green seal of approval that the forest has been sustainably managed. Not until 2016 did the USGBC recognize SFI, the Sustainable Forestry Initiative's certification, as a legitimate "sustainable" credential. SFI is the paper and logging industry group,

---

65 Edward Allen and Joseph Iano, *Fundamentals of Building Construction Materials and Methods* (Hoboken, NJ: John Wiley & Sons, 2004), 144–5.

66 *LEED for Homes Reference Guide*, 251.

67 www.rainforestfoundation.org.

68 Natural Resources Defense Council, "How to Buy Good Wood," accessed October 24, 2017, https://www.nrdc.org/stories/how-buy-good-wood.

The FSC-certified wood stamp.

In the LEED for Homes Rating System, there is one prerequisite pertaining to wood: *if* tropical wood is used intentionally (it's hard to imagine a scenario when it would be used unintentionally), it must be FSC-certified (unless the wood is reclaimed). Wood is considered tropical if it is grown in a moist tropical country that lies between the Tropic of Cancer and the Tropic of Capricorn. To be clear on what countries produce wood that would be classified as "tropical" (and therefore must be FSC-certified if it is grown there):

- All countries in Africa except Morocco, Tunisia, Algeria, Egypt, Libya
- All countries in Asia and Southeast Asia except Japan, North and South Korea, Russia
- All countries in Australia and Oceana except New Zealand

so certification from them could be viewed as akin to the fox guarding the henhouse. The industry group disagrees, and has proven otherwise. The USGBC now also recognizes the American Tree Farm System (ATFS) as a legitimate and credible certification system—a great move on the part of the USGBC, as it helps to expand the market for family forest owners and sustainable forestry.[69]

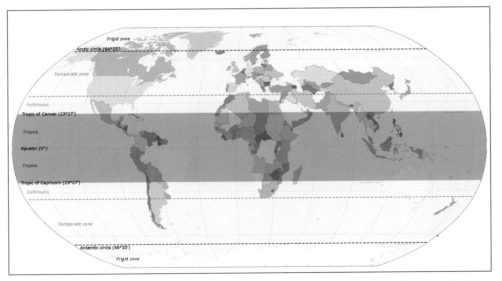

"Tropical" wood grows in between the Tropics of Cancer and Tropics of Capricorn.

---

69 Tom Martin, "A Win for Forest Conservation: US Green Building Council to recognize ATFS," *Huffington Post,* April 8, 2016.

- All countries in South America except Uruguay
- No countries in North America are included except Mexico, nor are countries in Europe or the Middle East

For non-tropical wood, like most wood used in home framing, LEED awards points for choosing FSC-certified wood, but does not require it. We asked our builder to include alternate bids for conventional wood and FSC-certified wood in every place we had wood—which was framing, cabinetry, doors, trim, and part of our exterior. (See material selections below on how this played out for us.)

LOCAL MATERIALS

We have all heard "buy local" or "think globally, act locally." Why? Choosing products from faraway places increases the transportation energy usage associated with constructing a new home. But what does "local" really mean? LEED defines local as products that were extracted, harvested, recovered, or manufactured within 500 miles of the home. That can be either driving distance or as the crow flies, whichever is shorter.

Obviously, materials that have to travel fewer miles to get to your house save transportation fuel compared to say, bamboo, which usually comes from Asia. Many people also care about locally produced products because they prefer to support their local economy. I know of a couple in Texas that wanted everything in their home to be 100 percent made-in-America. That proved to be pretty difficult for their designer, especially when it came to lighting fixtures. Even if something is assembled in America, many times components of

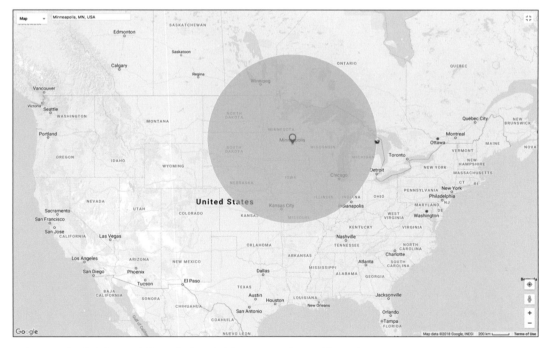

LEED's definition of "local" is within 500 miles of home.

the product come from overseas. For us, buying local was not a priority, because it just seemed like too difficult a constraint. If ever there were a choice of equal products, though, we would choose local.

All of our material choices were eligible for being considered "local" with the exception of paints, coatings, adhesives, and sealants. Finding out *where* each of our materials came from to determine if it was local proved to be a difficult process. We ended up with only one point in total for local products, attributable to our Sheetrock and our concrete foundation (which were a half point each).

Just as important as the materials we choose, we can have standards on materials to specifically *exclude*. Vinyl (PVC, or polyvinyl chloride) made that list for us. Vinyl is a significant source of volatile organic compounds (VOCs)—have you ever bought a new shower curtain and gotten a headache from the smell? From cradle to grave, vinyl is bad: it is highly toxic to produce, difficult to recycle, and releases dioxin when thrown away and a deadly smoke when burned. Vinyl contains phthalates, chemicals that disrupt the human endocrine system, especially in children.[70]

What home products contain vinyl, other than shower curtains? The list is long, but it includes exterior siding, replacement window frames, flooring, pipes, nylon and olefin carpet backing, and most egregious, wall coverings. Wall coverings, whose only function is to make walls look pretty, can make a home pretty unhealthy. The problem is that most standard wall coverings do not breathe—so condensation can get trapped behind them, leading to mold. Wallpaper adhesives can also off-gas. To me, cool looking walls versus high potential for mold is not a fair tradeoff, so we have no wallpaper. If those walls must be covered, healthier alternatives made from natural fibers are a better choice.

This section goes through the nine major material choices that confront every homebuilder and most remodelers. The first three—flooring, cabinetry, and countertops—are the most important and interesting from the standpoint of the design, look, and feel of the home. They are often changed in a remodel; that is why they are listed first. The next one—exterior siding—obviously has a large design element as well. The last five—interior walls, framing, roofing, insulation, and foundation—are more difficult to change in a remodel (and slightly less interesting to discuss). They are included nevertheless because they *do* have an effect on both the ecological footprint of the home as well as LEED certification.

Flooring

Choosing flooring probably takes the most time of any decision, since it has such an enormous impact on the look and feel of a home. In our previous condominium, we had chosen bamboo flooring for its beauty and purported sustainable properties, as it is a rapidly renewable grass and does not require chopping down trees. It is also listed as an "environmentally preferable" flooring material in the LEED rating sys-

---

70 Eric Corey Freed and Kevin Daum, *Green Sense for the Home: Rating the Real Payoff from 50 Green Home Projects* (Newtown, CT: The Taunton Press, 2010), 168.

Slate tile flooring. Photo credit: Paul Crosby.

tem, along with linoleum, cork, FSC-certified or reclaimed wood, sealed concrete, recycled-content flooring, and wool carpet. In reality, while bamboo is a rapidly renewable product, it requires a great deal of energy to be processed and transported across the Pacific Ocean. From a usability standpoint, it was a very hard wood underfoot but gashed and scraped easily. We also found it difficult to match with other materials, such as wood furniture. So, we were definitely not choosing bamboo flooring again.

What are the other choices? We considered wood, cork, carpet, and tile. But within each of these choices there are dozens of additional options, pros and cons, and varying levels of greenness.

Our main level, where we spend most of our waking time, was the biggest decision and one that we agonized over the most. One of the major influencing factors was the fact that we have hydronic (water-based) in-floor heating. This required us to understand the thermal properties of different materials. The other influencing factor was the openness of our main level: the only door on the entire floor is to the powder room. That meant any change in flooring could be used to define a change in room type or use, which we did not want—so it really needed to be the same material everywhere for continuity.

We first considered wood because wood is a renewable and biodegradable material, and it is beautiful. It can also be "green" by purchasing wood that is FSC-certified or reclaimed. But wood over in-floor heat is not ideal. First, it expands and contracts with varying temperatures. More importantly, though, wood exhibits a low thermal conductivity (high heat-insulating capacity) compared with materials such as stone and concrete. So a wood floor insulates *against* the in-floor heat being generated. Additionally, my aunt and uncle had to rip out their wood floors twice because of issues with their in-floor heating underneath. We wanted to avoid that problem.

We also considered cork flooring. Cork is generally thought to be a sustainable material because it is harvested from tree bark without killing the tree, and the bark regrows. Each tree can produce cork for about seven harvestings of its bark before it is unable to produce anymore. The problem is that cork oak trees really only grow in the Mediterranean Sea regions of Portugal, Spain, and North Africa—so it's up to the individual to decide whether this fits the definition of a "sustainable" material. The benefits of cork are that it is relatively soft under foot, it is a great sound insulator, and lasts a very long time—ours came with a fifty-year warranty (Wicanders brand). The downside is that its color can fade dramatically if covered by an area rug or exposed to sunlight. It's also a bit of an insulator over in-floor heat. We decided to use cork flooring only in my office above the garage. It was a way to have some cork to try out (it is beautiful) but not commit to it everywhere. We found an engineered cork floor, as opposed to cork tiles—a real enhancement in the look and feel of cork.

For the main level, then, we looked at stone tile because of its superior thermal conduc-

Cork floor in the office. Photo credit: Paul Crosby.

Reclaimed fir stairs. Photo credit: Paul Crosby

tivity on top of in-floor heat. Our architect frequently specifies twelve-inch square slate floor tile, so we were able to see what it looks like in other homes he designed (like his own). We really liked how it would hold the heat in the winter, remain cool to the touch in the summer, and how it felt grounded and earthy. The green part of slate flooring is that it is very durable and long lasting, and it does not off-gas. It does not need sanding, sealing, or really any maintenance except regular cleaning; it does not absorb water and is completely fireproof. The downside is that slate has to be quarried or mined. Most slate in this country comes from upstate New York and Vermont; ours is from Hilltop Slate, Inc.

in Middle Granville, New York. The decision to choose slate tile flooring was a balancing act between function, aesthetics, comfort, and energy efficiency.

Wanting to incorporate wood elsewhere for its beauty and warmth, we used reclaimed fir for our stair treads, where there is no in-floor heat and the treads are open to let in light and air. The fir was procured from old warehouses thanks to Duluth Timber Company. These open-stair treads are thick and durable, giving it a somewhat rustic look. The stairs get more beautiful with age, and any wear and tear on them only adds to the character of the wood. The stringers and risers (on the stairs to my office) are also reclaimed fir.

Reclaimed fir stairs up to office.

Sealed concrete floor in the lower level.

For the upstairs bedrooms, we debated using cork, wood, and carpet tiles. We ended up getting wall-to-wall wool carpeting with jute backing. It was primarily a comfort decision. The carpet provides great relief to the hard slate floor on the main level. Additionally, carpet is just nice in bedrooms. While wool carpeting is typically more expensive than nylon, the benefits are many: is more durable, softer to the touch, and naturally flame retardant.

For the basement, we chose sealed concrete (as well as for our garage, but garages are excluded here). That's mostly because we did not really want a basement—we didn't think we needed the space, and we did not

want a room that would potentially get wet and moldy. Our builders convinced us to have a basement, though, because we needed a mechanical room. Given that we are on a relatively small city lot, we did not want to take up yard space for a mechanical room. They also argued that it is the "cheapest" square footage we could build, because we had to build the foundation of the house anyway—so we might as well have a basement underneath. We acquiesced, but didn't know what we wanted in our basement and left the walls unfinished concrete as well. We knew leaving concrete exposed was a "green" technique, because you forgo using any additional materials. So, as opposed to a deliberate choice in going green for our basement floors, it was more of a lack of decision-making on what we wanted our basement to be. It also saves money.

Leaving the concrete unfinished worked great for our exercise room and the arts and crafts area. The other benefit is that if there is ever any leak or water issue in the basement, we will see it right away. Most mold issues

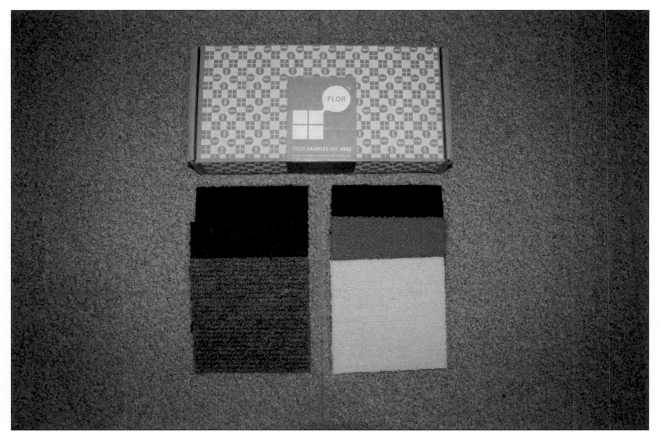

FLOR carpet and samples.

arise because water exists somewhere where it cannot be seen and cannot dry out quickly (it needs to within forty-eight hours). Basements that have wall-to-wall carpeting, for example, are at risk. For part of our basement, we installed FLOR carpet tiles. FLOR, formerly run by Ray Anderson, is one of the first companies in the United States to understand the ecology of commerce.[71] Their goal as a company is not only to become sustainable, but restorative. In addition to each of the carpet tiles made from recycled content, customers can send back their tiles for free for them to recycle. Compared to wall-to-wall carpeting, it is much easier to maintain and repair. If one area gets stained or wet, for example, we can replace just that one tile instead of having to tear up the entire carpet.

LEED for Homes awards points for flooring that meets any of its environmentally preferable criteria: it can be any combination of linoleum, cork, bamboo, FSC-certified or reclaimed wood, sealed concrete, wool or recycled-content flooring (45 percent for a

---

71 Ray Anderson's TED Talk discusses his company in more detail. He was very much influenced by Paul Hawken's *The Ecology of Commerce*, the book that is often credited with waking up the business community to issues of sustainability.

half point, 90 percent for a full point). For us then, only our slate tile did not meet the environmentally preferable criteria. The question is: did the size area of our concrete + cork + stairs + wool carpet add up to greater than 45 percent of the total floor area? The total was 52 percent, so we got a half point here.

Would we have done anything differently to get that percentage up to 90 percent? The only thing we could have done was to change out our slate tile to cork or reclaimed or FSC-certified wood. From a comfort, maintenance, and durability standpoint, the slate floors are tops—so we would have chosen it again, even though it did not give us that half a LEED point. LEED also rewards homes for 100 percent hard surface flooring (i.e., no carpet anywhere), because carpeting is discouraged—it traps dirt and contaminants. So, we gave up another half point for having carpeting upstairs.

Moving on to the local criteria, where did our flooring come from? While we only have one room with cork, cork is harvested in the Mediterranean area, so that would not count as local. Our slate tile comes from Upstate New York, which is more than 500 miles away—also not local (though it's at least the United States). Our wool carpet was made by Nature's Carpet, a division of Colin Campbell & Sons. The wool is New Zealand wool, and it was made in Australia, though we never knew that when we were choosing carpet. (Not only is the place of manufacture not advertised, it does not even say it anywhere on the website.)

Cabinetry

Tropical wood tends to be uniquely beautiful and durable: mahogany, teak, and ipé are

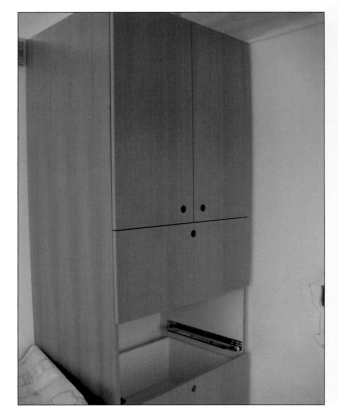

Fir veneer cabinetry.

some of the common tropical woods used in homes all over the world. We chose not to use any tropical woods, because, well, why? In the scheme of choices that are good or bad for the environment, it is pretty easy to choose non-tropical wood. Oak, pine, fir, cherry, and walnut are all abundantly grown in North America, and each of these types of wood has its own unique beauty.

Most of our interior wood cabinetry is fir veneer. It has a warm, orangey color and darkens over time. Using fir veneer over medium density fiberboard (MDF) requires much less of the fir tree than using solid fir. MDF also helps reduce bowing and warping with changing temperatures compared to solid wood, and is much less expensive.

We were already paying a 30 percent premium on our cabinetry to make sure it had no added urea formaldehyde (NAUF; see *Clean Air* chapter 4). To also have our cabinets FSC-certified would have cost us significantly more, and our cabinetmaker thought the quality was less consistent. So, we were not prepared to pay the additional amount for the FSC-certification. Over 90 percent of the other wood in our home was FSC-certified anyway, so we let that one go.

Where did our cabinetry come from? Damschen Wood manufactured all of our cabinetry in Hopkins, Minnesota—only about five miles away. However, to be considered "local," the wood must have been *harvested* within 500 miles of Minneapolis. Most of the core material in our cabinets came from Missoula, Montana—1,182 miles away. Not local.

Countertops

After flooring and cabinetry, countertops are probably the third biggest design decision for a home. We considered a lot of different types, including Cambria, granite, and a basic laminate. In my research, I had come across many

From top, clockwise: wheat board, Kirei board, sunflower board.

David Salmela outside his home in Duluth.

Richlite countertop installation.

150 Building a Sustainable Home

Maple butcher block kitchen island.

different types of countertops that contained recycled or reclaimed materials, such as wheat board (which we use for office desks), Kirei board (made from sorghum stalks), and sunflower seed hulls. While interesting, these products had not been time tested on the market for durability, and we did not love the look and feel.

One product that caught our attention was Richlite, because it has the look of honed granite but is not as hard or as cold, nor is it mined or quarried. Richlite, similar to PaperStone, a competing product, is made from 100 per-

cent post-consumer recycled paper and has no added urea formaldehyde. Richlite does cost about 10 to 15 percent more than honed granite. We thought it was worth it, though, not just for its superior environmental attributes, but also for its form and function. If it is scratched, it can be buffed out easily. It is the same material as used in epicurean cutting boards, skateboard parks, and even the exterior of David Salmela's own house—so we knew this was a very durable product. To me, durability outranks other sustainable attributes when it comes to countertops, since they undergo a fair amount of wear and tear, and replacing them can be a big, expensive effort. All of our countertops, with the exception of our maple butcher-block kitchen island, are black Richlite counters, so we earned another a half point here for LEED. Richlite has held up very well overtime; the only downsides are the cost and the weight—cabinetmakers have difficulty with it. It needs very little, if any maintenance, and its luster can be restored nicely with a food-grade butcher block oil.

Butcher block, on the other hand, absorbs stains and is not great around the kitchen sink, as the wood absorbs water and can start rotting. From a maintenance standpoint, butcher block needs to be sanded and oiled quite frequently. While beautiful and practical for lots of cooks in the kitchen, I'm not sure I would choose it again. Instead, I might opt for a more durable product like Richlite, manufactured stone (with a high recycled material content), or a countertop that is Cradle to Cradle Certified. Cradle to Cradle Certification is one of the more rigorous standards, rating products for safety, recycled content, recyclability, and manufacturing processes held to high standards of human health.[72] Where did our countertops come from? Richlite is made in Tacoma, Washington—more than 500 miles away. Not local. (We didn't have enough butcher-block in the house to warrant tracking that down.)

Exterior Siding

The exterior of our home is made up of three materials: brick, stucco, and reclaimed cypress. The reclaimed cypress is from Duluth

Reclaimed cypress from old pickle vats for the exterior façade. Photo credit: Karen Melvin.

Timber Company, a Duluth, Minnesota–based company that salvages wood from old warehouses, factories, trestles and tank stock throughout the United States. All of our exterior cypress is reclaimed from old pickle vats. It is very pretty and durable (for wood).

However, it is also more expensive than more typical exteriors like Hardie board or stucco. Initially, the design of the house

---

72 Cradle to Cradle Certified products are listed on the c2ccertified.org website; see https://www.c2ccertified.org/products/registry.

was planned to be almost entirely clad with reclaimed cypress, with black brick bookending the north and south sides. But during a value-engineering exercise, we pulled out some of the cypress siding—not only because it had a high up-front cost, but also because it requires annual painting to maintain its deep hue. So, we reduced the amount of cypress in favor of stucco. Stucco is low maintenance, but does not meet the reclaimed or FSC-certified LEED criteria. As a result, our cypress siding did not meet the 90 percent minimum requirement of our total exterior, so we did not get a point for using reclaimed material.

Duluth is well within the 500-mile range of Minneapolis, so I thought that might count as a local material. The old pickle vats, I found out, came from Bick's Pickles, based in Dunneville, Ontario—693 miles away. I was a little frustrated that this did not meet the "local" requirement, as our brick and stucco did. Since the reclaimed but not local cypress constitutes more than 10 percent of our exterior siding, though, we could not earn a LEED point for local sourcing, either.

Interior Walls and Ceilings/Drywall

While one might not think much about the gypsum board (also called drywall or Sheetrock), once I learned about it, this is a very easy way to participate in lowering our ecological footprint (and earn a half LEED point). Drywall (which covers most walls and ceilings in homes built after 1950) is made out of a gypsum core, with paper lining around it. Gypsum is a mined material, and while there is plenty of it, it takes energy to mine and

process it, and it is one material that can be endlessly recycled without losing quality. So, recycling gypsum waste reduces the need for quarrying and production of raw materials, and saves energy doing so.

All of our gypsum drywall is made from 100 percent post-industrial recycled drywall—which I specifically asked for, once I found out that there was no difference in cost nor in quality. While not available when we were building our home, there are now several drywall products that are Cradle to Cradle Certified.

Where was our drywall made? When we purchased our drywall, I also specifically requested that it be local, because our supplier told me that "local" was available for the same amount of money and the same quality. Olympic Wall Systems got it from Winroc, which was supplied by National Gypsum out of Fort Dodge, Iowa. Fort Dodge is 218 miles away—which qualifies as local (one out of two of our half points for local materials)!

Wood Framing, Sheathing, Trim, Doors

Among all the decisions that needed to be made, wood framing and trim was not something we thought about much—we left that to our builders. But because of issues with forest

FSC-certified wood framing.

mismanagement and our desire to support sustainably managed forests, we felt it was important to purchase and support FSC-certified wood. We asked for an alternate bid, and it came back at a 5 percent premium. That seemed reasonable to us, so all of our exterior wall wood framing, interior wall framing, roof framing, sheathing, trim, and doors are 100 percent FSC-certified.

See all those little black FSC-certified stamps? That 5 percent cost us about $4,000 extra. For most things for which we paid more, we are either rewarded with lower utility bills, a healthier home, or a cool design that we get to admire every day. However, FSC-certified wood does not provide any of those benefits. The only thing we got was a "feel good" that we were supporting sustainably managed forests. We also earned three LEED points for these choices, which, one could argue, made the difference between silver and gold level. So, while I would still recommend looking into sourcing sustainability-harvested wood (and require it for tropical wood), if you are

on a budget, it is not something I would recommend prioritizing.

Where did all of this wood come from? Shaw Stewart Lumber Company provided our lumber, and according to my contact there, the plywood came from Oregon, and the framing came from Idaho—both farther than the local definition of within 500 miles.

Where did the interior doors come from? Aaron Carlson Architectural Woodwork supplied the doors, and they are located in Minneapolis. But, I needed to find out where they got their wood. The doors were from Eggers Industries, based in Two Rivers, Wisconsin, which is local. But where did they get their wood? A very helpful man at Eggers Industries told me this: "The doors were FSC-certified particleboard with paint-grade birch veneer. The core is the only material in the construction of the doors that was harvested or recovered within 500 miles of your home. The core makes up 75 percent of the weight of the door." That's great, right? No. LEED for Homes requires that *90 percent* of a component needs to be local; we are at only 75 percent. It felt supportive of the local economy, but we did not earn a point for local doors.

Aaron Carlson also supplied our interior trim. Some is poplar, some is fir. This wood came from Metro Hardwoods out of Maple Grove, a suburb of Minneapolis (local). Where do they get their wood? An email back from their "green" spokesperson said, "We don't track the origin of wood unless it is requested in advance. I do know that the fir originates from the West Coast, so that would not be regional. The poplar is sourced from multiple regions so I can't confirm a specific region." We *did* request the source of wood in advance, because everyone on our team knew we were going for LEED certification, right? But somehow that got lost in translation. No point for local trim.

Made out of Douglas fir, our window frames are all H Windows, something our architect specified very early on, with no argument from us—they are great. When I asked them to provide an alternate bid for the frames to be FSC-certified, they gave us a quote that was about 50 percent higher than non FSC-certified. When I called them to understand how this could be, they told me that they had trouble even finding FSC-certified fir. (So the 50 percent was just a wild guess?) Apparently FSC-certified cherry wood was easy to find and typically does not cost more, but we could not get it for the fir. Our exposed beams and cabinetry were all fir, so cherry was not really an option because we did not want the red tone color to clash with the orange fir color. And while 5 percent more for FSC-certified wood seemed reasonable for the wood used for framing, we were not going to spend 50 percent more for the window frames to be FSC-certified. (FSC-certified Douglas fir is now much easier to source.)

Were the window frames local, at least? H Windows is based in Ashland, Wisconsin—less than 500 miles away, so that seemed to fit the local criteria. But there are many layers to window assembly, and just because the brand of the window is from a local company, that does not mean they sourced their material locally. Tracking this down for LEED, I found out that H Window Company got their fir wood from Colonial Craft out of Luck, Wisconsin—also less than 500 miles away. But, they sourced their wood from the forests of the West Coast. Not local.

Roofing

We wanted a flat roof because we wanted part of it to be a green roof—covered in plants (see *Landscaping* chapter 10). Our roofing material is EPDM (ethylene propylene diene monomer) membrane, a very durable, weather-resistant material often used in flat roofs. It has an added benefit of not polluting the runoff rainwater, but its recycled content is only between 0 to 5 percent, so it did not meet the environmentally preferable criteria of at least 25 percent post-consumer recycled content.

While I do not know where our EPDM was made, since it is partially made from petroleum-based products, I'm guessing it is not local (and spent no time trying to track that down). So we received no point for roofing, obviously!

Insulation

For many interior walls and floors where we wanted sound insulation, we used recycled cotton denim for its superior sound absorption as well its environmental qualities. The interior wall insulation was located in between the mechanical room and the living room floor above, and around the laundry room. Because it is more expensive than typical fiberglass insulation (which we did not use anywhere), we minimized our use of it. It contains about 80 percent recycled cotton denim materials, so it *would* have met the LEED criteria had we used it everywhere. Since spray foam was a vast majority of our insulation (see section on Insulation in *Energy* chapter 6), and spray foam does not contain 20 percent recycled content, we did not receive a point here.

Where did our insulation come from? While it was technically "manufactured" on site, it is derived from petroleum-based products. The extraction of the raw materials would not be local, so again, I did not spend time trying to track that down.

Concrete Foundation

Does anyone actually choose concrete? I had no idea. Concrete is a mixture of aggregates and paste. The aggregates are sand and gravel or crushed stone; the paste is water and portland cement.[73] LEED awards one point if the concrete incorporates at least 30 percent fly ash or slag. Fly ash is a fine, powdery residue from coal-fired electricity plants. Nelson Masonry, who supplied our concrete for our foundation, typically *does* use some percentage of fly ash, but only if the weather permits—apparently the higher the recycled content percentage, the longer it takes to "cure" (or dry). It would not have cost any more or less (though I would think it should be less, since less raw material is required) to incorporate a higher percent recycled content, but since our foundation was poured in November, we were told that the weather did not permit any recycled content.

Where did our concrete come from? Nelson Masonry got their cement products from Apple Valley Ready-Mix (AVR). AVR has nine manufacturing plants, all located in the Twin Cities area and definitely within 500 miles. So, we earned our other half LEED point here and can feel good about supporting a local business.

For these material selections, we ended up with six points: three for FSC-certified wood, one for locally made drywall and concrete, and a half point each for recycled countertops, recycled drywall, flooring, and choosing PEX for plumbing. Most of these choices we see every day, so it affects us every day. Functionally and aesthetically, we are happy with our choices, particularly the reclaimed wood and Richlite countertops. These are the "feel good" choices that remind us that we are helping the circular economy grow and wasting less.

Waste Management

A telltale sign of home construction and remodeling is the sight of that big waste dumpster outside—another tangible component of home building. "Waste" is an unwanted or undesired material. The concept of waste does not exist in nature—everything is part of a cycle that is a nutrient for another organism. Waste is therefore a human concept, addressed most commonly by the idea of being "thrown away." That's odd, though, isn't it? Where is "away"?

That concept of waste is being addressed with the well-known mantra, "Reduce, Reuse, Recycle." The order matters: first, reduce the amount you consume, then try to reuse something that might be considered waste, and then, if you still have something undesirable, try to recycle it. How are we doing? In 2014, the United States generated 258 million tons of municipal solid waste. Of that, 12.8 percent was combusted with energy recovery, 52.6

---

73 Portland Cement Association, "Cement & Concrete Basic Facts," accessed October 24, 2017, http://www.cement.org/cement-concrete-applications/cement-and-concrete-basics-faqs.

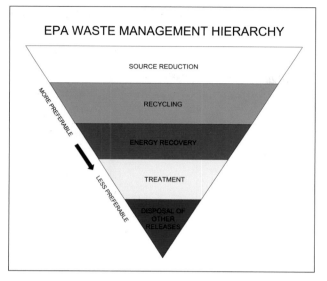

EPA WASTE MANAGEMENT HIERARCHY

SOURCE REDUCTION

RECYCLING

ENERGY RECOVERY

TREATMENT

DISPOSAL OF OTHER RELEASES

MORE PREFERABLE

LESS PREFERABLE

Source: US EPA.

was landfilled, and only 34.6 percent recycled or composted.[74] Not great!

The building industry is partly to blame. Construction and demolition wastes constitute about 40 percent of the total solid waste stream in the United States.[75] It has become part of best practices to recycle construction waste, and that is typically an easy point generator for LEED projects. But recycling is the last thing to do; we first need to try to reduce the use of materials, and then try to reuse them.

REDUCE

The concept of "reduce" in new home building simply means using fewer materials or no materials where they typically would be used. In the LEED rating system, there is no reward for *not* using certain materials. For example, the upper halves of all of our walls in the basement are all exposed concrete. We therefore used less drywall to finish the basement, which cost less and was better for the environment—but we did not earn any points.

Another example is our unique approach to cabinet and drawer pulls: we cut out a hole instead. This used less material, saved money, saved us a lot of time not having to choose the hardware, and now nobody rams their thigh on any cabinets in our house. But we did not get any LEED points for these things—probably because drawer pulls have a pretty small impact.

LEED does address what I learned can be a fairly wasteful practice: overestimating the amount of wood needed for framing the house, creating unnecessary wood waste. The credit, Material-Efficient Framing, sounded like a foreign language to me. "Framing" is what makes the house stand up, but it usually cannot be seen, unless the house is designed with deliberately exposed beams. Framing

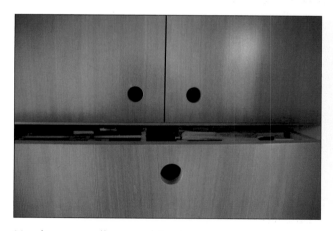

No drawer pulls on cabinetry.

---

74 US Environmental Protection Agency, "Advancing Sustainable Materials Management: Facts and Figures," https://www.epa.gov/smm/advancing-sustainable-materials-management-facts-and-figures.
75 *EED Reference Guide for Homes*, 233.

can also be a big component of the cost of the home. But what was inefficient about it? I could not get it through my head that builders might purposely order too much material and *plan* to *waste* some of it. But of course, if you think about it, they would: people can make measuring mistakes, and you would not want to run out of material during the middle of the job, because it would be more costly to reorder, and that could delay the project.

According to the *LEED for Homes Reference Guide,* a 1998 study by the Natural Resources Defense Council on home building in the United States showed that roughly one sixth of the wood that was delivered to building sites ended up going to the landfill.[76] And who paid for the extra, wasted wood? The homeowner! Nice: a LEED credit that by definition should *save* money.

The requirement? To limit the overall estimated "waste factor" to 10 percent or less. Waste factor is defined as the percentage of framing material ordered in excess of the estimated material needed for construction, and is calculated based on total material or total cost.[77]

When we began the project, we wanted to explore building our home using an Insulated Concrete Form (ICF) called Durisol, which was recommended to us by a local healthy home consultant. It is made primarily of recycled concrete and is meant to breathe—so you assume there *will* be moisture getting into the walls of the house, but the walls can dry out.

Not surprisingly, our builder and architect were adamantly united in opposition to this, primarily because wood allows for better and easier custom design, it is less expensive than ICFs, and they had much more experience using wood. Our builder went so far as to surmise that critters might easily get into and live in the Durisol ICF itself. In the end, we felt we had to go with their recommendation—after all, they were the experts, and they provided the warranty.

Complying with this prerequisite to limit the waste factor meant that the architect, engineer, and builder needed to work together to come up with a very accurate estimate of the amount of lumber needed for the job. This seems to be something that should *always* be done as a matter of good business practice. (Yet we all know not everyone employs good business practices—hence the reason for this credit.)

Would we be able to meet this prerequisite? The building project manager told me that they *always* estimate a 5 percent waste factor, which is clearly well below the 10 percent requirement. Additionally, our glulam[78] beams used for framing part of the home were ordered and prefabricated off-site, which meant that the on-site waste factor for those items would be zero percent. Ultimately, *we* did not save any money by ensuring the waste factor was less than 10 percent, but it could save you money by requesting this from your builder (and verifying).

---

76 *LEED Reference Guide for Homes,* 237.
77 Ibid.
78 Glulams get their name from glued, laminated wood. They are structurally engineered wood comprised of layers of lumber, bonded together with adhesives.

Prefabricated glulams support the entire home.

To earn LEED points for framing efficiencies, one option is to have the entire home framed at an off-site manufacturing facility. Off-site fabrication means either panelized construction, where the wall, roof, and floor components are all delivered to the job site pre-framed; or modular, prefabricated construction, commonly known as "prefab" (prefabricated) homes. My personal opinion is that prefab homes are appropriate (and fabulous) for some situations and some sites, but they are not for everyone. Additionally, I had been

reading about and researching prefab homes (they always look so great in *Dwell* magazine), but I kept hearing that they were not always as "affordable" as they were made out to be. The upside is that they are constructed quickly, but the biggest downside is their lack of customization—so it was not an option for us. Prefab practices have improved and become more affordable in the past decade, so they are worth checking out.

In order to realize framing efficiencies for on-site construction, the LEED rating system rewards the building team for actually creating detailed drawings from which one could order a fairly accurate amount of material. It seems to me that if we did *not* have detailed drawings, the house would not come together well. There may be mismatched or nonsymmetrical areas, there could be delays due to lack of materials, or a great deal of waste due to ordering too much material. We probably paid more for detailed drawings, but it was not driven by our desire to get our home LEED certified—it was a desire for a well-designed and constructed house. We hired an architect, so we did indeed have these drawings. For this, we got one point. We got another point for our builders creating a detailed cut list of lumber, which flowed directly from the detailed drawings.

Additional framing efficiencies that can be considered best practices for reducing waste include:

- Precut framing packages
- Open-web floor trusses
- Structural insulated panel (SIP) walls, roof, and floors
- Stud spacing greater than sixteen inches on center
- Ceiling joist spacing greater than sixteen inches on center
- Floor joist spacing greater than sixteen inches on center
- Roof rafter spacing greater than sixteen inches on center
  - Implementing two of the following:
  (a) size headers for actual loads;
  (b) use ladder blocking or drywall clips, or
  (c) use two-stud corners

For these practices, I needed to rely on Ben, our builder's project manager, to see with which items we actually complied. This was not a credit that I understood well—I only knew that it helps reduce overall waste. But it was not an area I felt strongly that we needed to achieve, since there are so many factors that go into framing a home properly. Insulation, ductwork, piping, and electrical installation all play into how a home is framed, not to mention structural integrity. Ben reviewed the list and confirmed that some of these things were their standard construction practice: precut framing packages, open-web floor trusses, and roof rafter spacing greater than sixteen inches on center. For the others, they would not do them, and we had to be okay with that; we still earned two and a half points here.

The one area we did question was whether to use structural insulated panels (SIPs), which can be used for walls, floors, or the roof. What are SIPs? According to SIPA (yes, there is a Structural Insulated Panel Association), "Structural insulated panels (SIPs) are a high performance building system for residential and light commercial construction. The panels consist of an insulating foam core sandwiched between two structural facings, typically oriented strand board (OSB). SIPs are manufactured under factory-controlled conditions and can be fabricated to fit nearly any building design. The result is a building system that is extremely strong, energy efficient and cost effective. Building with SIPs will save you time, money and labor."

This sounded good to us! And, LEED awards up to three points for SIPs because they provide superior and uniform insulation compared with more traditional construction methods, and can generate energy savings of 12 to 14 percent.[79] When we approached our architect with this persuasive argument, he was not supportive. Why? One of the main reasons is that SIPs require extremely detailed advance planning for electrical wiring and outlets, because they are precut at the factory. This is difficult to do, and any changes on site can be quite problematic. Even meticulously thought-out electrical plans might not work well once the house comes together, especially when you think of all the late-comer wiring requests for speakers, security systems, computer cables, even doorbells. The bottom line was pretty clear: for a custom-built home in 2008, we did not want to use SIPs. (Now, though, with wireless technology and Amazon's Alexa taking over the house, SIPs would probably make more sense.)

REUSE

In home building, there are no LEED credits for reuse. In larger commercial buildings, however, LEED strongly encourages reuse. A historic old Pillsbury flour mill located by the Mississippi River in downtown Minneapolis was one of our clients that I helped LEED certify (gold level, 2017). They reused 91 percent of the existing roof, walls, and floors—quite an accomplishment to turn an old flour mill into swanky artist lofts! In LEED for Homes, reusing old homes is not encouraged or addressed.

In any case, reusing materials is a great way to reduce waste. Before throwing unused materials in the dumpster, it's always a good idea to look at it with fresh eyes. Our builder did a great job salvaging unused lumber and saving it for us to use later. With extra stair stringers and treads made from reclaimed fir, we made several benches. With extra cypress tongue-in-groove siding from old pickle vats, we made raised-bed planters and a porch swing.

RECYCLE

After reducing and reusing materials, the final step is to recycle. Construction waste is a given—and is one of the reasons people criticize new construction, because there is so much of it. The National Association of Home Builders estimates that the construction of a typical 2,000 square foot home generates about 8,000 pounds of waste that occupies roughly 51 cubic yards of landfill space. The marketplace has come a long way, though, in developing products using construction waste, so more waste-hauler companies have options for recycling.

Reducing construction waste is just like trying to reduce waste as we live in our home. It has two components: planning ahead to minimize waste in the first place through purchasing the appropriate amount, and identifying ways to divert waste toward reusing or recycling. The reasons seem obvious: landfill space is diminishing, incineration produces pollutants, and waste of materials itself is costly and just, well, wasteful.

LEED has one prerequisite regarding waste management, and that is to investigate options for diversion for major components of construction, as well as to document the diversion rate. Diversion rate is a key

---

79 *LEED Reference Guide for Homes*, 242.

Extra reclaimed fir stair stringers were made into benches.

Photo Credit: Paul Croby

Extra reclaimed cypress found additional uses.

performance metric; it equals the amount of waste "diverted" from a landfill or incinerator, divided by the total construction waste—in weight or in volume. This was actually a great LEED requirement for our builder, because once I told them about this requirement, they found a waste management company that does recycle, and it did not cost any more than the company they had been using. Having discovered this, they switched to using this new company for all of their projects. That alone seemed worth the effort!

Aside from being required to document the waste diversion rate, LEED for Homes awards points for actually diverting waste from the landfill. In commercial LEED projects, the minimum diversion rate for a point is 50 percent. For residential projects, it is much more lenient, at 25 percent. The metric can be the "diversion rate," or, total construction waste must be less than two and a half pounds per square foot.[80] Atomic Recycling handled our waste and provided monthly reports. The easiest items for them to recycle were aggregate (asphalt and concrete), metals, and mixed wood. As shown in their final report, they were able to divert 68.3 percent of the total construction waste from landfills to recycling, which gave us two LEED points.[81]

Atomic Recycling recycles construction waste.

---

80 The newest version of LEED for Homes (LEED v4, released in 2016) requires more than just a high recycled diversion rate: projects need *total* construction waste to be less than what a "LEED Reference Home" would produce. Also, "alternative daily cover," which is material used to cover landfills at the end of each day to control odors, blowing litter, fires, and scavenging, can no longer be considered recycled. Under this new version, our home, and many other projects, would not have earned any LEED points for construction waste management. Kudos to USGBC for recognizing that total waste needs to be reduced, even if it is recycled. This should help drive further changes in the construction industry.

81 The GBCI (Green Business Certification, Inc.), the organization that administers LEED certification, also administers TRUE (Total Resource Use and Efficiency) Zero Waste Certification. TRUE Zero Waste and UL's Zero Waste verification programs are tailored for businesses and organizations; currently there is no zero waste certification for homes.

Construction Waste Diversion Rate: Project Summary		
Off-Site Source Separation by Material Type	% of Total Tons	Final Destination(s)
Fiber: Cardboard and Paper	0.8%	Pioneer Paper Stock Company
Aggregate: Asphalt, Concrete, and Masonry	19.8%	Barton Sand & Gravel & CS McCrossan Inc
Metals: Iron, Copper, Aluminum, and Brass	5.9%	Acme & American Iron & Gerdau Ameristeel & Interstate Batteries & Kirschbaum Krupp & Re-Alliance Steel & SCI & Shine Bros. Corp. & Spector Alloys
Mixed Wood	11.2%	General Biofuel Inc & Midwest Agrifuels LLC & Sylva Corporation Inc & Transfer N Transport LLC
Alternative Daily Cover	28.0%	Veolia ES Rolling Hills Landfill
Shingles	2.7%	Dem-Con Companies LLC & Elk River Waste Management
Total Recycled	**68.3%**	
Direct Landfill—Construction Waste	**31.7%**	Hennepin Energy Resource Co. (waste-to-energy) & Wast Management Burnsville & Elk River

What to Do with "Deconstruction" Waste?

The location choice for our home in Minneapolis gave us ten out of ten points (see Location, chapter 11). Due to development density, that is not an easy thing to do, unless one is prepared to tear down an existing house, which we did. We took down an old house: how could that be green? The reason we took it down was that the existing home did not take advantage of the views of the lake across the street, and did not really suit our needs—but the primary explanation is that the basement was really moldy. Mold usually does not go away. Even if we could have gotten rid of it, the process would have required the use of toxic chemicals that we would not want to be exposed to, so with our goal of having a healthy home, remodeling was not a viable option.

Reuse of old home built-ins and fixtures.

Before the demolition, we used a nonprofit organization called Deconstruction Services, which pulls out all the usable fixtures, appliances, cabinetry, and materials that can be sold for reuse (the proceeds benefit the nonprofit). Then, when the rest of the house was torn down, we made sure that anything that could be recycled was recycled (glass, wood, and concrete were all separated out). Though the neighborhood children thought it was fun to watch, it was still a heartache to witness the demolition of a home.

Nothing in the LEED for Homes Rating System addresses how to deconstruct a home. LEED did not penalize us for deconstructing a house; nor did we get any points for tearing it down in a manner as "green" as possible.

While Deconstruction Services no longer exists, an organization called Better Futures Minnesota provides deconstruction services and then sells reusable items from its ReUse Center. A friend of mine used their services to tear down an old home, which cost $11,000 (typically it is closer to $20,000 to pay a contractor to demolish the home). They paid another $1,100 to get everything that they donated appraised, and were able to realize a $46,000 tax deduction because of the large donation. While I am not an advocate of tearing down existing buildings, sometimes it needs to be done—and there is a way of doing it that is *less bad* and can be financially beneficial.

Old home being torn down.

For reducing waste through framing efficiencies and recycling construction debris, we earned five LEED points. Add that to the six we earned for purchasing "environmentally preferable" materials, plus one for "low emissions" (see *Clean Air* chapter 4), and we earned twelve out of sixteen possible points in LEED's Materials and Resources section.

Materials Dollars and Sense

GREENER CHOICE	DOLLARS	SENSE
FSC-certified tropical wood	Tropical wood costs more anyway; FSC may have premium	If you must use tropical wood, then make it FSC-certified
FSC-certified non-tropical wood	Extra 5–25 percent MEDIUM COST	Not worth it unless you really care, or it's the same price and quality NOT ENOUGH SENSE
Reclaimed wood	Can be extra cost, unless you find it yourself ☺	Worth it if you like the look and feel
Concrete containing recycled material	NO INCREMENTAL COST	Do it if you can
Recycled drywall	NO INCREMENTAL COST	DO IT!
Recycled cotton denim insulation	More expensive than fiberglass, less than spray foam	Good for interior wall sound insulation; not recommended for exterior walls
Richlite/recycled countertops	Typically 10 percent more than granite	Only if you like the look and feel
Local materials	Variable	If you can find them, go for it!
Reduce materials; limit framing waste factor to less than 10 percent	May save money	DO IT!
Reuse construction material	May save money	DO IT!
Recycle construction waste	NO INCREMENTAL COST	DO IT!

CHAPTER 10: LANDSCAPING

It was the bees that showed me how to move between different flowers—to drink the nectar and gather pollen from both. It is this dance of cross-pollination that can produce a new species of knowledge, a new way of being in the world. After all, there aren't two worlds, there is just this one good green earth.

—Robin Wall Kimmerer, *Braiding Sweet Grass* (Milkweed Editions, 2013)

This topic of landscaping matches up only in part to the LEED section on "Sustainable Sites." Worth twenty-two points and requiring at least five, I'm omitting several of the LEED credits because some of them are just not that interesting, would not do much to feed our soul, and there were not really any choices for us to consider. Things like "erosion control during construction" (a prerequisite) and "minimize disturbed area of the site" were accomplished as a matter of course, and there were no additional choices to be made. "Non-toxic pest control" is important, but it was standard construction practice, and we have no story.

The interesting parts of landscaping fall into three categories (of course): what you plant (and do not plant), the hardscape (decks, patios, driveways), and a green roof, which deserves its own section due to its stupendous-ness. The choices for plantings, hardscape, and a green roof can all work symbiotically to address three critically important issues that can contribute to a sustainable site: reducing the demand for irrigation, managing surface water runoff, and reducing the heat island effect. Do these sound boring? Read on.

Irrigation demand. Reducing demand for irrigation can significantly decrease potable water usage and save money. According to the EPA, outdoor water used for landscaping accounts for 30 percent of the 320 gallons of water used per day by the average American family. The *Water Efficiency* chapter discusses reducing outdoor water usage through efficient irrigation *systems*. Here, the plantings themselves can reduce the *need* for irrigation. Determining *actual* irrigation demand reduction is a complicated formula, requiring the calculation of the baseline irrigation usage, using assumptions about baseline evapotranspiration rates, which represents the rate of water loss for a particular climate. Other variables include things you might learn if you have a degree in landscape architecture (maybe): landscape coefficient (the volume of water lost via evapotranspiration), the species factor (the water requirements of different plant species), the microclimate factor (environmental conditions specific to the landscape, including temperature, wind, and humidity), irrigation efficiency, and other things most of us do not understand. When I showed the formula to our irrigation subcontractors to see if they could tackle it, their brows furrowed. But the calculations do not matter so much, as long as we understand which plants require a lot of water, and choose those plants that require minimal, if any, irrigation.

Surface water management. Managing surface water runoff—rain and melting snow that flows off streets, rooftops, and lawns—is actually a pretty big problem for many urban areas, including Minneapolis. Because water can damage property, most developers treat water as something to get off their site, and therefore do not design features—like swales or cisterns—to handle the water on-site. Imagine a densely developed area of driveways, roads, and rooftops, and not much vegetation. Where does all the water go? It can quickly overload the stormwater management system, which is a complex system of underground pipes that drains into local bodies of water, such as lakes where we swim and fish, and rivers from which we get our drinking water. Water is a universal solvent, meaning it can absorb and dissolve many contaminants—salts, oils, pesticides, fertilizers, pet and yard waste—along the way. Contaminating our water is not a good thing. We don't think too much about what happens to all the

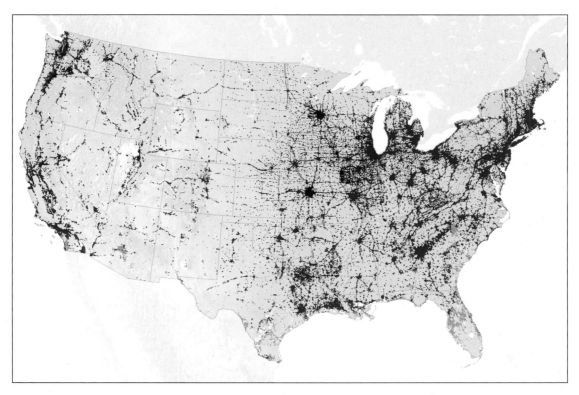

Map showing the urban heat island effect (explained on next page) where cities are 2–5 degrees warmer than neighboring areas. Photo credit: Joshua Stevens, NASA Earth Observatory.

runoff after it goes into that scary black grate in the street, but we should! Cities started recognizing this, and many now require that new developments incorporate features that keep some percentage of water runoff on the property—that's what surface water management means. This practice helps reduce the quantity of water flowing into the storm system, as well as the quality of water, since vegetation helps filter out the contaminants.

Heat island effect. The heat island effect refers to the phenomenon that occurs in cities everywhere: urban areas are hotter than the suburbs and the exurbs. The reason for this is that higher density developed areas have much more hardscape—pavement and buildings—which absorbs the sun's heat and radiates it to the surrounding areas. This problem is exacerbated by additional heat sources in the city like car and truck exhaust and air conditioners. Then, it becomes circular, because it increases the demand for air conditioning, which increases the heat outside. What does it matter if it's warmer? First, more air conditioning requires more electricity, which is costly and produces more greenhouse gases and smog. Second, it is disruptive to microclimates and habitats. Third, it's just not that pleasant for humans, plants, or animals to be so hot.

Several landscape design strategies can be used to help mitigate the heat island effect, manage water on-site, and reduce the need for irrigation. The two primary variables where we can make greener choices are plantings and hardscape.

Plantings

The options for plantings are numerous and can be confusing. Most people shop for plants and find what they like at the plant nursery, or just press the easy button and cover their yard with conventional lawns. But there are many other things to consider. What does the plant look like in the winter? What kind of maintenance does it require? How much water, trimming, sun, and shade does it need? Does it spread? How big does it get? I am very far from having a green thumb, but my mom has ten of them and I have grown to appreciate how interesting and beautiful a backyard can be, and, without too much work, a little more sustainable. But first, just as important as what *to* plant is what *not* to plant.

Invasive Species

The only prerequisite for landscaping in LEED is to *not* introduce any invasive plant species on your property. What is an invasive species? The term refers to non-indigenous or "nonnative" plants that have a tendency to spread or grow in population such that they damage the environment, human health, or the ability for other species to co-exist. Buckthorn, common in our neighborhood, is an example of an invasive species. The Minnesota Department of Natural Resources lists buckthorn as a "restricted noxious weed," as it out-competes native plants for nutrients, light, and moisture, and it is very hard to control without toxic herbicides.

Since invasive plant species vary by region, I needed to first find the list of local invasive plants, against which we had to compare our own list of plants we were introducing: techny arborvitae, serviceberries, a few more white pines and birches, and native wildflowers and grasses (coreopsis, wild geranium, wild blue

Buckthorn is considered an invasive species. Photo credit: Richard Webb, Bugwood.org.

phlox, meadow parsnip, dendranthema, long-fellow fescue). I obtained the list of invasive species from the Minnesota Board of Water and Soil Resources,[82] and we were in the clear for this prerequisite—though we did have to remove a large buckthorn "hedge."

Turf Grass

What is it about lawns that we all love? People think lawns are easy, inexpensive, and low maintenance. They most definitely are not—we just have the infrastructure in place to support them. Lawns require more irrigation than other plants, need regular mowing—which burns fossil fuels (unless you have an electric or manual mower)—and require chemicals and fertilizers for those who want a weed-free green lawn. All of these are bad for the environment, bad for our health, and costly. It would be great to have no grass: nothing to mow, nothing to fertilize, nothing to irrigate. The LEED rating system encourages planting drought-tolerant turf and limiting the amount of turf as a percent of the designed landscape.

---

82 Lists of invasive species can be found through most states' department of natural resources. Minnesota's is at http://www.dnr.state.mn.us/invasives/terrestrialplants/index.html.

Before: backyard as initially landscaped. Photo credit: Karen Melvin.

After: new backyard provided outdoor living space and flowers. Almost all of our turf grass was replaced.

We initially considered drought-tolerant turf. From what I learned, some species are indeed more drought tolerant than others, but those species might not be the typical soft grass in which your kids (or you) want to frolic. Additionally, it seems that you can actually train your lawn to be more drought tolerant through techniques like aeration, mowing, and proper watering. The biggest consideration, though, came to which grass type is best for our climate. Our landscapers recommended Kentucky bluegrass, which is the most common and best known cool-season grass. It actually can survive a drought by just going dormant. I learned that fine fescue, a cool season grass that is drought tolerant, does not tolerate wear and tear. That would not work so well for us. So, while we did not choose drought-tolerant turf, we did limit the amount of "conventional" turf we planted, for the reasons I mention above. We still felt the need to have grass, because we had two little kids, and that's just how it has to be, right?

LEED awards one point for having turf grass be less than 60 percent of the total softscape (area that is not the house, driveway, patio, etc.), two points for less than 40 percent, and three points for less than 20 percent. We were not point-searching; we were just trying to design a landscape that worked for our family. We ended up with 47 percent conventional turf and one LEED point. That 47 percent turned out to be too high, as the backyard grass was always wet and weedy. Seven years later, we ripped almost all of our backyard grass, added hardscape, and planted more flowers.

If you are now convinced to get rid of some, if not all, of your turf grass, what do you plant in your yard instead? Drought-tolerant plants.

DROUGHT-TOLERANT PLANTS

What, exactly, is a drought-tolerant plant? I used to live in Arizona, so I think of them as cacti—prickly pear, saguaros, teddy bear cholla, etc. Were we supposed to plant those in Minnesota? Those plants would die from too much moisture. Most native trees, shrubs, and plants would be considered "drought-tolerant," because they survive in your particular climate without supplemental watering. And that is the main point—design landscaping that requires less potable water, often referred to as "xeriscaping."

We started out with several river birches thriving on our property without any extra irrigation on our part, but they were definitely getting extra water from our wet soil as well as from the underground river running beneath our house. We planted another birch (Heritage variety), but I would not count that one among the drought-tolerant plants. We planted three white pines and five serviceberries, which are considered drought-tolerant. We planted a row of techny arborvitae to provide a natural fence around the edges of our property. Those do not count as drought-tolerant, because I could not find them on any list—and we installed drip irrigation for them.

We also had a large area of our landscaping devoted to native prairie grasses and wildflowers—an area that is not irrigated, so, by definition, it is drought-tolerant. In order to get this area established, we had 738 tiny plant plugs installed: little blue stem, coreopsis, aster, daisies, and phlox. Due to this, about 90 percent of our plantings were considered to be drought-tolerant, giving us two LEED points.

After a few years, we replaced our native wildflowers and grasses with other tried-and-true drought-tolerant plants. Here's how the garden unfolds: in the spring, little white anemones are the first flowering perennials, around late April. Then purple wild geraniums bloom, and they stay as low growing plants, blooming all summer and into fall. Next come the yellow coreopsis, in late May, then the dark red and bright pink echinacea, or coneflowers, shine their happy face in June. Rudbeckia (black-eyed Susans) blossom in July, presenting us with a full rainbow of color for the rest of the summer. The purple asters come out in September, and in October the coneflowers lose their petals. That's our front yard.

Our backyard, which we changed out after seven years, is similar but also has many varieties of sedum, including autumn fire. Autumn fire is glorious: bright green in the summer, changing to orange, then red, then maroon in late fall. We were also recently introduced to spiderwort, a beautiful flowering purple plant with bright green/yellow leaves, and amsonia, which turns to gorgeous golden-yellow in late autumn. These plants required no additional watering (rainfall was sufficient) and virtu-

Drought-tolerant wildflowers.

ally no maintenance. The colors bring beauty to our lives every day, and the bees, butterflies, and birds couldn't be happier.

Another category of drought-tolerant plants that cannot be overlooked is edibles. We have raspberries, strawberries, one plum tree, and an herb garden outside the kitchen door. We also have a raised-bed vegetable garden with kale, peppers, tomatoes, and cucum-bers, but only the kale can be considered drought-tolerant. Being able to walk outside and grab fresh yummy food off the vine is truly the definition of feeding your soul.

Hardscape

Hardscape includes all sidewalks, patios, decking, and driveways on the site. There are two ecological issues with hardscape: it does not absorb rainwater, so it creates more problems for stormwater management, and it can add to the heat island effect (unless it is white, which most hardscape is not).

LEED awards points for reducing the heat island effect if you shade your hardscapes with trees, or you install light-colored materials or vegetation for at least 50 percent of sidewalks, patios, and driveways. Acceptable strategies include white or gray concrete, open pavers, and any material with a solar reflectance index (SRI) of at least 29. SRI is a measurement of how much light energy a material reflects, on a scale of 0 to 100, where an SRI of 100 is white and 0 is black. This figure is useful in comparing different materials, because darker materials absorb more heat, worsening the heat island effect.

Our hardscapes include the driveway and our patios on east and west sides. Our driveway is made of asphalt. This does not count as light-colored material, and does contribute to the heat island effect. We explored pavers (which were very expensive up front as well as for ongoing maintenance), concrete (our neighbors have this and it is very difficult to

Butterflies are attracted to the cone flowers.

Drought-tolerant sedum and asters.

Amsonia cut from our garden in the fall.

Sedum and Nepeta plants attracting bees.

repair), and even a grass driveway (not very practical for Minnesota). We also looked at permeable pavers, which at the time were still

Tomatoes, kale, and cucumbers love that black brick wall.

Fall harvest.

fairly new to the market, and we didn't love what was out there. Rain and snow make permeable pavers a little risky, since the water can soak in, then freeze, and make the pavers pop out or crack. Vast Enterprises makes a permeable paver out of recycled materials, but to me, they gave off a certain smell, and we were not sure how well they would perform long-term. We reluctantly went with the asphalt driveway because of cost and convenience—the main reasons for almost everything we do that is not sustainable.

For hardscape patio products, we initially considered wood, because who doesn't like a wood deck? We don't: with vivid memories of slivers in my feet from when I was little, and pulling slivers out of my daughters' feet after visiting their grandparents, wood was nixed. We considered slate for the outside, because we have slate tile floor inside, and it would look cool to have it match—but the price was too high. We ended up with gray concrete pavers, sticking with stone as a grounding material that connected well with our interior, and qualifying as light-colored. In a concrete study by the Portland Cement Association, all concretes tested had a SRI of 36 or higher, exceeding the LEED minimum of 29. With our lighter-colored pavers and other aggregate rock comprising just over 53 percent of our hardscape, we qualified for one LEED point.

In reality, the concrete pavers do not feel like they are mitigating the heat island effect; in the summer it is extra hot in our backyard. That could be exacerbated by the fact that we have a black brick wall facing south, absorbing and radiating the heat. But in the early spring and late fall months, we love this feature, as our backyard is significantly warmer than the front—so our ability to enjoy the outdoors in the spring and fall is extended a few more weeks because of this.

Green Roof

A green roof combines the variables of plantings and hardscape, as it transforms what normally is hardscape (the roof) into vegetation. The size and shape of the roof is a big design decision, if you are building new. Initially, we wanted a green roof everywhere, which requires a flat or slightly sloped roof. I love the idea of a bird flying overhead, not knowing there is a building below, being able to find food and water almost anywhere she lands. When we priced it out, we realized it was not affordable for our entire home. Since our soil is mushy, not only would we have had to pay for the green roof, but we also would have had to pay for additional pilings to support the extra weight of the roof. They can get pretty heavy: the saturated weight of matured vegetation on a green roof weighs between twenty-six and twenty-nine pounds per square foot. Additionally, I had no idea what kind of maintenance it would require, but knowing that I might need to access it to weed it seemed likely. So, we decided to locate the green roof in the one spot where we can see *and* access it: outside my office, on top of the other half of the garage. Later, we decided to also put it on top of the little breezeway that connects the garage and mudroom to the rest of the house, because we can see it from the hallway outside our bedrooms.

I had seen some examples of green roofs where soil is placed on the roof and seeded, and then you have to wait for the plants to grow and bloom. These were customized green roofs, which start out looking brown and are quite expensive. Fortunately, I had stumbled across the LiveRoof system, a national company that partners with local nurseries to grow the plants ahead of time in 2x1-foot trays. The trays, full of a variety of low-growing plants, are then easily placed on the roof and look good from day one. You can customize the plants, but it generally is wise to let the grower recommend which species work best for your

Sedum varieties on the green roof.

climate and the relative shade and sun the area receives. We worked with Doug Danielson from Bachman's Wholesale Nursery, and he recommended the Carefree Mix, which has eight different varieties of sedum, providing a mix of textures and colors that evolve year round. The plants are hardy, drought-tolerant, and spread easily. It magically transformed the view.

A green roof has many other benefits as well. First, it helps insulate the roof, meaning less need for heating or cooling in the space beneath it. In our case it is above our garage, which is not that important for keeping warm or cool, but it's still a benefit. Second, it reduces the heat island effect—making it much cooler compared to the black EPDM roof that had been there initially. I noticed the difference in my office immediately, and less air conditioning is needed to keep the office cool in the summer. Third, it reduces the stormwater runoff, as it absorbs and filters most of the water on the roof when it rains. Even in huge downpours, there is no erosion or annoying splashing at the bottom of the gutter.

A financial benefit of the green roof is that it helped reduce our stormwater utility fee. Ever since March 2005, the city's costs for providing stormwater management have been listed as a separate line item on customers' water bills (not all municipalities do this). The portion of our fee attributed to stormwater management

Green roof outside my office. Photo credit: Paul Crosby.

Smaller green roof over breezeway, connecting the house to the garage and office.

was $13.86 per month; it has risen to $15.45 per month over the past eight years. The city offers a stormwater utility fee credit program as an incentive to reduce the quality and/or quantity of stormwater runoff. After filling out the application and showing that we managed much of our stormwater on-site, they approved a monthly stormwater credit of $5.32 per month (which has risen to $5.56 per month). While not a huge amount, over time, it adds up: we have saved over $500.

Finally, and this is the biggest financial benefit, a green roof extends the life of the roof by two to three times. How? Since it covers the roof membrane, it protects it from weathering and cracking over time. When we moved into our home, I figured I had a good twelve to fifteen years to prove this out. After two years, though, we got to test a green roof's protective capabilities in another way: Minneapolis suffered a serious hailstorm in May 2011. While the plants were slightly limp and lifeless, they survived, and prevented the roof membrane

Roofing company installing the LiveRoof trays.

underneath from incurring any hail damage. So, while most of the roof needed replacement (insurance mostly covered it, but it was still a huge hassle), our green roof stayed put—a very unexpected early benefit.

With the rest of our black EPDM roof still needing replacement, we had the choice of white or black—there was no cost difference.

We decided to go with a white roof, because it also helps reduce the local heat island effect due to its reflective qualities.[83] While many people think Minneapolis is too cold for a white roof to be beneficial, I disagree. A black roof *might* help keep our home warmer in the winter, but it is often covered in snow anyway. A black roof absorbing the sun's warmth *may*

---

83 In order to mitigate the urban heat island effect, many cities like Chicago have ordinances that require roofs to have a higher SRI (solar reflective index) than typical darker roofs. More and more, white and green roofs are being installed as strategies to comply with these ordinances.

help keep the home warmer in the late fall, but in the spring, it only makes the snow and ice on the roof melt faster—accelerating the water runoff from the roof. (That's bad from a stormwater management perspective—we want to *decelerate* water runoff.) Conversely, the white roof *does* help keep it cooler in the summer.

So what's the real payback? If a typical roof needs replacement in fifteen years, then the payback time period is at *most* fifteen years. The cost of having to replace your roof is the avoided cost. With the improved insulation, reduced cooling load in my office, and the reduction in water bill, the payback is probably between ten and twelve years. A ten-year payback does not necessarily justify the expense, but who looks at a garden and needs it to have a financial return? The fact that it is beautiful year-round, attracts birds and butterflies, and keeps my office cooler—these are the real paybacks.

Maintenance of our green roof has been fairly minimal. We go out and weed it about twice per year, and because it is a small, contained area, it does not take more than an hour or two. We have never irrigated it (except when it was first installed), never fertilized it, and have not had to replant it until 2017—so for eight years it was pretty much self-sufficient. 2017, a few of the species had died off, so we just took some sedum clippings and spread them around. The clippings took root quite easily; we were advised to add fertilizer in the spring.

How does LEED treat a green roof? It rewards you with points only if it actually does something to manage surface water on-site, and LEED believes you must have at least 50 percent of the roof vegetated (and even then, it's only half a point; we would get a full point for 100 percent vegetated roof). Because our green roof is less than 50 percent of the entire roof, it did not contribute any LEED points.

It did, however, help in achieving a point for "Surface Water Management." Our site was designed to manage runoff from the roof. The top of my office drains onto the green roof, so that area is managed. On the main part of the house, there are two downspouts, each draining into a twenty-four inch catch basin.

Green roof changes colors all year round and evolves over time.

Under those catch basins are more drainage design elements: on the south side, a drain tile carries the water to a naturally occurring vegetated swale along our property line; on the north side, it goes to a perforated sleeve that slowly releases the water underground, underneath our wildflower garden. So, the green roof did help us earn two LEED points for surface water management.

Beyond the green roof, surface water management is further controlled by having what is called a "permeable lot"—at least 70 percent of the site, not including the roof or the area under the roof, has to allow water to be absorbed, so that it does not overload the storm sewer system. Square footage that is permeable includes any areas that are vegetative landscape (grass, trees, shrubs), permeable paving, and any impermeable surfaces that direct all runoff toward an appropriate permanent infiltration feature, like a swale, rain garden, or cistern. While we did not have permeable pavers or a cistern, 92 percent of our lot can be categorized as permeable, which gave us three LEED points (and still a wet lot). Did it cost more to get these points? I think we would have done these measures regardless of LEED, because the water running off the roof needs somewhere to go other than our foundation and basement. It's an important durability requirement, and I'm glad it was addressed.

The green roof was suffering, so we added sedum clippings (before and after).

Yard Work as Viewed from Heaven

The following overheard conversation between God and St. Francis has been circulating on the web:

God: Hey, St. Francis, you know all about gardens and nature; what in the world is going on down there in the United States? What happened to the dandelions, violets, thistles, and the stuff I started eons ago? I had a perfect no-maintenance garden plan. Those plants grow in any type of soil, withstand drought, and multiply with abandon. The nectar from the long-lasting blossoms attracts butterflies, honeybees, and flocks of songbirds. I expected to see a vast garden of color by now. All I see are patches of green.

St. Francis: It's the tribes that settled there, Lord. They are called the Suburbanites. They started calling your flowers "weeds" and went to great lengths to kill them and replace them with grass.

God: Grass? But it is so boring; it's not colorful. It doesn't attract butterflies, bees, or birds, only grubs and sod worms. It's temperamental with temperatures. Do these Suburbanites really want grass growing there?

St. Francis: Apparently not, Lord. As soon as it has grown a little, they cut it . . . sometimes two times a week.

God: They cut it? Do they bale it like hay?

St. Francis: Not exactly, Lord. Most of them rake it up and put it in bags.

God: They bag it? Why? Is it a cash crop? Do they sell it?

St. Francis: No sir, just the opposite. They pay to throw it away.

God: Now let me get this straight . . . they fertilize it to make it grow and when it does grow, they cut it off and pay to throw it away?

 St. Francis: Yes, sir.

God: These Suburbanites must be relieved in the summer when we cut back on the rain and turn up the heat. That surely slows the growth and saves them a lot of work.

St. Francis: You aren't going to believe this Lord, but when the grass stops growing so fast, they drag out hoses and pay more money to water it, so they can continue to mow it and pay to get rid of it.

God: What nonsense! At least they kept some of the trees. That was a sheer stroke of genius, if I do say so myself. The trees grow leaves in the spring to provide beauty and shade in the summer. In the autumn they fall to the ground and form a natural blanket to keep the moisture in the soil and protect the trees and bushes. Plus, as they rot, the leaves become compost to enhance the soil. It's a natural circle of life.

St. Francis: You'd better sit down, Lord. As soon as the leaves fall, the Suburbanites rake them into great piles and pay to have them hauled away.

God: No way! What do they do to protect the shrubs and tree roots in the winter to keep the soil moist and loose?

St. Francis: After throwing the leaves away, they go out and buy something called mulch. They haul it home and spread it around in place of the leaves.

God: And where do they get this mulch?

St. Francis: They cut down the trees and grind them up to make mulch.

God: Enough! I don't want to think about this anymore. St. Catherine, you're in charge of the arts. What movie have you scheduled for us tonight?

St. Catherine: *Dumb and Dumber*, Lord. It's a really stupid movie about . . .

God: Never mind—I think I just heard the whole story from St. Francis!

CHAPTER 11: LOCATION

The three most important things in real estate are location, location, and location. This final chapter of *For Our Soul* addresses the most important attribute of a home. The location of your home affects your daily commute to work or school, where you buy groceries, your shopping patterns, friends and neighbors, and cultural activities.

My favorite thing about our home is its location, as it is near many community resources, across the street from a lake and neighborhood park, connected to many miles of bicycle and running trails, and easy, quick access to downtown. When we initially decided we were done with high-density condo living and wanted a house, we looked in the suburbs, where you can typically get more land and house for the money. We quickly realized this did not fit with our lifestyle, and fortunately found a home much closer to the city. While location does not have an immediate impact on our health or our wealth, it has a huge impact on our soul—and that can be positive or negative.

Location also happens to be one of the first LEED credit categories addressed in the LEED for Homes Rating System, as development can promote environmentally responsible land-use patterns; conversely, be it can be a detriment to a neighborhood. Attempting to earn the ten

LEED location points can be tricky, because the choice of location is so personal and is based on market availability and affordability—mostly factors outside individual control. We chose our location without having any idea what the LEED criteria were. As I read through the five location-related credits, they were all enlightening to me with respect to how much location choice actually does impact our ecological footprint.

The first three sections, Site Selection, Preferred Locations, and Infrastructure, are simply about encouraging people to develop on land that is more suitable for a home. We are *not* supposed to develop on a site that meets any of the following criteria:

- Land whose elevation is at or below the 100-year floodplain as defined by the Federal Emergency Management Agency (FEMA) (*ours is not, though sometimes I wonder*)
- Land that is specifically identified as habitat for any species on federal or state threatened or endangered lists (*not*)
- Land within 100 feet of any water, including wetlands (*barely not*)
- Land that prior to acquisition was public parkland, unless there was

some trade for public land (*definitely not*)

- Land that contains "prime soils," "unique soils," or "soils of state significance," as identified in state Natural Resources Conservation Service soil surveys[84] (*luckily not—we would have had no idea!*)

Where *do* you develop? LEED encourages building a home near or within existing communities. The idea is that there is less environmental impact if we build on or near previously developed sites, as opposed to farmland, wetlands, etc. New remote developments require extensive expansion of basic infrastructure and community services, and typically force residents to rely solely on cars for all transportation needs.[85] That's bad for the environment, bad for neighborhood connections, and bad for your health—because you can't walk or bike anywhere. So, LEED awards one point for "edge development"— building along the edge of already developed land; two points for "infill development"— at least 75 percent of the perimeter borders previously developed land; and an additional point for building on previously developed land[86] (which we did). You can rack up even another point for selecting a lot that is within a half mile of existing water service lines and sewer service lines, because places that already have utilities and roads reduce both the environmental impact and the economic cost of extending infrastructure.

So, the best strategy for having the least amount of detrimental impact on the environment is to build a new home on a previously developed infill lot. That can be difficult to find and expensive to purchase. Absolutely these LEED credits cost more. But location impacts everything. The importance of this concept needs to be understood by builders and developers, as location choices can encroach on habitat corridors, recreational open spaces, and wildlife sanctuaries. Many suburban and exurban developments ignored these things, and we are paying the price: exurban development is one of the primary causes of loss of land and habitat.[87]

The other major component of a location is about access: access to community resources, access to mass transit, and access to open spaces. Why? Because close access means we will be in our car less, which means less pollution, and we may even exercise more and live a healthier lifestyle. We live across the street from a trail where we can walk or bike to a pharmacy, grocery store, several restaurants, an urgent care clinic, a dry cleaners, and a workout facility. LEED awards varying level of points for living within a quarter mile of four basic community resources, a half mile of seven basic community resources, or a half mile of transit services that offer thirty or more transit rides per weekday (combined bus, rail, and ferry).

---

84 *LEED Reference Guide for Homes*, 55.
85 *LEED Reference Guide for Homes*, 60.
86 *LEED Reference Guide for Homes*, 59.
87 Michale Glennon and Heidi Kretser, "Impacts to Wildlife from Low Density, Exurban Development," Adirondack Communities & Conservation Program, Technical Paper No. 3, October 2005, viii.

Original house we purchased.

"Basic community resources" include the following: arts and entertainment center, bank, community or civic center, convenience store, daycare center, fire station, fitness center or gym, laundry or dry cleaner, library, medical or dental office, pharmacy, police station, post office, place of worship, restaurant, school, supermarket, other service retail, or major employment center. I counted sixteen basic community resources near us, but I had to mess around on Google Maps for a while to see if we met the distance requirement of being within a half-mile. I found that *all* of these are outside the range of a half-mile, but within the range of one mile. So to me, they are close enough to walk, but not for LEED points. This seemed a bit arbitrary, but alas, we got zero points for having great access to community resources.

For access to transit, I had to figure out how many bus stops are within a half-mile of our house (we are not near rail, yet, nor a ferry) and count the number of average daily rides offered per weekday. The MetroTransit bus has two routes that are within a half-mile of our home, and they run every fifteen to twenty minutes during rush hours and every thirty minutes during non-rush hours. By my calculations, the total number of transit rides near our home equals 192, which would more than qualify us for three LEED points, under the bucket of "Outstanding Community Resources."

Lastly, access to open space is rewarded, so long as we are within a half-mile of a publicly accessible or community-based open space that is at least three quarters acre in size, consisting predominantly of land that is planted with grass, shrubs, and trees. This includes parks, play areas, and ponds if they border a walking or bicycle path. This is hands-down the number one thing we love about our house. Not the fact that it is energy efficient, water efficient, healthy, new, and what we consider to be a cool design, but the fact that we are across the street from a park, across the street from a lake, and across the street from walking and bicycle paths that can take us to the city, the river, or out into the sub-

urbs. Granted, we are fortunate to live in a city like Minneapolis that has one of the best park systems in the country and was recently rated the number one bicycling city by *Bicycling* magazine.

To me, the benefits are obvious. We like to play outside. The *LEED for Homes Reference Guide* makes it clear why it is important: publicly accessible green spaces promote outdoor activity and recreation and provide calming and restorative settings, community gathering places, and space for environmental education. Open spaces also facilitate outdoor activity, leading to improved health.[88] Could this mean that LEED recognizes things that are good for our souls?

So, due to our *one* choice of location, we earned all ten out of ten possible points, and just over 11 percent of the total we needed for gold rating. Did we pay more for these points? No, not incrementally. We would have chosen this location whether or not we wanted to get LEED certified. But buying previously developed land that is close to transit and community resources and near parks and trails typically does cost more. So we did pay a premium. But the benefits are immeasurable.

---

88 *LEED Reference Guide for Homes*, 76.

EPILOGUE

CHAPTER 12: THE WORST GREEN DECISIONS WE MADE

This may be the chapter you turned to first, because everyone likes to hear how and where we screwed up. I don't blame you; failing is how we learn, and I readily admit to failure. There is no perfect house. Life evolves, and there is no way to anticipate how your home can meet all of your needs. We had to make so many decisions that inevitably, in hindsight, we can see that we would do some things differently if we had it to do again. Three are worth highlighting: two that were an attempt to be more sustainable, but did not work out as expected, and one that worked out well but is just flat-out *not* green.

Irrigation Well

If you've been reading this book, you know we have a very wet lot—so much so that there is water running beneath our house, our sump pump always runs, and we had to put pilings under our home to support it so it won't sink. When we looked into cisterns to collect rainwater, it did not make sense financially or practically, because we would have had to put more pilings in the wet ground to support the cisterns. Since we already had ample water

under our house, in order to save water and money on irrigation, the logical conclusion was to drill a well and add a small pump.

From a cost/benefit perspective, this decision was not a slam dunk: it would cost $6,500 to install the well and pump, and we estimated we would save about $500 annually on our water bill—so, about a thirteen-year payback. I figured we would be in our house a long time, and I would feel less guilty watering our plants from water that was already there, rather than using potable water from the city. Jim was never too supportive of this, but I persisted and got my way. It would be financially beneficial, I argued, maybe even before year thirteen, if water prices increase!

One issue we had not been cognizant of was that our well water contains iron, and once iron is exposed to oxygen, it leaves a reddish-brown stain on every surface it touches. This would be an issue, because the water from the sprinklers, especially on windy days, would dampen the edges of our house, patio, and driveway. Our irrigation provider told us that we would need something called "Rid O' Rust" as a well-water additive to prevent rust

Standing water on our lot, even during dry days.

stains. The Rid O' Rust system consisted of a thirty-gallon tank, located in our mechanical room, which was rigged to pipe into our irrigation system during operation. For a one-time fee of $1,800 for the Rid O' Rust system and pump, our problem was solved. That additional cost only added another three and a half years to our payback timeframe!

I wondered, though, what is Rid O' Rust, and is it toxic? It is made with oxalic acid, and while not flammable, it is rated as "Danger—corrosive poison."[89] So that did not seem so good, but our contractor assured us we would never be in direct contact with it: once it was mixed with the water, it would be so diluted that it would not cause any harm. That sounded logical, so we paid the additional money and installed the system.

I first started not loving our "green" decision to use well water when our annual bill

---

89 Rid O' Rust Material Data Safety Sheet, Pro Products LLC, http://www.ridorust.net/E_AmerHy_RidORust_ PowderRustStainRemover.pdf.

for ten gallons of Rid O' Rust, plus labor, was coming in at $345. That was cutting into our cost savings on irrigation. If we thought we were saving $500 on annual water bills, we were really only saving $155. That made the financials look even worse—bringing it to a fifty-three-year payback. (I did not tell Jim this part, and if he reads this book, he's just finding this out now.)

We had an additional problem: whenever the irrigation system was on, which was in the middle of the night (a better time to water, since in the daytime the water evaporates more quickly), the system produced this loud ticking noise—waking up any guest that might be staying at our home. Since guests did not stay at our home very frequently, we figured we could live with that.

Given that the Rid O' Rust tank was in our mechanical room, we did not make it a practice to check its level. Once, we ran out of Rid O' Rust, and indeed our concrete pavers and patio furniture turned reddish-brown. We had to use another version of Rid O' Rust to scrub out the stains—which was difficult and not entirely successful. Jim's patience with our well was running thin, and I had to agree with him. The decision was flat-out *not* financially beneficial, not operationally beneficial, created more hassles and problems than it was worth, and did not even get us any LEED points! After three years of living with it, we decommissioned our irrigation pump and now use good old inexpensive city water.

How did *that* play out for us financially? I analyzed our water usage before and after we used city water for irrigation. Our $500 estimate was actually off by 50 percent; we pay about $750 per year for irrigation. (Fig-

Irrigation pump for the well.

uring that out is no easy task—does any homeowner know how much they pay for irrigation?) Compared to using well water, we are now actually spending an extra $405 per year for city water. So now we know the real financials: if we still used the well, that $405 of annual savings would have gotten us to a twenty-year payback on our investment, which does not seem worth the hassle. While we still have the non-functioning well—it looks pretty forlorn among the flowers and trees—we are glad to be done with it. It could come in handy, though, for a doomsday scenario—we'll just have to run it through our RO/DI system somehow.

Native Prairie

I was excited about our "native prairie," plantings of native wildflowers and grasses that were to be the highlight of our landscaping. I had seen pictures of beautiful white daisies and yellow coreopsis billowing among tall grasses, conjuring up a rustic, meadow-like look and feel. A native prairie is a very sustainable choice compared to lawns. It requires no irrigation (saving water), no mowing (reducing air and noise pollution), and is sort of a return to how the land used to be—its natural state. On top of that, we would not need to fertilize the area, reducing any run-off of chemicals into our lakes and rivers. The wildflowers also attract birds, bees, and butterflies—wildlife that is essential to our ecosystem. Our landscape architect showed us photos of established prairie gardens, and we were sold. "Native" was all the rage—let's get back to what used to be there.

Our landscapers told us that it would not look great for a few years and to have patience while it "establishes itself." While we did not any introduce invasive plants on purpose, I found I spent a good part of the summer trying to weed them out: dandelions, thistles, grass-like weeds, and clovers—all of which grow freely and abundantly in the park across the street. The first year, it looked horrible. I did not want to use pesticides, so I weeded. This part of our yard was supposed to be "low maintenance"; it was not. The daisies were

Native prairie not looking so good.

the only thing that looked good, but they did not bloom for very long. The second year, it

Daisies looked great for a short period of time.

The best our native prairie ever looked.

started looking a little better, but I still had to weed constantly.

Toward the end of the second summer, we had been on a camping trip, and I came home with a case of the shingles—so I wasn't exactly staying on top of the weeding. A few weeks later, we received a letter from the City of Minneapolis. It was a citation, informing us that we were in violation of a city ordinance that requires all grass to be less than eight inches tall. Apparently, tall grass is a nuisance and demonstrates negligent treatment of property. We had a nice little lawn in the front of the house that we mowed once a week, so clearly we were not negligent. When I called the city to protest the citation and let them know how righteous we were with the native prairie, I was met with the standard response: "Ma'am, we can't treat you different than anybody else. You're in violation of city code and you need to comply." If we did not chop down all the grasses within the next two weeks, the city would not only have fined us a few hundred dollars, they would also have mowed everything down for us and sent us the bill. All those coreopsis, asters, blue phlox, and wild geranium plants we had been tending to (and spent a fair amount of money on) would be killed on the spot.

After being pissed off for a few weeks, I found I actually appreciated the city for calling it like it was: an eyesore full of weeds. It gave us the opportunity to change our landscape, for the better. Besides, I had come to my own conclusion: do not try to replicate a native prairie unless you have a lot of land for it (it looks weird in small spaces), *and* a lot of time on your hands to not only be able to

Dead native prairie.

Nepeta (catmint) on the street-side of the arborvitae—huge improvement over weeds and grasses.

distinguish between native grasses and invasive weeds, but also to pull out the latter. Daily.

To fix our problem, first, we had to kill all the native grasses, because the weeds were so mixed in with them (we were able to save some of the flowering plants). That was sad. Now, though, we have a wide variety of wildflowers growing among mulch instead of all the weeds and grasses, and it does look a lot better. We put nepeta (catmint) on one side of arborvitae. These are very hardy, beautiful purple flowering plants—a huge improvement over a motley group of grasses. Lesson learned, but it was quite an expensive mistake!

Looking back, I'm not sure why we had been so enamored with the "native prairies" that seemed to be popping up next to trails in Minneapolis. If you think about it, hardly anything is truly native, because we are always adapting and evolving. *We* certainly are not native to this land. Don't we want adaptive and resilient plants? As Frederic Rich so eloquently explains, "The gardener does not look for some hypothetical past time when the ecosystem was wholly native and natural, but instead asks only whether the mix of plants is healthy, sustainable, and resilient."[90]

Snowmelt

We have already discussed a few areas where Jim and I could not agree, like low-flow showerheads. I wish we had them, but it was a smaller battle to lose. The bigger battle I lost was the snowmelt in our front entryway. And by snowmelt, I do not mean those crystal flakes or

90 Frederic Rich, *Getting to Green: Saving Nature: A Bipartisan Solution* (New York: W.W. Norton, 2016), 176.

Installing the ability to heat the outside!

pellets that you can buy from Home Depot and spread on your driveway as a de-icing agent. I mean the kind of system that actually melts snow and ice from underneath, using heat energy. "We cannot heat the outside!" I yelled.

Our front entry faces north, gets no sun, and becomes a hazardous sheet of ice in the winter (November through April). It is very difficult to shovel it off. Even our builders thought we should add snowmelt to that area (but they got paid more for it). In reality, we do not use it much, and when we do use it, it really does improve the front entryway. It has prevented many wipeouts—by my kids, our parents, the postal service carrier, etc. The installation did not cost much extra, as we already had in-floor heat installed in the adjacent spaces. Since we do not use it often, we do not spend much money operating it (though I have no idea exactly how much). So, it was probably worth it. But I still cringe when I see that "on" button—it is pretty much the *opposite* of a green feature.

Through all of this, I have learned that it takes huge focus and effort to design and build a sustainable home. But then, once that is done, how we *live* in our homes can continue make a difference for our health, wealth, and soul.

CHAPTER 13: THE BOTTOM LINE

When I talk about building a sustainable home, business, school, etc., the pushback I receive is always: yes, but it costs more! That is a myth that many of us in green building are trying hard to dispel (in addition to the myths that you have to sacrifice comfort and beauty, and that green is a political statement—it's not).

To address this misconception, this short chapter bottom lines the top priorities of building a sustainable home into three groups: (1) No Additional Cost; (2) Additional Up-front Costs, but Worth It for Your Wealth; and (3) Additional Up-front Costs, but Worth It for Your Health. Those under the first category are the no-brainers. For the second category, the truth is, if the home is mortgaged, which most are, the up-front costs are wrapped up in principal and interest payments—so the money savings are not only worth it in the long run, they help your cash flow starting day one. And for the third category, efforts to stay healthy and prevent illness pay off in overall happiness and quality of life, as well as monetarily. These are the top strategies that I believe should be standard construction practice for all homes. The bottom line: it does not have to cost more.

No Additional Cost

1. Specify low-flow fixtures: faucets with flow rates of 1.5 gallons per minute or less, showerheads with flow rates of 2.0 gallons per minute or less, and toilets as dual-flush, or with flush rates of 1.3 gallons per flush or less. This will save about 20 percent on your water bill, and you will *not* notice a difference in water pressure.

2. Specify materials (paints, adhesives, sealants) with no VOCs (volatile organic compounds), and look for Ecologo and Green Seal certifications. This keeps the air from being harmful to your health, and there is no difference in quality.

3. All appliances and electronics should be Energy Star labeled. This will save money on your energy bills, and there is no difference in performance.

4. Purchase electric instead of gas appliances. This reduces the need to burn fossil fuels in your home, which is healthier for your lungs, and as electricity from the grid is getting cleaner and cleaner, you will be

part of our economy's clean energy transformation.

5. Choose a waste subcontractor that recycles construction waste and reports back the diversion rate. This helps the circular economy and reduces landfill waste.

6. Specify drywall and concrete that is both local and has a high recycled content. This decreases embedded energy in your materials, and again, there is no difference in quality.

7. For landscaping, limit the amount of turf grass and introduce drought-tolerant plants. This will save water and energy (and money) from reduced mowing, less fertilizing, less irrigation, and it will attract pollinators. (This may or may not cost more, depending on how it is accomplished.)

8. For project planning, involve all architects, contractors, and subcontractors in an initial meeting to discuss goals and durability risks. This can save time and prevent miscommunication and expensive change orders from happening later in the process.

Additional Up-front Costs, but Worth It for Your Wealth

1. Purchase or replace light bulbs with LED bulbs. These are always the lowest-hanging fruit with typical paybacks in energy bill savings of less than one year. You also will not have to replace them for years, saving time, hassle, and replacement costs.

2. Specify closed-cell spray foam insulation for all exterior walls and roofs. This helps improve the structural integrity of the home and is the best insulator for colder climates. It can save you about 20 percent on your energy bill.

3. Specify triple pane windows with one coating of low-E glass, if possible. For a small percent more in cost (ours cost an additional 8 percent), you get more insulated windows (ours were 25 percent better). This decreases energy bills and makes the home more comfortable, because it will be quieter and less drafty.

4. Purchase the most efficient HVAC system and water heater you can find. These two components comprise over 50 percent of your home energy bills, so they can save you a significant amount of money. Preventive maintenance plans also reduce repair and replacement costs.

5. Assuming numbers one through four are accomplished, then consider solar electric energy (photovoltaics) for your roof. You will be producing electricity where you use it, for free, forever—saving money on your electric bill and increasing the value of your home.

Additional Up-front Costs, but Worth It for Your Health

1. Filter your water—preferably all of it, because you bathe and wash clothes

in it, but if you can't, then just filter your drinking water through a reverse osmosis deionizing process ($1,000–$5,000 plus annual filters).

2. Ventilate and filter your air (building code, so no incremental cost), preferably with at least MERV 11 filters ($10–$30/year more cost, depending on number of filters and frequency of changing them).

3. Specify materials (cabinetry, flooring, countertops, flooring) that do not off-gas formaldehyde: specify NAUF (non-added urea formaldehyde) or TSCA Title VI compliant (this may not actually cost more).

4. Test for radon gas ($40), and mitigate if it is above recommended levels ($1,500).

5. Choose a location (if you can) that is in proximity to your work, school, activities, etc., and that lets you get outside to enjoy nature. This could cost more, but the resale value should increase.

The Top Three Best and Worst Things about LEED for Homes

Worst

1. It's a pain in the rear to go through all the documentation and verification; it is not easily accessible or designed for the average homeowner (but the local LEED for Homes Provider helps with that).
2. The cost of LEED registration and certification required by the United States Green Building Council can be in the thousands of dollars, and it is unclear whether the market will pay for this upon resale.
3. LEED for Homes does not address how you live in the house beyond the initial education of homeowner (LEED for Existing Buildings, a different rating system, does address this, but it was designed for commercial, not residential, buildings).

Best

1. Going through the LEED certification process requires an independent Green Rater to ensure the house is built and sealed as it should be—which serves as quality assurance.
2. LEED certification provides a framework, strategies, and metrics that inform how and why to build a high-performance green building.
3. LEED certification communicates, in one word, that your home was designed, built *and third-party verified* to be more sustainable—which means there is real substance behind the claim; it is not just greenwashing.

Chapter 14:
Beyond LEED: Moon Shot

We can just as easily have an economy that is based on healing the future rather than stealing from it.

—Paul Hawken, *Drawdown: The Most Comprehensive Plan Ever Proposed to Reverse Global Warming*

Everything I have addressed in this book around building a more sustainable home is better than the conventional alternative—an important and meaningful step that can save you money, improve your health, and nourish your soul. The green building principles espoused by the LEED rating system are certainly an improvement over standard construction practice. Even as building codes become more stringent, LEED evolves to continuously improve.

Certification programs are useful because they require meeting certain performance standards, which is then verified by a third party. Without verification, it's kind of like saying, "Yeah, I went to college. I audited all the classes and did really well. I just didn't want to have to pay for that piece of paper that says I have a college degree. But I did all the same work; I got the same education." Really? Architects and builders frequently argue against LEED certifying a project, because they say they *already* design to LEED standards. As someone who has led the LEED certification of over two million square feet of space, I can tell you that is simply not true. The critics that say you are just paying for a plaque do not understand LEED.

As LEED certification has grown, so have other building certifications that go beyond LEED standards. Passive House certification has a singular focus, going beyond LEED in one area only: energy usage. Whereas LEED certified buildings are about 25 percent more energy efficient, buildings designed to the Passive House Institute's 2015 standards consume 86 percent less energy for heating and 46 percent less energy for cooling (depending on climate zone and building type) when compared to code-compliant buildings, and typically cost 5 to 10 percent more to build.[91] There are over 4,200 Passive House–certified buildings in the world, but only ninety in the United States.[92] The Passive House is based on building-science principles, which match up

---

91 See http://www.phius.org/home-page and http://www.phius.org/what-is-passive-building/passive-house-faqs.

92 Passivehouse-database.org, accessed November 6, 2017.

well with the first four sections in the *Energy* chapter and LEED's prescriptions for reducing the need for energy: orientation to the sun, insulation, windows, and air infiltration.

Kathryn Johnson of Minneapolis is in the middle of building her family's soon-to-be-certified Passive House. Meeting with her over lunch, I was able to find out more about her motivations for doing so. Her parents are back-to-the-land type of people; they grew their own food and canned it. Her German heritage instilled in her a love for efficiency. She and her husband had always wanted to build and live in a Passive House. Why? "The power goes out a lot, and you start to think about how you want to live. You think hard about what is the appropriate way to have a house built. We want to be off-gridable. Not that we are preppers, but we just don't want to be stressed about it. Part of it is knowing what most of your expenses will be—that predictability is lovely."

They will probably get to net zero energy (meaning, consuming very little energy, and the energy that is consumed is produced by renewable energy onsite), but that is not their primary goal. Their number one goal is energy independence—to not have to rely upon the grid. They will not have one drop of natural gas in the house. It's too dangerous, she said. Combining the Passive House design principles with ground-source heat pumps, electric appliances, and solar panels, they will meet their goal. She added, "This is just one home where we can make a difference. We cannot make a difference in the greater world; I can't stop a war; I can't change climate; but I can set an example by showing that it can be done."[93]

Another building certification program that goes well beyond LEED in every area is the Living Building Challenge. Published in 2006 and owned and administered by International Living Future Institute, the Living Building Challenge is a framework and certification program with three paths: Living, Petal, and Zero Energy (which goes beyond Passive House), all of which can be achieved for either homes or nonresidential buildings. As the most rigorous green building certification program, Living Building Challenge visualizes the ideal for the built environment. Living Certification helps to create buildings that are regenerative, self-sufficient, produce more energy than they consume, and collect and treat all water on site. Part of its beauty is that it is based on twelve consecutive months of *actual* performance data, as opposed to designed or predicted performance—but that's also part of what makes it challenging. Certification is difficult to achieve: as of late 2017, only seventy-three buildings have achieved certification through the Living Building Challenge.[94]

I had the opportunity to speak with Paul Holland, a venture capitalist who lives in Portola Valley, California, who with his wife, Linda Yates, built Tah Mah Lah[95]—touted as one of the greenest homes in America. They were

---

93 Interview with Kathryn Johnson at Birchwood Café, September 22, 2017; for more see her blog at www.sweetpassivehouse.wordpress.com.

94 https://living-future.org/contact-us/faq/.

95 www.tahmahlah.com.

motivated by their love of nature and their desire to model what green living can look and feel like. With enough solar panels to power their entire home and their electric cars, they truly are net zero energy. Their house is comprised of four natural materials that are primarily locally sourced, unpainted, and recycled or reclaimed: wood, metal, glass, and stone. There are no oil-based products in the house—no natural gas, no plastics. "We live guilt-free," he told me. With their LEED platinum certified home, they have shown that we can go a lot further toward sustainability with our homes, without sacrificing comfort or beauty.

Building a Sustainable Home really has two meanings: (1) building, as in the physical design and construction of a home (what most of this book is about), and (2) building, as in working toward making changes over time (hopefully what this book inspires). Developing a more sustainable lifestyle does not happen overnight. It takes a lot of work. While I would not call a LEED certified home a "sustainable home," it is on the right path. A Passive House is also on the right path.

The building community's thinking continues to evolve over time—and mine has too. A decade ago, when we were initially building our home, it was all about efficiency. We chose a natural gas-powered dryer and a back-up gas boiler with a very high efficiency rating. We thought we were doing really well. Now, though, I would give up some efficiency in favor of clean energy—which means transforming all gas-powered equipment to electric. As technology develops, prices come down, and electricity generation becomes more and more powered by clean and renewable resources like wind and solar, our goals *can* be more aspirational. I would encourage anyone involved in a building project, whether it's a home or an office building or a school, to aim high. If net zero energy is not within reach now, make the building net zero energy-ready. And when it comes to furnishings and furniture, be intentional about the choices you make, with a sustainability lens.

Solar panels power the home and electric cars at Tah Mah Lah (photo credit to Tahmahlah).

When I talk about sustainability, I know I have not addressed key issues around equality and justice. I am not discounting those at all. Abuse of power is at the root of these problems. And when we abuse the system of nature that supports our lives, we are putting in jeopardy our public health. So I am prioritizing what is known as *environmental sustainability*, because without that—without clean air, clean water, and food—we do not get to fight for equality and justice. For our economy to become environmentally sustainable, then, we have to work toward three BHAGs:

Goal #1: *100 percent of energy is supplied by renewable energy sources.* First, we need to be less wasteful with our energy and implement energy efficient technologies and practices that have demonstrated success. For the power we do need, we need to migrate away from natural gas, gasoline, and coal, to electricity: electric homes, electric vehicles, electric factories. Then, we can continue cleaning up the electrical grid and power it with non-fossil fuels like solar, wind, and hydro. (If we can figure out energy, we can figure out water, too.)

Goal #2: *Zero percent of toxic chemicals that pose a threat to human health are released to air, water, or land.*[96] As defined by the EPA's Toxic Release Inventory Program, this is primarily an issue for industry.

Goal #3: *100 percent of waste is either recycled or composted.* The current waste diversion rate in the United States is only 35 percent, so we have a long way to go. Thinking about products in terms of their entire life cycle can get us on the path toward a circular economy, where outputs from one industry are inputs for another. If we start paying more attention to how products are designed and produced, from cradle-to-cradle[97] instead of cradle-to-grave, we can become more like nature, where there is no such thing as waste.

These three goals encompass all industries. While I have focused on the home and building industry, the industries of food, clothing, and transportation are working on becoming more sustainable as well—at least some businesses are, because they are discovering it is the only way to be *financially sustainable*. We, as consumers, can be intentional about our choices. The power we have as individuals is that we can vote with our wallets and support those businesses that are more sustainable. Our free market-based economic system gives us that power, which we can all use to make a meaningful difference.

Building a sustainable home can be part of our society's transformation toward a more sustainable future. We have the technology; we have the knowledge; I believe we can do this. Developing into a sustainable economy is, without a doubt, the moon shot of our time.

---

96 See www.epa.gov/tri/NationalAnalysis. In 2015, of the nearly 26 billion pounds of total chemical waste managed at TRI-covered industrial facilities (excluding metal mines), approximately 92 percent was not released into the environment due to the use of preferred waste management practices such as recycling, energy recovery, and treatment.

97 William McDonough and Michael Branugart, *Cradle to Cradle: Remaking the Way We Make Things* (New York: North Point Press, 2002).

Photo credit: Karen Melvin.

The LEED Checklist

LEED for Homes Simplified Project Checklist, version 2008			
Innovation and Design Process (ID)	**(No Minimum Points Required)**	**Max Points**	**Our Points**
1. Integrated Project Planning	1.1 Preliminary Rating	Prereq	Y
	1.2 Integrated Project Team	1	1
	1.3 Professional Credentialed with Respect to LEED for Homes	1	0
	1.4 Design Charrette	1	0
	1.5 Building Orientation for Solar Design	1	0
2. Durability Management Process	2.1 Durability Planning	Prereq	Y
	2.2 Durability Management	Prereq	Y
	2.3 Third-Party Durability Management Verification	3	3
3. Innovative or Regional Design	3.1 Exemplary Performance WE2.1	1	1
	3.2 Exemplar Performance WE2.1	1	1
	3.3. Building Performance Partnership	1	1
	3.4 Exemplary Performance EA9.2 - Energy Star Clothes Washer	1	1
	Sub-total for ID Category	**11**	**8**
Location and Linkages (LL)	**(No Minimum Points Required)** OR	**Max Points**	**Our Points**
1. LEED ND	1. LEED for Neighborhood Development LL2-6	10	0
2. Site Selection	2. Site Selection	2	2
3. Preferred Location	3.1 Edge Development LL3.2	1	0
	3.2 Infill	2	2
	3.3 Previously Developed	1	1
4. Infrastructure	4. Existing Infrastructure	1	1
5. Community Resources/Transit	5.1 Basic Community Resources/Transit LL 5.2, 5.3	1	0
	5.2 Extensive Community Resources/Transit LL 5.3	2	0
	5.3 Outstanding Community Resources/Transit	3	3
6. Access to Open Space	6. Access to Open Space	1	1
	Sub-total for LL Category	**10**	**10**
Sustainable Sites (SS)	**(Minimum of 5 SS Points Required)** OR	**Max Points**	**Our Points**
1. Site Stewardship	1.1 Erosion Controls During Construction	Prereq	Y
	1.2 Minimize Disturbed Area of Site	1	0
2. Landscaping	2.1 No Invasive Plants	Prereq	Y
	2.2 Basic Landscaping Design SS 2.5	2	0
	2.3 Limit Conventional Turf SS 2.5	3	1
	2.4 Drought Tolerant Plants SS 2.5	2	2
	2.5 Reduce Overall Irrigation Demand by at Least 20%	4	0
3. Local Heat Island Effects	3. Reduce Local Heat Island Effects	1	0
4. Surface Water Management	4.1 Permeable Lot	4	3
	4.2 Permanent Erosion Controls	1	1
	4.3 Management of Run-off from Roof	2	2
5. Nontoxic Pest Control	5 Pest Control Alternatives	2	2
6. Compact Development	6.1 Moderate Density SS 6.2, 6.3	2	0
	6.2 High Density SS 6.3	3	0
	6.3 Very High Density	4	0
	Sub-total for SS Category	**22**	**11**
Water Efficiency (WE)	**(Minimum of 3 WE Points Required)** OR	**Max Points**	**Our Points**
1. Water Reuse	1.1 Rainwater Harvesting System WE 1.3	4	0
	1.2 Graywater Reuse System WE 1.3	1	0
	1.3 Use of Municipal Recycled Water System	3	0
2. Irrigation System	2.1 High Efficiency Irrigation System WE 2.3	3	3
	2.2 Third Party Inspection WE 2.3	1	1
	2.3 Reduce Overall Irrigation Demand by at Least 45%	4	0
3. Indoor Water Use	3.1 High-Efficiency Fixtures and Fittings	3	1
	3.2 Very High-Efficiency Fixtures and Fittings	6	2
	Sub-total for WE Category	**15**	**7**
Energy and Atmosphere (EA)	**(Minimum of 0 EA Points Required)**	**Max Points**	**Our Points**
1. Optimize Energy Performance	1.1 Performance of ENERGY STAR for Homes	Prereq	Y
	1.2 Exceptional Energy Performance	34	25.5
7. Water Heating	7.1 Efficient Hot Water Distribution	2	0
	7.2 Pipe Insulation	1	0
11. Residential Refrigerant Management	11.1 Refrigerant Charge Test	Prereq	Y
	11.2 Appropriate HVAC Refrigerants	1	1
	Sub-total for EA Category	**38**	**26.5**
Materials and Resources (MR)	**(Minimum of 2 MR Points Required)** OR	**Max Points**	**Our Points**
1. Material-Efficient Framing	1.1 Framing Order Waste Factor Limit MR 1.5	Prereq	Y
	1.2 Detailed Framing Documents MR 1.5	1	1
	1.3 Detailed Cut List and Lumber Order MR 1.5	1	1
	1.4 Framing Efficiencies	3	2.5
	1.5 Off-site Fabrication	4	0
2. Environmentally Preferable Products	2.1 FSC Certified Tropical Wood	Prereq	Y
	2.2 Environmentally Preferable Products	8	7
	3.1 Construction Waste Management Planning	Prereq	Y
	3.2 Construction Waste Reduction	3	2
	Sub-total for MR Category	**16**	**13.5**

Indoor Environmental Quality (EQ)	(Minimum of 6 EQ Points Required)	OR	Max Points	Our Points
1. ENERGY STAR with IAP	1. ENERGY STAR with Indoor Air Package		13	0
2. Combustion Venting	2.1 Basic Combustion Venting Measures	EQ1	Prereq	Y
	2.2 Enhanced Combustion Venting Measures	EQ1	2	0
3. Moisture Control	3. Moisture Control Load	EQ1	1	1
4. Outdoor Air Ventilation	4.1 Basic Outdoor Air Ventilation	EQ1	Prereq	Y
	4.2 Enhanced Outdoor Air Ventilation		1	2
	4.3 Third-Party Performance Testing		1	1
5. Local Exhaust	5.1 Basic Local Exhaust	EQ1	Prereq	Y
	5.2 Enhanced Local Exhaust		1	1
	5.3 Third-Party Performance Testing		1	1
6. Distribution of Space Heating & Cooling	6.1 Room-by-Room Load Calculations	EQ1	Prereq	Y
	6.2 Return Air Flow / Room by Room Controls	EQ1	1	1
	6.3 Third-Party Performance Test / Multiple Zones	EQ1	2	2
7. Air Filtering	7.1 Good Filters	EQ1	Prereq	Y
	7.2 Better Filters	EQ7.3	1	0
	7.3 Best Filters		2	2
8. Contaminant Control	8.1 Indoor Contaminant Control During Construction	EQ1	1	1
	8.2 Indoor Contaminant Control		2	1
	8.3 Preoccupancy Flush	EQ1	1	1
9. Radon Protection	9.1 Radon-Resistant Construction in High-Risk Areas	EQ1	Prereq	Y
	9.2 Radon-Resistant Construction in Moderate-Risk Areas	EQ1	1	0
10. Garage Pollutant Protection	10.1 No HVAC in Garage	EQ1	Prereq	Y
	10.2 Minimize Pollutants from Garage	EQ1, 10.4	2	2
	10.3 Exhaust Fan in Garage	EQ1, 10.4	1	0
	10.4 Detached Garage or No Garage	EQ1	3	0
	Sub-total for EQ Category		21	16

Awareness & Education (AE)	(Minimum of 0 AE Points Required)		Max Points	Our Points
1. Education of Homeowner or Tenant	1.1 Basic Operations Training		Prereq	Y
	1.2 Enhanced Training		1	1
	1.3 Public Awareness		1	1
2. Education of Building Manager	2 Education of Building Manager		1	0
	Sub-total for AE Category		3	2
Total Points			**136**	**94**

	Adjusted Certification Thresholds: Certified	61.5	
	Silver	76.5	
	Gold	91.5	
	Platinum	106.5	

Acknowledgments

This book has been a long work in progress; there are too many people to thank over the course of the past ten years! I have to start by thanking my literary agent, Michael Croy, and my editor, Abigail Gehring at Skyhorse Publishing, for trusting and encouraging me throughout this process.

Going back many years . . . I owe gratitude to the entire home building design and construction team—beginning with Malini Srivastava, our dedicated project architect, whom I had met earlier due to a mutual interest in green building. She encouraged us to call David Salmela, our brilliant architect. Working with David and Malini was a pure delight. The architect/homeowner relationship is quite intimate, and though we miss talking to David as much as we did in 2007–2008, we feel a bit of his presence in our house every day.

The people that built our home, Streeter & Associates, are to be commended for their attention to detail and focus on quality: Mark Olson and Mark Backman are two of the best carpenters you could ask for; Kevin Streeter is a wealth of knowledge; and Ben Dunlap, our project manager, helped us every step of the way—even through some of the more difficult moments. Travis Van Liere and Stephanie Grotta of Coen + Partners were thoughtful and creative in helping us think through our landscaping. And thanks Jim Cusack at UMR Geothermal and Jason Gaspard at Select Mechanical for giving me indispensable lessons in HVAC design.

Our home would not be LEED certified without our LEED for Homes Providers, Ed Von Thoma and Pat O'Malley of Building Knowledge, Inc., and our Green Rater, Jimmie Sparks from the Neighborhood Energy Connection—truly knowledgeable and committed professionals.

Not everyone has the opportunity to build a home. Building a home, or renovating one, can be a daunting task. To know that we could do it, I have to thank my mom and dad, Susan and Gary Rappaport, who demonstrated (twice) that it was possible to make the dream of building a new home come true. I was witness to the plans, the discussions, the changes, and have benefited from living in these homes—where they instilled in me the values of excellence, hard work, and the importance of design and functionality.

I am grateful to my sister, Rabbi Debra Rappaport, who, back in the 1990s, recommended that I read Paul Hawken's *The Ecology of Commerce*, a foundational book for me that should be required business school curriculum (and was certainly missing from my MBA!). In writing this book, her supportive words encouraged me to find my voice: "if you've got something to say, sister, say it!"

Finally, I would like to thank my family for their never-ending support and love. I am eternally thankful to Jim for being my life partner and building a home and life together; I am truly blessed. And to my two wonderful daughters: I can only hope that my work improves your future. With love and gratitude, this book is dedicated to you.

Index

A
adhesives, 35–37
aerators, in faucets, 127–128, 129
AFUE, 90
air, 26–46
air filtration, 39–42, 202
air flush, pre-occupancy, 45–46
air fresheners, 26–27
air infiltration, 81–84
air ventilation, 43–46
American Clay, 32–34
American Tree Farm System (ATFS), 140
Anderson, Ray, 147
appliances, 96–97, 200
architects, 12
ASHRAE standards, 43, 89

B
bamboo, 143
bathing, 128–129
buckthorn, 171
builders, 12
butcher block, 151, 152

C
cabinetry, 29–30, 148–149
candles, scented, 26–27
carbon dioxide, 64
carbon filtration, 19, 22
carpet, 31–32, 146
carpet tiles, 147
ceilings, 153
Chapin, Carol, 55
chlorine, 19
chrysanthemums, 44
clay plaster, 32–34
Cleaning Product Right to Know Act (California), 56
cleaning products, 51–56
cleanliness, 47–57
clerestory, 71
clothes washing, 96–97
coal, 64
coatings
   interior, 32–35

community resources, 188
computers, 66, 96–97
concrete, 201
concrete floor, 146–147
concrete floor sealant, 36–37
concrete foundation, 156
contaminant control, 48–51
cooking, 66
cooling, 66, 84–90, 201
copper pipes, 93
cork flooring, 143–144
cost/benefits analysis, 61
costs, 12
cotton denim insulation, 80
countertops, 149–152
CRI (Carpet and Rug Institute), 31
cypress, 152–153

D
Danielson, Doug, 179
deconstruction waste, 165–166
demolition, 165–166
design, and energy consumption, 69–73
diversion rate, waste, 161–164
doors, 153–155
drought-tolerant plants, 173–174
dryer, 96–97
drywall, 153, 201
durability, 130–134

E
Ecowarm, 88–89
education, homeowner, 133–134
electric, solar, 103–108
electronics, 66, 96–97, 200
energy, 63–115
energy consumption, 65–69
   air infiltration and, 81–84
   appliances and, 96–97
   design and, 69–73
   home size and, 69–70
   HVAC and, 84–90
   insulation and, 75–81
   lighting and, 97–103

orientation of home and, 70–73
    renewable energy and, 65–66, 84, 86–87, 103–110
    water heating and, 90–96
    windows and, 73–75
energy independence, 204
energy production, 66
energy recovery ventilator (ERV), 43
Energy Star, 66, 68, 96–97, 200
Environmental Protection Agency (EPA), 17–18
Environmental Working Group (EWG), 26–27, 53, 55
exterior finishes, 37–39
exterior siding, 152–153

F
fiberboard, 148
filtration
    air, 39–42, 202
    water, 18–19, 21–25, 201–202
financing, of energy efficiency, 112–113
finishes, exterior, 37–39
fir, 145
fir veneer, 148
floor heating, 88–89
flooring, 31–32, 142–148
FloorScore, 32
floor sealant, 36–37
FLOR, 147
fluoride, 19, 20–21
Forest Stewardship Council, 139–140
formaldehyde, 28–30, 77
fossil fuels, 27, 63–65, 200
foundation, 156
fragrances, 26–27
framing, 153–155, 157–158, 159–160
FSC-certified wood, 139–140, 148–149, 154

G
garage, 50–51
gas generator, 132
gasoline, 64
generator, 132
geo-exchange systems, 86
geothermal, 66, 86–87
grass, 171–173
graywater reuse, 121–122, 129
green, defined, 5
Green Label Plus, 31–32
GREENGUARD, 34
Green Rater, 67
green roof, 155, 178–184
Green Seal, 34–35

ground-source heat pump, 86–87

H
hardscape, 174–178
harvesting, of rainwater, 117–121
Hawken, Paul, 203
health, 6, 15–57
heating, 66, 84–90, 108–110, 201
heat island effect, 168, 169, 170
heat recovery ventilator (HRV), 43–45
heavy metals, 64
HEPA filter, 42–43
herbicides, in water, 18
HERS, 66–67, 111
Holland, Paul, 204–205
Home Equity Line of Credit (HELOC), 112
homeowner education, 133–134
home size
    energy consumption and, 69–70
Homes That Heal and Those That Don't (Thomson), 26
home value, 12
hot water distribution, 90–92
hot water heating, 66, 87–88, 90–96
houseplants, 44
humidity control, 47–48
Hurricane Katrina, 28–29

I
indoors, time spent in, 15
indoor water use, 125–129
inorganic contaminants, in water, 18
insulation, 37, 75–81, 92–93, 155–156, 201
integrated project planning, 133, 201
interior coatings, 32–35
interior paints, 32–35
interior walls, 153
invasive species, 170–171
irrigation, 122–125, 129, 168–169, 193–195

J
Johnson, Kathryn, 204

K
Kimmerer, Robin Wall, 168

L
lacquers, 35
landscaping, 168–185, 201
    green roof and, 178–184
    hardscape and, 174–178
    plantings and, 170–174

LaPorte, Paula Baker, 26
laundry, 96–97
lawn, 171–173
LEDs (light emitting diodes), 98–101
LEED
    accreditation, 11
    background of, 9–11
    categories, 10
    certification levels, 10, 11
    checklist, 208–209
    costs, 12
    performance standards in, 8
    reasons for, 11–13
LEED for Homes Reference Guide, 8–9
lighting, 66, 97–103, 113, 201
local materials, 141–156
location, 186–189, 202
low-E coating, 74–75

M
Material-Efficient Framing, 157–158
materials
    cabinetry, 148–149
    ceiling, 149–153
    countertop, 149–153
    from demolition, 165–166
    door, 153–155
    exterior siding, 149–153
    flooring, 142–148
    foundation, 156
    framing, 153–155
    insulation, 155–156
    interior walls, 149–153
    local, 141–156
    purchasing, 137–156
    reclaimed, 138–140
    recycled, 138–139
    recycling, 161–166
    reduction of use of, 157–161
    reusing, 161
    roofing, 155
    sheathing, 153–155
    trim, 153–155
    waste management with, 156–166, 201
McDonough, William, 137
medium density fiberboard (MDF), 148
MERV rating, 42–43
metals, heavy, 64
microbial contaminants, in water, 18
moisture control, 47–48
mold, 47–48

Morris, Robert D., 116
mudroom, 49
municipal recycled water, 122, 129

N
Nadel, Steven, 114
native prairie, 124, 173, 195–198
natural gas, 63–65
NAUF, 29–30

O
off-gassing, 27–39
open space, 189
organic chemical contaminants, in water, 18
orientation, energy consumption and, 70–73
outdoor air ventilation, 43–46
outdoor water use, 122–125, 129

P
paint, interior, 32–35
Passive House, 65, 203–204
permeable lot, 183
pesticides, in water, 18
PEX piping, 92–93
pipe insulation, 92–93. *See also* insulation
plantings, 170–174
plants, 44
plaster, clay, 32–34
pools, 109
pre-occupancy air flush, 45–46
Prescriptions for a Healthy Home (LaPorte), 26
project planning, integrated, 133, 201
propane, 64
Property Assessed Clean Energy (PACE), 112
purchasing materials, 137–156

R
R-value, 75–79, 83, 92–94
radioactive contaminants, in water, 18
radon, 39–42, 202
rainwater harvesting, 117–121, 129
recirculation pump, 91–92
reclaimed materials, 138–140
recycle, 161–166
recycled water, 122, 129
reduce, 157–161
refrigeration, 66, 96–97
renewable energy, 65–66, 84, 86–87, 103–110, 206
resale value, 12
resiliency, 130–133
reuse, 161

reverse osmosis, 19, 21–25
Rich, Frederic, 135
Richlite, 151–152
roof, green, 155, 178–183
roofing, 155
runoff, 169–170, 182–183

S
Safer Choice, 55
Salmela, David, 69, 151
Santer, Ben, 65n36
scented candles, 26–27
SDS/MSDS, 27, 55, 77
sealants, 35–37
sedum, 174, 176, 178, 179, 182, 183
sheathing, 153–155
showers, 128–129, 200
siding, 152–153
Simple Green, 55–56
sinks, 126–128, 129, 200
size, home
    energy consumption and, 69–70
skylight, 71–73
slate flooring, 144–145
snowmelt, 198–199
solar electric, 103–108, 201
solar heat gain coefficient (SHGC), 74
solar thermal, 108–110
soul, 7, 135–189
Sparks, Jimmie, 12, 45
spray foam insulation, 77–80, 201
steel, galvanized, 37–38
stone flooring, 144–145
structural insulated panels (SIPs), 160–161
stucco, 153
surface water management, 169–170, 182–183
sustainability, defined, 5–6
swimming pools, 109

T
Tah Mah Lah, 204–205
tankless water heaters, 95
third-party verification, 11–12, 131
Thomson, Athena, 26
toilets, 125–126, 129
Toxic Substances Control Act, 30
transit, 188–189
trim, 153–155
turf grass, 171–173

U
U-factor, 74
United States Green Building Council (USGBC), 9
urban heat island effect, 168, 169, 170

V
vacuum system, 49–50
ventilation, 43–46, 66, 84–90, 201, 202
verification, third-party, 11–12
vinyl, 27, 92, 142
volatile organic compounds (VOCs), 31–39, 142, 200

W
walls, interior, 153
Warmboard, 88
washing machine, 96–97
waste diversion, 161–164
waste factor, 158
waste management, with building materials, 156–166, 201
water, 17–25
water, recycled, 122, 129
water deficit, 116
water efficiency, 116–129
water filtration, 18–19, 21–25, 201–202
water fluoridation, 20–21
water heating, 66, 87–88, 90–96, 201
water quality standards, 17–18
water reuse, 117–122
water runoff, 169–170, 182–183
WaterSense, 123, 128
water use, 116–117
    indoor, 125–129
    outdoor, 122–125, 129
wealth, 6–7, 59–134
well irrigation, 193–195
Wilson, Alex, 109
wind energy, 110
windows, 73–75, 155, 201
wood, FSC-certified, 139–140, 148–149, 154
wood finish lacquers, 35
wood flooring, 143
wood framing, 153–155
wood sealant, 38–39
wool carpet, 146

Y
Yates, Linda, 204–205